Lead Like A Woman

Your Essential Guide for True Confidence, Career Clarity, Vibrant Wellbeing and Leadership Success

Megan Dalla-Camina and Michelle McQuaid

First published in 2016 by Lead Like A Woman Pty Ltd

Publication data:

Title: Lead Like A Woman: Your Essential Guide for True Confidence, Career Clarity, Vibrant Wellbeing and Leadership Success

Authors: Megan Dalla-Camina and Michelle McQuaid

ISBN: 978 0 9945970 0 7

Disclaimer

The material in this book is of the nature of general comment only and does not represent professional advice. You should use this information as you see fit, and at your own risk. It is not intended to provide specific guidance for particular circumstances. Your situation may not be exactly suited to the examples here; in fact, it's likely that they won't be the same, and you should adjust your use of the information and recommendations accordingly. The authors and publisher assume no responsibility for your actions.

The authors have taken every reasonable precaution to verify the materials in this book and assume no liability for the content herein to the extent legally permissible.

Cover Design: Nikki Hassett, Bliss Creative

Typesetting: That's Creative!

Back Cover Photography: Ali Novis Photography & Alise Black

To all the women who are open hearted
and brave enough to go on this journey

and

To all the men who support them.

Contents

Introduction 9

Chapter One: Being an authentic leader 29

Chapter Two: Closing the confidence gap 61

Chapter Three: Building your personal brand 111

Chapter Four: Mindfully maintaining wellbeing 173

Chapter Five: Cultivating grit and grace 217

Chapter Six: Creating positive organizational change 257

Afterword: Our dream for you 289

Acknowledgements 291

Notes 297

Lead Like A Woman

Introduction

You might recognize this story. It's one that has played out in the minds and lives of millions of women around the world for decades. Meet Mary. She is highly skilled, capable, reliable, and professional. She works with tenacity and kindness. She moved up the ladder in her organization slowly but surely, until she reached mid-management where she has sat for a long time, still making a solid contribution, but essentially sidelined from the really hot jobs. Reflecting on her career, she's resigned to this and thinks to herself, "who am I to want better, they clearly don't think I'm worthy of a more senior role, so I guess they're right." And as she ruminates on that thought, again and again, her confidence slips just a little bit lower, as she bows her head and gets back to work.

Or another story that might sound familiar. Meet Sarah. She has pushed and driven and strived for more than a decade to reach the top of her profession. And she is there, at the table, leaning in with the best of them (mostly men) and outwardly, she is a celebrated success. She's part of the inner circle, on the A team, blowing all her targets out of the water, and on the fast track for even bigger jobs with more pressure, more responsibility, and more rewards. But Sarah has a dirty little secret. She hates it. Loathes it. She wakes up every morning gritting her teeth and wondering what she'll have to do to endure the day. She puts on her business suit like she's putting on armor, like a cloak of masculine power that will protect her as she strides through her long, long day, without a glimmer of her authentic self along for the ride. And in her rare idle moments, she longs for something better.

Or perhaps you might relate to Amy. She works hard. Too hard. She looks after everyone at work and everyone at home. She's had her head down for so long, just getting through it all, that she doesn't even recognize herself when she looks in the mirror. She long ago lost any sense of passion or purpose, let alone a vision of what she wanted for her life. And even though she is deeply unhappy with her lot, she can't see past her exhaustion to even contemplate what a better career or life could look like. She's worn down and burnt out. And all she dreams about is throwing in the job and hiding under the covers until something better comes along. And really, anything would be better than this.

You may recognize these women. You might even be one of these women. In our decades of working as executives in multinational organizations, as researchers, coaches, and as business owners running leadership development programs in Fortune 500 companies, we have seen thousands of versions of these stories.

We see women putting on the cloak of masculine traits so they can survive in a world created by men, for men, even though they are desperate to show up as women. We see women driving themselves so hard to succeed that they have lost any semblance of their essential self or the life they had once dreamt about. We see women who just don't know who they are anymore, completely out of touch with their strengths, their passion, and their purpose, lost and forgotten in the seemingly endless climb to the middle. And we see women who are so sick of having to fit into systems that have done little to value and honor their unique contributions that they have left all together—to create their own business where they can be real, authentic, and lead how they long too.

We also see the flip side. The organizations struggling to meet their business targets, keep good people in leadership roles, and create cultures that inspire, enable, and empower people to be their best. We see CEOs who are personally committed to gender diversity as a strategy, yet are completely frustrated with their inability to make inroads into their diversity targets, to cultivate middle management as change agents, or to achieve any real breakthroughs for women or their gender goals.

And we see men who are so sick of having to conform to gender roles that were built in the dark ages, where they have only one contribution to make—the provider—and where success looks the same as it always has. Be ever available, show no emotion, man up and lead like a warrior—how very exhausting and disempowering for them too.

But it doesn't have to be this way. Because we have also seen the life changing moments when these same women realize that there's another way to be in the world, when they have the information, tools, strategies, and permission to choose something better for themselves. We have seen the transformations of women who were stuck in their career, who longed to lead but didn't know how to do it authentically, who found their inner confidence, and strength, and changed not only their life, but also the lives of hundreds of other women just like them.

We have also seen the change that takes place when leaders in organizations, male and female, give women the permission to show up in a unique way that is a revolution in thought and action.

And we have seen the relief on the faces of men, many of them leaders in these organizations, when they are shown that there's a softer, more authentic, more balanced way for them to show up, that will not only make them happier, but more successful, especially in terms of their impact on people as well as profits.

It's a pretty simple revolution, and we'd love you to join us. What is it?

It's about women leading like women. Allowing women to show up and use their feminine traits like compassion, collaboration, empathy, vulnerability, and intuition and see them for what they are—natural strengths—and value them in workplaces.

It's a revolution about enabling women with an evidence-based roadmap to step into a new leadership paradigm, one based on a balance of feminine and masculine traits, that closes the confidence gap, creates careers that matter, nurtures wellbeing, and cultivates the grit and grace to sustain these behaviors.

It's a revolution of change in workplaces around the world enabling them to embrace the authentic skills and capabilities of all genders, and supporting people to bring their unique strengths, abilities, leadership, and humanity to business.

It's a revolution of optimism and collaboration, not negativity and aggression as we have seen for far too long. It's about unity, not division. It's about transcending what has held us back, as women, as men, and as businesses, and creating something better for us all, and for generations to come.

And whilst it's about inclusiveness and a journey for everyone, it starts with us as women, stepping into our power. Because it's a revolution of healing and hope—imagining all that can be possible when we truly come home to ourselves, and lead as only women can—with strength, with courage, with creativity, and yes, with good men and our sisters celebrating every step of the journey.

The revolution is here. Are you ready?

How we got here: our stories

We'd like to share with you a little of our stories up front so you have a sense of how we got here. We have both had interesting journeys that have brought us to this moment, winding paths as opposed to straight lines, and filled with many, many opportunities for self-reflection, challenge, and growth. Perhaps like you, we spent most of our careers being the good girls we'd been groomed to be. Making smart choices. Working hard. Doing what was expected of us. And from the outside, most of the time it looked like we had it all together. We were held up as modern day success stories. But the real story is always the one behind the story. Because whilst we both might have looked like we always had our stuff together, there were critical times in both of our journeys when we were crumbling inside. Were we the only people feeling this way?

Megan's story

They say you keep getting sent the same lesson until you learn it. For Megan, her day of awakening came when she was thirty-five. Just back from yet another trip to New York, feeling tired, run down, stressed, and over it, she drove into her office car park one morning and called her mother on the phone. "I just don't think I can do this for one more minute," she sighed through the phone, speaking of course about her job, and expecting the usual pep talk from her mom, who was ever supportive of her crazy career and schedule. What came next shocked Megan to her core, "Of course you can't Megan," she said, "You have no life."

You have no life. How did she get here? She was thirty-five, and had one of the biggest marketing director roles in the country. She had spent the past fifteen years working her way through some of the most respected organizations in the world, and was managing thirteen countries and dozens of team members by the time she was twenty-six; she'd lived on a plane for the best part of the last decade setting billion dollar business strategies and executing marketing strategies worth tens of millions of dollars; she had completed her first Masters degree in business, won global awards, counseled global chairmen, and shared the stage with leaders of countries. And in between all of that, she had gotten married, had a beautiful baby, gotten divorced, and become a single parent.

No wonder she was exhausted and completely burnt out. Sure, over the past ten years she had had more than one signal that her work and lifestyle wasn't sustainable, but it was nothing that a day's rest or more coffee couldn't fix. Until they couldn't. That morning in the car park, she knew in an instant that it was time to make a change. Not consider a change. Not mull one over. But to make a radical decision that she had been dreaming of, quietly, silently, secretly, for as long as she could remember.

So that morning, after she hung up the phone, she walked into her CEOs office and said the two words that would change her life. *I'm done.* Over the next few weeks, Megan and her CEO pieced together a plan that enabled her to take two months leave to get well and refocus, and then come back in a newly created role as director of strategy, including remits for gender diversity and organizational culture and change. She negotiated to do this role in a part-time and flexible capacity. And she made a plan to get her life on track.

Over the next decade, that is exactly what Megan did. It took conscious effort and a mindful practice to go from being a complete workaholic (eighty hour weeks anyone?) to living a more intentional life, but over time—with the new skills she was learning through her yoga teacher training and second Masters degree in Wellness and Positive Psychology—she built the life she was seeking. Whilst still leading business strategy, she moved her work more and more to focus on diversity, women in business, and positive leadership strategies. She became increasingly productive, happier, sparked her long-lost creativity to write her first book, and reconnected with friends. And most importantly, she created the space and energy to focus on her most important relationship, with her son.

As a strategist and coach, speaker, writer and researcher, now in her own business, she uses the tools and skills she learned to empower thousands of women around the world to step into their power and create careers and lives in which they can thrive, and enable organizations to create leaders and change that matters. And through doing this, she has connected with a purpose so deep that it inspires her everyday. Is it still a journey? Absolutely. Is it always easy? Not by a long shot. Megan still gets bitten by the drive and strive mindset that fueled her career for fifteen years. She is intentional about what she says yes to and prioritizes her self care. But by making the commitment to herself that she will walk her purposeful path with grace and ease, she lives the life of her creation and is grateful for that everyday.

Michelle's story

For Michelle, the wake-up call came in 2006. She was living in New York, with her beautiful, young family, was in good health, and six months earlier had landed her dream job as a global brand director for one of the world's largest firms and was busy traveling around the world. But for all she had to be grateful for, it was getting harder and harder each morning to find the energy to get out of bed.

Increasingly plagued by fears that she wasn't really good enough, smart enough, or worthy enough to deserve the life she had, Michelle was sure that it would take just one mistake for others to also figure it out. As a result, she was exhausted from trying to keep up the façade of her life. Everything felt gray and flat. And while there were the odd glimmers of joy, they just never seemed to last.

Of course, this wasn't an overnight phenomenon. After starting life in a violent, highly dysfunctional family, Michelle dreamed of being happy when she grew up. Intelligent, resourceful, and determined to prove she was good enough, she left home at sixteen, managed to get herself through college, and landed a job in public relations. With her head down and working hard, over the next decade she steadily moved up, up, and up the career ladder, and along the way married a good man, and started a family. But despite the outward signs of success, in her quieter or more desperate moments Michelle realized that on the inside she remained plagued by fear and self-doubt. No matter what she achieved professionally or personally, it just never felt like it was enough.

So as she sat slumped one night in her New York apartment

numbing herself with mindless TV, it took her a few minutes to tune into the Harvard professor who was being interviewed about the emerging science of positive psychology and happiness. The idea that researchers were trying to discover an evidence-based roadmap for consistently flourishing in life soon had her bolting upright. Could this be what she'd been unable to figure out?

In the weeks, months and years that followed, Michelle devoured all the research she could find and even completed her Masters of Applied Positive Psychology under the field's founder, Professor Martin Seligman. And slowly, but surely, as she began to apply everything she was learning, the colors in her life started returning. She discovered her strengths—the things she was good at and actually enjoyed doing—and began to find more ways to weave these into her work. She learned to make peace with her voices of self-doubt and instead discovered what it was to feel truly confident. And she began to realize the small changes she could make to maintain the kind of energy and vibrancy that she'd been craving. Far more than simply being happy, she found the courage to show up whole-heartedly through the highs and lows that are a natural part of every life.

As a result, Michelle's career took off to new heights. She went on to negotiate roles that were better aligned with her sense of purpose; she was given unexpected promotions and pay rises whilst managing to keep every Friday free to play with her pre-school aged kids. And when she was ready to start her own business teaching the skills she'd learned to others—although she'd never been so scared in her life—Michelle found that the positive psychology skills she's discovered have made it possible to keep putting one foot in front of the other.

Of course, that doesn't mean it all goes perfectly. She's still human, and there are days when the work could be delivered better, she could be a more patient and attentive mother, and when she wants to devour a glass of wine and box of chocolates. There are also days when she's needed to help a sibling to recover from a serious drug addiction, a friend to finally escape from an abusive relationship, and when she has had to bury people she has loved. But instead of feeling like she may forever sink under the weight or endlessly berate herself about not being good enough, she's come to appreciate that even the darkest moments of life can bring lessons of light, if we're able to be open enough.

We share these stories with you so you can see the real journey, not just the glossy one. As you work your way through this book, you may feel the story creep in, "well it's OK for *them* to do what they do, but I *could never* live my dream." We hope that by sharing a little of our path and some of the obstacles we have faced, you will see that we are just as real as you are and have had perhaps many of the same challenges around finding our purpose, overcoming self-doubt, creating wellbeing and balance, and showing up with grace. And by doing so, give you the hope that you can create the career, life and leadership success that you long for.

So after all of that, just how did we come to create *Lead Like A Woman*?

Lead Like A Woman

A year and a half after Michelle left the corporate world, and six months after Megan did, we were sitting in a café in Carmel, California, before heading off on a writing retreat. Drinking our hot chocolates, warmed out of the cool December Cali weather, we had an idea. In reality, it was more an explosion of a decade's learning, experience, repressed frustration, and illuminating vision of how things could be different for women at work. As you can probably see from our stories, we had lived first hand what it's like working in male dominated businesses as young hot shot women itching to make a difference; as still young managers swimming through the sea of politics, expectations, deadlines and budgets as we managed big teams with even bigger requirements; and as female executives sitting around board room tables filled with middle-aged men, most with good intentions, but little idea how to really help a woman succeed in an environment built by men, for men.

We knew there had to be a better way. What if, we thought, we built a leadership program for women that took them on a holistic journey that not only showed them the science of how to lead and manage themselves effectively, but ignited the spirit as well? What if we could construct an experience that would shine a light on the forces shaping a new wave of leadership that would change the game for how women show up and the opportunities they have when they do? What if we could take the still relatively new science from positive psychology and combine it with neurobiology, gender science, behavioral economics, and wellbeing practices, to literally teach a new model for how we work, live, and lead? What if we took the work we had been doing in our executive roles for the past few years around Positive Leadership, with everything else we knew, to really make a difference? And what if we could create a joyful, heartfelt, and soul-stirring quest for women at all stages of their careers to make, whatever comes next, seriously life changing?

And with those thoughts, in our cozy café in Cali, *Lead Like A Woman* was born.

About the book

This book is about enabling women to lead, but not in the traditional way we have come to know. Our mission is to enable women to lead like women. To stand in their power, to show up authentically and to shine on their own terms. That may sound lofty. It may sound soft. It may seem impossible from where you currently sit, or for where your organization is right now. And it may seem ludicrous as you look around you and see scores of women leading anything other than authentically. After all, they don't have the permission, the role models to demonstrate what this would even look like, or a roadmap to follow. So how can they?

That is what this book is all about. Laying out the roadmap, shining a light on role models, and demonstrating what authentic, confident, vibrant leadership for women can be. Of course, you don't need to be anointed a leader to lead. Everyone has the capacity for leadership, irrespective of where you currently sit in a business or organizational structure. And this journey is as much about leading yourself as it is about leading others. So wherever you find yourself is exactly the right place to begin this exploration of who you really are and how you show up, in your career, your life, and your leadership.

Trust us: we get it. We don't just talk about research and develop these women—as you can see from our stories—we were these women. Which is why we are here, writing this book and doing this work, to make it better for all of us. We have now been working in the leadership development and women's personal and professional empowerment space for more than a decade. First through our corporate executive roles and then through our own businesses guiding thousands of women through the *Lead*

Like A Woman journey. As you will see as you get into the content of this book, this journey is a unique one: a powerful roadmap creating a new leadership paradigm designed for women, but that also includes men and those we all lead.

The journey to create the roadmap has been as interesting as the content. As we started to work and play with our methodology many years ago, and witnessed the way women responded to and used the teachings, we started to see a very clear and consistent path emerge. There was a particular way that women were applying the teachings that deepened not only the learning, but also their ability to make real life changes. And what they were doing was sticking and sticking like glue.

If you have ever been through leadership development, or in fact, development of any kind, you will know how all too rare this is. More often than not, you sit in a training program for a day or two, and no matter how interesting you find the content, in a few weeks you are back to your existing patterns of behavior and the class content is all but forgotten.

In the years of working with the *Lead Like A Woman* journey, with thousands of women, the exact opposite of that normal pattern has happened. We have seen women having incredible a-ha moments, playing with certain concepts and theories with dramatic outcomes and journaling answers to the questions we pose, just like in this book, that have completely changed the way they show up not only in their work life but in their personal life as well. And no matter how much we believe in the content and the journey map, even we have been humbled and stunned with the outcomes.

Part of that is the content itself. The unique blend of science and spirit, research and practice, on which this journey is founded.

Part of it is the fusion of positive psychology, neuroscience, leadership development, gender science, behavioral economics, and wellbeing practices that we have integrated in a truly groundbreaking way. But it's not just the pieces of content that matter. The way the journey is designed is of vital importance as the themes build on each other and uncover an ever-deepening level of understanding of self and how we are in the world. Whilst the contents of this book do not have to be followed in a linear manner to understand or appreciate each component, it is desirable for the best results.

The other part of it is the soulful journey you are about to embark on. Through weaving the spiritual and the inspirational together with the science, we have created an experience that not only engages your mind in a rational and pragmatic way, but that also gets you connected somewhere way, way deeper. For some, this is on an emotional level and for others; it's somewhere deep down in your soul. Either way, it's a place that we don't often talk about or mention in the confines of our business and working lives, but that we are so desperately longing for and insatiable for when we finally get a taste of it. And it's a place we trust you are excited to get to.

The Lead Like A Woman journey

Let us frame the journey you are about to embark on. In chapter one, we step into the world of authentic leadership. Just what does new leadership look like? The rise of feminine traits in business is a phenomenon that will not only change how we as women lead but in how business is done. We share with you the exciting research about the future of leadership, and look at just what it takes to *lead like a woman*. We explore gender mindsets and the concept of presence, both of which influence how you show up in your leadership and career. And finally, we look at the choices you have around just how you will lead.

In chapter two, we will close the confidence gap. Let's face it from speaking up in a meeting, to putting ourselves forward for a new role; from offering an alternate perspective in the boardroom, to negotiating for a pay rise in our performance review, the limiting stories and beliefs that many women struggle with impacts everything we do. Rather than trying to blame, shame or tame your self-doubt we'll show you how you can leverage your strengths, befriend your inner kind girl, reframe success, and align your mind and body to feel truly confident.

In chapter three, we will journey into your life vision, purpose, and career through the lens of your personal brand. Whether you've intentionally shaped your brand or left it to chance, the reality is that we're all known for something, and this impacts everything from your career to your ability to live the life you're most wanting. So together we're going to get clear on your life vision, what gives you purpose, your career plan, and what this means for your personal brand. And we will lay the path for the critical relationships—from your mentors, sponsors, and wider networks—you'll need to realize your career and leadership goals.

In chapter four, we will explore the tested ways you can mindfully maintain your wellbeing. It is really hard to show up as an authentic leader without the vibrant energy that comes from looking after yourself, body, mind, and soul. We will leave the hype behind and take you through what the science says, as well as many stories of what it actually takes to be well, to be mindful and to leverage busy-proof ways to get to consistently thriving. We can't wait to see you on the other side of this work, healthy, radiant, and truly flourishing.

And then in chapter five, we will show you the latest findings and practices from the science of grit, that ability to persist toward long terms goals you are deeply passionate about. We will help you to improve your resilience by understanding the upside of stress and introduce you to the power of grace and ease so you can leave behind your drive, strive, and push through mentality. And we will teach you how you can use flow and focus in equal measure to achieve a career and life that perhaps you hadn't dared conceptualize.

Finally, in chapter six, we close with our visionary view of what organizations need to do to truly support and engage you on your leadership journey. We'll take an honest look at why the conversation on gender equality has become stuck in so many places, and propose a new way we can all collectively move forward. We'll give you the tools you need to create lasting change for yourself, your team, and your workplaces. We'll even show you how to start your own revolution.

The tools

As we set out to create this book, we wanted to ensure that it wasn't just interesting to read, but that like our programs, it provided real, actionable tools that you can reflect on and implement to support your journey. We know that reading can be exciting and informative, but the real change happens when you take action. So we encourage you to not only read and enjoy the writing, but to also do the work so you can realize the outcomes you are truly seeking.

In each chapter you will see some common themes:

- *Playsheets:* You will see throughout the book at the end of many sections there are what we call *playsheets*. These are coaching questions that will support your inquiry process. We encourage you to buy a journal and work through each question in your own time. You will see the reference to www.leadlikeawoman.net/bookplaysheets throughout, where you will find all the playsheets and resources we mention available for free download (use the code LLAWPLAY referred to in the back of this book). Feel free to share them with others.

- *The key ideas:* The brief section at the end of each chapter summarizes the core themes from each section you have been through. Use this as a reminder, a refresher, and to further embed the key ideas.
- *For you:* As a woman reading this book, this section highlights key actions you can take to move to deeper levels of understanding, along with tools and resources for further learning.
- *For leaders:* We recognize that as well as individual women reading this book, many leaders will also be on this journey. This section poses questions for leaders to think about, in how to apply the concepts from each chapter for women in their teams.
- *Reflection questions:* In the final part of each chapter you will find a number of questions for reflection, that you may wish to use for journaling to further discover the true, the good, and the possible in each area of focus.

The invitation

Our invitation for you as you read this book, think about the questions we ask and reflect on the teachings we highlight, is this: *What will you do with it?* It's easy to read a book such as this and say to yourself "I already know that" when in fact, you may consciously know it, but you aren't actually doing anything with it. It's very easy to dismiss new ideas, new thoughts, or indeed a new paradigm, for fear of what it will mean if you actually absorb it and take it on board. That would mean making a change. Real change.

Perhaps changing your beliefs, the stories you tell yourself about how you lead or indeed who you follow. Perhaps taking a real and honest look at the traits you embody, where you are leading with your masculine traits, and where the feminine may or may not be present. Looking at what is really serving you, and how you may be helping or hindering those around you. And taking a broader view on the impact you could truly have, if you had the courage to show up authentically, with grace, taking full responsibility for your career, your life, and your leadership, and choosing to lead your way.

Dr. Brené Brown, best-selling author of books *Daring Greatly* and *Rising Strong*, and research professor at the University of Houston Graduate College of Social Work says, "You can have courage or comfort, but you can't have both." As you read this book, we invite you to think about what path you are taking. Will you remain comfortable, attached perhaps to your current ways of thinking and behaving? Will you sit in a mindset that things just are the way they are and you can't change them, or yourself? Or will you go with courage, and embrace the chance to embark on a new journey of leadership that will help you achieve things you had never imagined possible for yourself?

We hope you choose courage. We hope that you come into this journey with an open mind and an open heart. That it helps you become more of who you really are, and get more of what you truly want. And we hope that in ways beyond what you can see today, it helps you step into your authentic leadership power, and to truly lead like a woman. We are here to support you every step of the way. And there are thousands upon thousands of women and men all around the world, who are right this very moment, rising up with courage beside you.

Let's begin.

1

Being An Authentic Leader

What would it be like to show up for work every day bringing the very best of yourself to your role? Imagine going through your day tomorrow feeling fully engaged, alive, passionate, and invested, not only in the work you were doing but in how you were doing it.

What would it feel like to have the freedom to lead exactly like you long to, using all of your unique strengths and talents, and being valued for them? And imagine having both the permission and the ability to throw off the cloak, remove the mask, and step out of your leadership shadow, stepping into the light of who you are longing to be in the world.

Just imagine.

This is why we are here. This is why we are on the *Lead Like A Woman* journey. And this is exactly why we are starting the journey with a discussion on authentic leadership.

It is what it is . . . or is it?

There is so much talk in and around organizations today about women and work; diversity and inclusion, the number of women in leadership positions, the talent pipeline, the gender pay gap, flexible work, parental leave, unconscious bias, targets, quotas, off ramps and on ramps, leaning in, and the list goes on. The volume on these discussions has been turned up so loud in recent years that it's hard to believe there is any actual work going on, or that women have the time or energy to concern themselves with anything other than this debate and drama with their place in the world.

Websites, magazines, and newspapers are constantly blaring the latest report, article, book, comment or cover story on the statistics of how bad things are, or how much worse they're going to get. About how little progress women have made. About how much discrimination there is in the workplace, and just how terribly bad we, as women, have it. And by default, how the men are out to hold us back, so you better watch out! It's enough to make you want to hide under the bed and stay there until the next millennium.

To illustrate just how convoluted and confusing the current discourse can be, let's look at one of the most common narratives—stemming from a large body of research that exists in the gender and psychology spaces—the correlation between likeability and success for women. Now we could have chosen any number of topics that also have significant bodies of research and rigorous debate to illustrate our point, including the ambition gap, unconscious bias, issues of confidence, and many others. But for the sake of brevity and your sanity, we will demonstrate our point with just one hot topic.

For more than a decade, one of the most visible gender workplace discussions has been about the "fact" that women can be either competent or likeable, but never both. Research on the dynamics of warmth and competence from psychologists Susan Fisk, Amy Cuddy and Peter Glick among others, paint a daunting picture of what it can be like for women at work when it comes to subjective perception and the impact that has on employability, succession, and leadership.

It appears that we are constantly judging each other on two core facets of human behavior; how warm we think you are, and how competent we think you are and can be. The first is important because we are trying to assess if we can trust you or not, and therefore whether we should stay or flee. The later is important so that we can determine whether you are capable of doing what you say you will. These decision points dramatically shape our human bias and have significant consequences when it comes to the workplace, particularly for women.

From research in multiple countries and with thousands of people, the researchers have found that women are held to a higher standard than men when it comes to being able to hold both warmth and competence perceptions, and they are typically inversely correlated for women, meaning that when you are viewed as one, you are automatically counted out for the other. These judgments, of course, lead to stereotypes, which for women land us primarily in one of two categories; competent but cold, putting us firmly in the *too bossy, too aggressive,* and *what a complete bitch* category; or the *warm* and *likeable* but *incompetent* category, which often happens for women when they become working mothers, and can lead to a lack of opportunities due to perceived capabilities and being too nice.

Competence stereotypes lead to fear and envy while warmth perceptions elicit pity. Both lead to discrimination. Think of the new mother returning from parental leave who instantly receives the paternalistic prejudice experienced by warm but incompetent groups, *traditional* types of women, she is treated affectionately, but her efficacy is undermined which impacts her future viability for roles, promotions, and hot jobs. Or the older female worker, senior in rank, exceptionally competent and decidedly *non-traditional* as far as gender stereotypes go, who elicits social backlash for her perceived coldness and suffers forms of discrimination and exclusion because of it.

These biases that stem from the reported likeability/success matrix for women at work, and the rampant dialogue that exists around it, ripples through organizations and shows up in pervasive issues such as the gender pay gap, how we need to *fix the women*, how women should dress and speak, the need to address the ambition gap, unconscious bias and many other diversity discussions and programs. It contributes to many women holding a mindset that their gender is a liability and a hindrance, not just for their likeability and competence, but also for their career success in general. And that mindset is a major problem that shows up practically in talent pipelines, succession plans, and the lack of women around boardroom tables.

But what if that entire body of research and a decade's worth of discussion was not entirely accurate? What if we, as women, have become firmly embedded in a particular mindset around our gender and its limitations based on stories that were not completely true, out of date, or just not relevant to many of us? It's a fascinating question to ask because asking it could change everything about how you show up, how you work, how you lead, and what's possible for your career.

So, consider this: There is another body of research starting to emerge, which suggests that the research around warmth and competence, or success and likeability for women, may not be entirely accurate. Contribution to this discussion is particularly compelling from Jack Zenger and Joseph Folkman of Zenger/

Folkman, a leadership development consultancy that looks at analysis from thousands of 360-degree reviews analyzing peer, subordinate, and manager feedback. Their research shows that women actually rate higher than men on twelve out of the sixteen competencies that impact effective leadership, including all of the questions that point to likeability. They also show that women become more likeable the more senior they become, whereas men take a likeability hit as they move through the ranks.

So there's that.

And in her new best-selling book, *Presence: Bringing Your Boldest Self to Your Biggest Challenges,* Associate Professor Amy Cuddy from Harvard Business School, one of the researchers mentioned previously, suggests regardless of gender we can actually be viewed as both warm and competent. The key she suggests is the presence that comes from being acutely attuned to our most sincere selves so we can be honest, genuinely connect with others and fully represent our abilities. It's what synchronizes our thoughts, physical and facial expressions, and behaviors, so people feel safe with us. It's what enables us to communicate with passion, confidence, and comfortable enthusiasm whilst still owning any nerves that we might have. It's the medium through which trust develops and ideas travel. More on that later, but for now, it all adds to the question of how valid the previous research findings are for everybody.

It's also interesting to think that one of the leading voices in this current narrative that women can't be both likeable and successful is Sheryl Sandberg, COO of Facebook and author of, *Lean In: Women, Work and the Will to Lead,* which has become the greatest phenomena in the women's leadership space in decades. We have the greatest respect for Sandberg. We agree with her on many (but not all) aspects of her work, and we are grateful that she has planted gender equality firmly where it belongs, in the center of the popular discourse about what our workplaces need to look like for women to thrive.

But we can't help but note the irony; even though she didn't author the research studies, here is Sandberg arguing so strongly for the case that women can't be both warm and competent, or liked and successful when she herself has both covered in spades. From her TED talk to her *Lean In* movement, her articles in the *New York Times,* to appearing on stages all over the world as the face for her revolution, and particularly as the second most powerful person at Facebook, she is well liked, and from all objectives measures, highly competent. So clearly, there are outliers, many of them, that completely disprove the research and show that maybe we can pull it off, this being a woman, being successful and not being a hated thing. Go figure.

Kind of makes you want to scratch your head a little right? Here's the thing: When it comes to the "facts", we know it's not all bad for women. We know that just as one research report tells you that women lack ambition and need to be fixed if they aspire to leadership, that another report is going to declare there is no science to the ambition gap, and everything is just fine. We know that one report will say we are making great progress in the talent pipeline while another says that no progress has been made at all. We know that you only have to look around you, in your workplace, the media, and at high profile leaders to see a swath of senior women, who are actually both likeable and competent, have no shortage of ambition and have successfully climbed their way to the top. And we know that for as long as there is any discrepancy in the numbers of women and men in leadership roles, that this dialogue in its various forms will continue— and according to the World Economic Forum, that will be for the next 117 years—so you better buckle in for the long haul.

So in our minds, and those of many other researchers, there is a big question mark over the discussion about how gender holds women back. In many ways it all comes down to which part of the conversation you want to buy into.

Why does it matter? Because it directly influences how you show up, how you view your capability and the trajectory of not only what you believe you can achieve in your career, but the way you feel in it as well. So we want you to consider this: If you are currently sitting with one of the above belief sets, perhaps that you can't be both successful and likeable, we want you to open yourself up to the idea that perhaps the information on which you have based your mindset may not be completely accurate. That even the best research only tells us what works for some of the people some of the time. That there may be other facets that haven't been widely measured that can explain what is going on. And that there may, in fact, be a mindset that could serve you better as you show up to be the kind of leader you want to be and to have the kind of impact you hope to have.

Now before we get on to the next section, we want to be clear that we are not for one moment suggesting that there aren't real and formidable challenges for women at work, particularly for those women who, like we did, aspire to leadership roles. As we've already shared we both worked in some of the biggest multinational companies in the world, all male dominated, and in multiple countries including Australia, China, Japan, Singapore, India, France, the Middle East, Germany, the United Kingdom and the United States. We have lived through the realities, the struggles, and the barriers that women can face. We are also researchers, and have studied in depth the hundreds, if not thousands, of reports across the spectrum of workplace issues. And we are leadership development teachers and coaches, having worked directly with thousands of women in the trenches of business and government. So we fully appreciate that there are real challenges for women at work and in getting to parity for women in leadership and assure you that we aren't writing this book with blinders on.

But what we are very conscious of and what we would like to instill in you as you continue this chapter is this: Regardless of which version of the research you believe to be true, or even if you see truth in both points of view, *you have a choice* about where you invest your energy in the current discourse, how you absorb the statistics, and what you choose to do with the public narrative about women and work.

So the question we'd love you to ponder is, which mindset will you choose for your career, your leadership journey, and the world in which you live?

What's your gender mindset?

Alia Crum a psychologist at Columbia University, has one thought that sits at the center of, and motivates, all of her research: How you think about something can transform its effect on you. Said another way, the effect you expect is the effect that you get. She has tested this theory in all manner of research subjects; from highly active hotel housekeepers who, when primed to consciously see their work as exercise rather than straining physical activity, lost weight and became healthier; to people undergoing a shake tasting study who, when drinking the exact same milkshake but primed to believe it was a decadent full fat indulgence, experienced significantly different effects on their hormone and satiety levels than when they thought it was a low fat shake.

Crum's provocative hypothesis is that when two outcomes are possible—in the first case above, the health benefits of exercise or the strain of physical labor—what a person expects directly influences the outcomes they will wind up with. In both studies, the effect most participants expected was exactly the effect they got. And profoundly, absolutely nothing else changed in the experiments other than their mindset.

So what does this mean for gender and what exactly is a gender mindset? If you think about mindset as the filter through which you view life, that is based on your beliefs about how the world works and is shaped by your experiences, then you can begin to see how the gender mindset you choose can impact how you show up at work, and the outcomes you're able to achieve. As our mindsets get activated—by a memory, a situation you find yourself in, or a remark someone makes—it sets off a cascade of thoughts, emotions, and goals that bias how you respond to life. It's quite important then to be intentional and mindful about the choices we're making.

In our workshops, programs, coaching, and corporate leadership development programs, as well as our own personal experiences, we have come to see that there are three primary mindsets that determine how women view their gender and its impact on their careers.

Mindset 1 – Gender is negative. This mindset is rooted in the belief that being female has negative consequences on your career, makes it harder to progress, and limits leadership success. This mindset buys into and perpetuates the findings of all the research studies that report how hard it is for women to get ahead. The bias is negative. Thought patterns include:

- I am limited in my ability to succeed because I am a woman.
- Gender norms and stereotypes negatively impact how I am perceived.
- At work I must fit into expected and often male modes of behavior to get ahead.
- I will be paid less and given fewer opportunities to progress.

Mindset 2 – Gender is neutral. This mindset is based on the belief that your gender has no impact on your performance at work, ability to progress or leadership success. This mindset simply does not see gender as an issue, making the bias neutral. Thought patterns can include:

- I succeed on my own terms.
- I don't buy into gender stereotypes or their impact on how I am viewed.
- My work environment has the same impact on me as my male counterparts.
- I don't believe my gender has any correlation to the opportunities available to me.

Mindset 3 – Gender is positive. This mindset is based on the belief that being female is actually a benefit in the workplace, and that inherent female character traits are of great value to work, leadership, and success. These traits are seen as an asset, not detraction, to positive workplace outcomes. The bias is, therefore, positive. Thought patterns include:

- My natural feminine traits and characteristics are strengths to be valued.
- I'm not limited by gender norms and being a woman is an asset.
- At work I do not need to fit in or change myself to comply with male modes of behavior.
- My gender enhances the opportunities available to me at work.

Of these mindsets, from both the research and our own observation, we see that *Mindset 1 – Gender is negative*, is the most common. Given where we started this chapter, relaying that the current narrative and discourse around women and work is full of statistics and opinions about how hard it is for women to succeed at work, this is not a surprise.

We also find a large number of women in *Mindset 2 – Gender is neutral.* Megan found herself in this mindset for a large part of her career, pretty much blind to the fact that being female had any consequences, negative or positive, on her ability to succeed at work. She worked hard and played by the rules of the businesses she was in and rose through the ranks swiftly and seemingly with ease. It wasn't until she hit senior management and got a real taste of what it's like to be a female leader in staunchly male dominated workplaces, that she started to see that perhaps things weren't so gender neutral after all.

Michelle, on the other hand, who had a similar and speedy rise to the top, found herself more in *Mindset 3 – Gender is positive.* As she recounts when we have this discussion, for a large part of her management journey in one of the world's largest professional services firms, she was well aware that both her gender and her feminine traits were assets in many ways that helped her career. She intentionally drew on these—even when male leaders told her that she was too nice to succeed—to carve the path she most wanted.

Mindsets are not black-and-white truths about the world. They are based on evidence, but they are also stances we choose to take toward life. Having a mindset that acknowledges that your gender can be an asset does not discount that there may also be very real challenges in your workplace. You don't need to talk yourself out of the gender imbalance you might see at work; you're simply choosing to put your focus on the opportunities you also see because of your gender or in yourself. The mindset shift that matters is the one that allows you to hold a more balanced view of the impact of gender in the workplace—to fear it less, to trust yourself to handle it—to use it as a resource for engaging with life.

Mindset over matter

Greg Walton is a psychologist at Stanford University, who has spent the last decade researching how you effectively alter people's mindsets. Whilst most of us might think that to change someone's mind you need lengthy and detailed programs, Walton has found that you can actually alter someone's mindset with one brief intervention, often not lasting more than an hour. One of the main ways he does this is by offering up an alternate perspective to an issue, working out how that applies for the person in question, and testing the mindset shift over time. Pretty simple, and often with profound results.

When we run our *Lead Like A Woman* program in a face-to-face workshop, we begin with exactly this kind of mindset intervention. In the workbooks the women receive, we have a list of one hundred character traits on a page. We ask the women first to think about and mark the traits they believe are most required for leaders in their organization and to share their observations in small groups. Typically they select traits such as driven, ambitious, dominant, independent, focused, and arrogant.

We then share the research we will cover shortly that shows which of these traits have been classified by 32,000 people all over the world as masculine, feminine or neutral, irrespective of whether they are embodied by a man or a woman. They take a few minutes to absorb this new knowledge. As this sinks in, we observe them exchanging knowing looks and rolling their eyes as they realize most of the traits they believe are required for leaders in their organization are masculine. And yes, we even see some actual scoffing, as if to say, "Yeah, well that's pretty clear isn't it!"

Then we ask them to think about the *best* leaders they have worked with; the leaders who, regardless of gender are the most effective and have had the greatest positive impact on them directly. Looking at the list with fresh eyes we see the women mark down traits such as nurturing, empathetic, collaborative, intuitive, and caring. This time, we see the look of surprise, wonder, and realization on the women's faces. Most of them had never for a moment thought that the most effective leadership traits amongst the men and women they admired were *feminine traits*. A few minutes before, that seemed almost implausible. As we will see in the research, this realization of the women is not unique to them, because in fact, most people say that these are the traits they want in their leaders today.

Finally, we ask the women this question; how could these traits apply to you and your leadership style? This is where the mindset shift really starts to come in. For the majority of the women, they have never even entertained the thought that these feminine traits, things that are inherent to their gender, could actually be an asset that could help them be better, more effective and yes, more authentic leaders.

As these thoughts sink in, the energy in the room shifts. The walls come down. The women noticeably relax, open, and soften. They breathe more deeply and exhale more fully. And our work then really begins.

This simple exercise of reviewing the value of feminine traits and reflecting on how they can leverage these to be effective leaders is enough to start shifting the mindsets of the women. But the effects are not just short term. When we have checked in on the women more than a year later, they are still showing up in *Mindset 3* and believing that their gender was a significant advantage to their work, leadership, life, and success.

Tuning into your mindset

The first step in working effectively with your mindset to support your journey is to understand where you are currently. Think about these questions, and work your way through the following process as a journaling exercise, which you can download at www.leadlikeawoman.net/bookplaysheets:

- Firstly, start to notice your thoughts and beliefs around how your career and leadership style is influenced by your gender. Just like a habit, the thoughts you have can be so ingrained in your everyday life that you don't actually see them as a choice, or that you can change them. Start to be mindful by looking at how your current gender mindset shows up in your work and life.

- Begin to notice how you think and talk about being a woman. Do you go through your day with no thoughts popping up about your gender and its impact on your work, placing you in the *Mindset 2 – gender is neutral* category? Or do you notice yourself throughout the day having limiting thoughts around being a woman at work, or perhaps even gender positive thoughts? How do these thoughts make you feel? Do they bug you, energize you, or exhaust you?
- Start to look for gender mindsets in your workplace and in the relationships you have. How do you react to other women, or even men, at work when you notice their gender mindsets showing up? When someone gets promoted or lands a spot on a hot project, do you find yourself having gender related thoughts as a contributing factor in their success?
- What are the messages in your workplace about gender, and how you are supposed to act because you are a woman? Look for the obvious signs in policies or programs, but also the more submissive signs in language and subtext. How do you feel about what you witness? Once you start actively seeking out gender mindsets, as we talk about in this chapter, you will see them everywhere.
- Openly journal about your observations, thoughts, feelings, and frustrations about what you have noticed in the outside world, as well as your internal narrative, about gender mindsets. Note the impact these gender mindsets are having

on how you show up at work and in life. Are they serving you well or are they holding you back?

A new kind of leadership

The research we referred to earlier reveals unequivocally that what people want from their leaders today is changing, and changing dramatically. And the good news is, women have never been better placed to lead, as we transition from an old style of leadership based on command and control, short term thinking and aggression, to one that is more in tune with feminine sensibilities of relating and empowering, sustainable thinking, and collaboration. In fact, we are wonderfully wired to do so.

But let's start with where we are so you can get a full grasp of the current leadership issue. If the loudest alarm bell of the past decade, blaring that the world was in leadership trouble was the global financial crisis of 2008, the World Economic Forum (WEF) is calling out a forward-looking warning sign. Each year the WEF asks its Global Agenda Council Members to identify the issues they believe will have the greatest impact on the world over the coming twelve to eighteen months. They generate the Top Ten Trends, which is a forecast of the social, economic, and political flash points that reside on our collective horizon.

In 2014, *lack of values in leadership* was number seven out of ten on the list, and more specifically, the kind of values in leadership was stated as a primary concern. That was troubling enough. But turn to the 2015 report, which calls out *lack of leadership* as number three on the list, with a shocking eighty-six per cent of respondents agreeing that we have a leadership crisis in the world today. From a business perspective, only twenty-three per cent of survey respondents have confidence in leaders of international organizations to effectively implement the mandate of their organization.

When the World Economic Forum declares that there is a global crisis of confidence in leadership today, you know we have a problem. The time for incremental change has long come and gone. New leadership is no longer a nice to have: It is now an imperative. And women have a staring role to play in this new future.

The rise of the feminine

Coming out of the global financial crisis in 2008, researchers John Gerzema and Michael D'Antonio were writing the book *Spend Shift: How the Post Crisis Values Revolution is Changing the Way We Buy, Sell, and Live*, analyzing what the *new normal* behaviors were as the economic and social dust was settling. As they were working on their research, they noticed a trend forming that they hadn't expected and couldn't quite articulate (certainly not in research or data terms). Many of the behaviors they were witnessing were what people were referring to as feminine traits. Deciding that they wanted to explore this in an analytical way, they embarked on an ambitious research project for their next book, *The Athena Doctrine: How Women and the Men Who Think Like Them Will Rule the Future,* which explores the rise of feminine skills and competencies and their impact on leadership, policy, and innovation.

In the research, they asked 64,000 women and men in thirteen countries to classify 125 human traits; half of the sample by gender and the other half by which traits were most important to leadership, success, morality, and happiness today (these were the same traits we give to the women in our workshops). The countries they researched represented sixty-five per cent of global GDP and included Brazil, Canada, China, Chile, France, Germany, India, Indonesia, Japan, Mexico, South Korea, the United Kingdom and the United States. What they found was pretty exceptional and perhaps surprising considering the male dominated cultures of many of these countries: people consistently picked what they considered *feminine traits* or values—such as selflessness, empathy, collaboration, flexibility, and patience—as the most important traits for leadership.

The majority of people researched also rejected masculine notions of control, aggression, and black-and-white thinking notions that traditionally underlie many of our business, political, and social structures. In their survey, eighty-one per cent of people said that man or woman, you need both masculine and feminine traits to thrive in today's world, which is a massive global values shift. And the headline of the research that grabbed our attention when we first read it, and that stuns audiences when we present it, is that two-thirds of people thought the world would be a better place if men thought more like women.

As a woman reading this book, just think about the reality of what this research may mean. For as long as we can remember, feminine traits have been undervalued, dismissed, and have had no place in our work environments. Leading with intuition, kindness, humility, and empathy has up until now not been encouraged for women in many organizations and absolutely contributes to the prevalence of *gender mindset 1* as we covered earlier.

But there is a significant and world changing shift taking place right now. A shift that is not only acknowledging the value of our natural, inherent and authentic feminine traits and how they serve both leadership and the greater good, but that is also blatantly stating, by men, women, and the next generation, that a balance of the feminine and masculine is what the world needs to actually thrive. If there were ever a permission slip to step fully into who we are, and to own our authentic power as women, this is it.

The WEF report we visited earlier also looked at what traits were needed, by raising the question: What kind of skills do our leaders need today to address the issues we face in the world? They identified these key virtues: A global interdisciplinary perspective; long-term, empirical planning; strong communication skills; a prioritization of social justice and wellbeing over financial growth; empathy; courage; morality; and a collaborative nature. Can you see the pattern emerging? Again feminine traits—such as empathy and collaboration over dominant and self-reliant; long-term planning over short- term financial gain; and a focus on humanity and wellbeing, not just profits—are emerging as the ascendant traits for great leadership.

And in case you needed even more evidence (and perhaps permission), for the value of feminine traits, consider a recent study from Stanford Business School, that examined the promotion rates of 132 MBA graduates over an eight year period following graduation. The researchers found that women who can combine masculine and feminine traits effectively did better than everyone else, including the men. These women were promoted 1.5 times more often than most men, twice as often as feminine men, three times as often as purely masculine women, and 1.5 times as often as purely feminine women.

The path is being laid. For so long women have felt forced to either take a back seat due to their feminine traits or entrench themselves in masculine traits in order to move forward, fitting a model of leadership and into a workplace culture, that seemed to value them in isolation. What we are now seeing, what is becoming glaringly obvious, is that the way for women to truly thrive at work and in their lives, is to honor themselves, celebrate their own strengths, define their own meaning of success, and get to work on their own terms.

Being authentic leaders

What this all points to, in case you missed it like we did for a long time, is a giant big permission slip for you as a woman to finally show up authentically. To bring your full self to the table. And to stop trying to twist yourself like a pretzel into what either the market, your company, or your boss thinks you should be.

Being authentic at work has been found to fuel optimal levels of self-esteem, to help us feel friendly towards others, to elevate our performance, and to improve our wellbeing. But it's not just good for us. It appears that when we act on our true values, beliefs, and strengths, it helps others to do the same, improving the wellbeing and performance of our teams. And it's why our feminine traits are valued so highly.

We can get all tied up in empirical research and mythical conversations about what the authentic self is and what that means for how you lead authentically. But we won't do that here. By all means go and read *Jung* and search the research logs if you want to go there. But for our purposes, all you need to know is that being authentic means showing up as who you truly are. No cloaks, no masks, no leaving parts of your self at the office door each morning. It's just about being yourself, without excuses or apology, and having that be more than enough. Because it is. And you are. And it's how the world needs you to lead.

Leading with presence

As we read earlier, Cuddy believes that the best way for us to step into our authenticity and personal power is through cultivating more moments of what she calls *presence*. As she articulates: "Presence is the state of being attuned to and able to comfortably express our true thoughts, feelings, values and potential. It emerges when we feel personally powerful, which allows us to be acutely attuned to our most sincere selves. It's what makes us compelling. We are no longer fighting ourselves: we are being ourselves."

As you think about how you want to show up as a woman, as a leader, and what authentic leadership may look like for you, we want you to consider your own presence. Presence is what allows you to approach stressful situations without anxiety, fear, and dread and leave them without regret, doubt, and frustration. Instead you can go forth, knowing that you did everything you could. That you showed people who you really are. That you showed yourself who you really are.

The good news Cuddy assures us is that we all have moments of presence. The challenge, however, is that most of us don't yet know how to summon that presence when it escapes us at life's critical moments. You can work on becoming more present by: Identifying the values, traits, and strengths that represent your authentic best self; believing these stories even when threatened by self-doubt or perceived social judgment; showing up and genuinely connecting with others in ways that make them feel safe. It is confidence without arrogance, courage even in the face of fear, and connection without the need to control.

Megan discovered the power of presence first hand as an executive at an international technology company, when she was asked to advise the CEO and her general management peers on the best approach for building a more positive culture and improving engagement for 15,000 employees. It didn't take her long to realize that their best hope was to harness the cutting edge science of positive psychology that she'd been playing with personally for some time, but she also knew that her predominantly engineering minded peers were likely to be highly skeptical. After all the company culture was very conservative, leadership development was driven from corporate headquarters in New York, and they were in the middle of a spending and training freeze.

Drowning in self-doubt and worried about what her fellow GMs would say afterwards, the anxiety and uncertainty Megan experienced leading up to this presentation was almost enough to make her shelve the idea entirely. It would have been so easy for Megan to recommend a safer option and slip back into her old, masculine, dominant style of leadership as she did. But she knew she owed herself, her CEO, her colleagues, and every other employee in the company the opportunity of showing up to work more authentically.

By reminding herself of her values, her strengths, and her belief in this approach, instead of stepping into the meeting feeling overwhelmed by dread, she confidently presented her recommendation. She was present, able to listen, and felt no need to defend what she was proposing. Knowing that she'd done all she could to make the idea stick, the subsequent approval of her idea and more than half a million dollars in funding for the pilot round of positive leadership development were an important lesson about what's really possible when we step into our power and presence.

Being our most authentic selves works. Think about the questions below from Professor Laura Morgan Roberts an organizational behavior professor and widely recognized expert on the ways people develop positive, authentic identities on the job. Work your way through them as a journaling exercise, which you can download at www.leadlikeawoman.net/bookplaysheets:

- What are the stories you tell about who you are at work? Just for a moment violate all the norms of humility and think about the times at work when you were really growing and developing into your full potential, when you were engaged in virtuous actions, and when you felt good about yourself, and were validated by others. Who are you when you're at your best? Try to create at least three concrete, specific examples of the experiences that have felt *natural or right* and how they have led to your success at work.
- Based on these stories what three words best describe you as an individual?
- What do these stories suggest is unique about you and that leads you to your happiest times and best performance?
- What are the attitudes, beliefs, and behaviors that enable your best self at work?
- What are the attitudes, beliefs, and behaviors that block your best self at work?
- What changes would you like to make in your current role, relationships, and future career plans to help you consistently be more of your best self at work?

Leading with vulnerability

Seth Godin legendary business thought leader and major ruckus creator said this: "Everyone you interact with is changed forever. The only questions are, how will they be different, and how different will they be." Think about how profound that statement is. The way you choose to show up each and every day, regardless of the position you hold, impacts not only your life but also the lives of everyone you come into contact with.

This doesn't mean that in order to be a good leader you have to have all the answers. Or even that you should pretend to. In fact, research suggests that great leaders do exactly the opposite. For example, Dr. Brené Brown, who we met earlier and who is one of the world's leading researchers on authenticity, has found that one of the critical components for great leadership is the willingness to be vulnerable with others.

Of course, vulnerability is far easier to read about, than it is to do. After all vulnerability is the first thing we look for in others and generally the last thing we're willing to show. In others, it's courage and daring, but in us it often feels like shame and weakness. Showing up and genuinely being seen for all our worthiness can be tough. Being real takes courage.

It also makes us more relatable and trustworthy. Being vulnerable means rather than needing to always be the expert, that we can ask questions when we don't know something; instead of trying to do it all, that we can ask for help when we're struggling; and when things go wrong, that we're willing to ask for feedback, take accountability and learn from it. When you allow yourself to be seen for the strength and struggle you really are studies have found people at work may feel closer to you, be more willing to share advice, and your team may begin to feel more horizontal. Brown has also found that vulnerability is the birthplace of love, belonging, joy, courage, empathy, and creativity.

As leaders, vulnerability requires us to own how we're feeling, to be attuned to the emotional landscape of others, and to be willing to sit in the discomfort this can bring. It means accepting that uncertainty, risk, and emotional exposure don't need to be outrun or outsmarted. It means consistently choosing what is courageous over what's comfortable. Perhaps this is why Godin suggests that if we're not uncomfortable in our work as a leader, it's almost certain we're not reaching our full potential.

Brown suggests that vulnerability starts with the willingness to be honest about what gets in the way of being our most authentic selves at work. What's the fear that holds us back? Where and why do we want to be braver?

Then she recommends figuring out what's our armor? Are we hiding our true selves behind perfectionism? Intellectualizing? Cynicism? Numbing? Control? While this armor feels like it's keeping us safe, it's actually shielding us from the chance to feel truly worthy of connection. So what if you put it down for a moment? What if instead of feeling the need to protect yourself, you accepted that we are each imperfect, but wired for struggle, learning and growth, and absolutely worthy of being respected, valued and loved? And by the way, in case you were wondering, this all means that you are good enough, just as you are, right now.

The truth of it is that in work and in life there are no guarantees about the outcomes that we'll achieve. Instead of striving for perfectionism or worrying about what others might think, great leaders allow themselves to be truly seen. It is their courage to be imperfect that makes them both authentic and effective.

We invite you to reflect on what we have covered in this section and what it could mean for you as an authentic leader; a new vision for leadership that embraces feminine traits and empowers women to lead as women; an approach to gender mindsets that frame our beliefs about how we show up and the actions we take when we do; a new concept called presence that teaches us to focus less on what other people think of us and more on what we think of ourselves; and finally the power of vulnerability and having the courage to express it.

Think about the questions below and work your way through them as a journaling exercise, which you can download at www.leadlikeawoman.net/bookplaysheets:

- On a scale of one (not at all) to ten (absolutely) how comfortable are you with truly being vulnerable and seen for who you are at work? Try to be as honest as you can with yourself.
- How does this willingness to be vulnerable impact your work and your relationships? How does it impact your ability to lead others?
- What gets in the way of being your most authentic self at work? What's the fear that holds you back? Where and why do you want to be braver?
- What's your preferred armor when you want to hide your true self at work? Perfectionism? Intellectualizing? Cynicism? Numbing? Control? What might this be costing you in terms of opportunities for genuine connection or learning?
- If instead of feeling the need to protect yourself, you accepted that we are each imperfect, but wired for struggle, learning and growth, and so absolutely worthy of being respected,

valued and loved, could you put down this armor in the areas you want to be braver? If you truly made peace with the idea that imperfection simply means you're learning like every other human being on the planet, could you accept that you are perfectly good enough? If this feels like a big ask, what could you do to experiment with these ideas and see what unfolded?

- What is one small way you could start allowing yourself to be seen more authentically at work?

If thinking about the kind of authentic leader you really want to be has left you feeling slightly nervous, don't despair. Brown notes that in fifteen years she's not met one transformational leader who did not do discomfort. Leadership she suggests is about choosing to do what is courageous over what is comfortable. So if you're feeling a little vulnerable or afraid about what's ahead, know that you are exactly where you're meant to be, and that in the chapters ahead we give you everything you need to navigate the highs and lows of your journey to authenticity.

The key ideas

- Everyone has the capacity for leadership; no matter what your role or your place in an organization. The *Lead Like A Woman* journey is as much about leading yourself as it is about leading others, and you can start from where you are right here, right now.
- The discourse around women and work, including whether women can be both likeable and successful, can impact women's mindset and behavior at work, in their careers, and how they lead.
- We all have a gender mindset that influences the lens with which we see the world, and how we show up in it. Whilst there are three identified gender mindsets, we can flex and change where we sit on that continuum to better serve us.
- Research shows us that what the world is seeking from leaders is changing, and feminine traits are ascendant in what people want to see in leadership today. Women are uniquely placed to leverage their feminine traits to embody new leadership styles.
- Presence is what allows you to approach stressful situations without anxiety, fear, and dread and leave them without regret, doubt, and frustration. Instead, you can go forth, knowing that you did everything you could. That you showed yourself and others who you really are.
- One of the critical components for authentic leadership is the willingness to be vulnerable with others. When you allow yourself to be seen for the strength and struggle you really are, studies have found it makes you more relatable and trustworthy and that it is the birthplace of love, belonging,

joy, courage, empathy, and creativity.

Leading you

- How authentic do you feel in your current leadership style? Reflect on how much you feel like your true self at work each day, and where you might be putting on a mask, and why.
- Where is your current gender mindset? Think about the aspects of the three mindsets we have outlined and look at where you are on the continuum. Is this where you are thriving or do you need to make some adjustments? Reflect on the questions posed in that section and get the worksheet at www.leadlikeawoman.net/bookplaysheets.
- What mix of traits are you showing up with right now? Head to www.leadlikeawoman.net/bookplaysheets and download the feminine and masculine traits worksheet to identify which traits you are using now, and where you might like to make some adjustments to feel more authentic.
- How do you feel about the concept of *presence*? Can you identify the values, traits, and strengths that represent your authentic best self; believe these stories even when threatened by self-doubt or perceived social judgment; and show up and genuinely connect with others in ways that make them feel safe?
- How vulnerable are you willing to be? Can you accept the idea that being imperfect means you're learning like every other human being on the planet? Can you make peace with the belief that this means you are perfectly good enough? What can you do to allow yourself to be more authentically seen by others at work?

- How do you want to lead? Journal on the traits and qualities you want to embody as the most authentic version of yourself, and what you need to do to show up like that each and every day.

Leading others

- How does your leadership style encourage or discourage your team members from showing up as their most authentic selves? How authentic are you in the way that you lead? How can you encourage your team to feel safe to show up as the most real versions of themselves?
- What gender mindsets do you witness in your team and organization? Is gender seen as a limiting factor for women in your business? Is this perpetuated through the cultural narrative? What are the gender norms for both men and women in your team? Reflect on where you sit as a leader in the gender mindsets, and which ones are prevalent throughout your team and peer group.
- What mix of traits are evident in the leadership style of your team? Do you skew more toward the masculine, or are the feminine traits we have seen in the research encouraged and rewarded? What can you do as a leader to acknowledge and reward a balance of traits that are shown to be more effective in sought after leadership styles?
- Host a roundtable or virtual session with your team to facilitate an open leadership dialogue. What do they need to bring more of their authentic leadership to the fore at work? How can you better support them to bring their best selves to work? And how can you better demonstrate what true authentic leadership looks like so that you can role model it for your team?

Reflection questions

- Think about a high-point moment—a time that is particularly memorable and stands out—when you really felt like you were showing up authentically at work and achieving great things as a result. It might be a big or small moment, recent or a while ago, it doesn't matter. Just take yourself back to the last time you really felt you were being true to who you are at work, and when it was serving you well. What were you doing? What was making it possible for you to show up authentically? What were you able to achieve as a result?
- If you were able to have more authentic leadership moments like this at work each day what would the months ahead look like? What beliefs would you be investing in about the impact your gender has at work? Which feminine or masculine traits would you be leveraging? How would your sense of presence help you navigate challenging situations? How would your willingness to be vulnerable improve the joy and trust you experienced with others?
- If there was one small thing you could do in the next one to two days to start being a more authentic leader, what would that be?

2

Closing The Confidence Gap

Confidence. Sometimes we have it . . . and sometimes we don't. We didn't know whether to be relieved or dismayed when we started hearing the confessions of women who look like they've got this whole confidence thing sorted, only to discover that deep down they were struggling just like the rest of us. When the German Chancellor, Angela Merkel, or the head of the International Monetary Fund, Christine Lagarde admit that their feelings of self-doubt have them exhaustively preparing and over preparing so they feel completely on top of everything, what hope do the rest of us have?

The truth is we're in good company. Fifty per cent of female managers and thirty-one per cent of male managers admit to feelings of self-doubt. But with a growing body of research finding that when it comes to our success at work confidence is more important than competence, you won't be surprised to learn that finding ways to feel authentically confident is the next step on our *Lead Like A Woman* journey.

What confidence really is and why it matters

At this stage in our workshops, we ask the women to introduce themselves to as many people as they can like they believe confident men do at work. With no further instruction needed, they're quickly moving around the room with hearty handshakes, backslapping, and loud laughter. In room after room when we debrief this exercise, they observe that these introductions feel transactional, impersonal, and rushed, as they try to appear assertive, decisive, and commanding.

Then we ask them to introduce themselves to as many people as they can like they believe confident women do at work. Again, with no further instruction they start slowly moving around the room—in fact, most of them struggle to meet more than one person this time—looking into people's eyes, nodding intently, and asking in-depth questions. When we debrief this part of the exercise, every room acknowledges that these introductions felt warmer, slower, and more connected, but that they met fewer people. What every group observes is that confidence in women often looks different than it does in men.

One of the biggest challenges we've found is that many of us mistakenly believe that confidence requires us to behave like assertive jerks, demanding we get what we deserve, talking over the top of other people, and dismissing ideas that aren't our own. While this behavior may sometimes work, it's not actually what's required for confidence. Instead, researchers are finding that confidence is simply the ability to turn your thoughts into action. It's what allows you to start acting, and risking and failing, and to stop mumbling and apologizing, and hesitating. With it you can take on the world; without it, you remain stuck on the starting block of your own potential.

It's not actually bravado, but their ability to turn their thoughts into action that allows so many of our male colleagues to willingly risk their careers on new challenges, confidently ask for more money, and gamely put themselves forward for promotions even when they're not quite ready. And the lack of confidence is also why despite now being more educated than many of our male colleagues, women generally ask four times less frequently for pay rises, negotiate salaries of thirty per cent less, and won't put ourselves forward for promotions unless we meet one hundred per cent of the qualifications necessary for a new role.

Why we struggle with confidence

But if confidence is as simple as turning our thoughts into action, why do we hesitate and hold ourselves back at work more frequently than our male colleagues? Why do we find feeling confident so challenging? These are some of the questions researchers are still hotly debating. Some researchers chalk this up to biology, noting that while the brains of women and men are vastly more alike than they are different, there are some variances in structure and chemistry that encourage unique patterns of thinking and behaving that may affect confidence.

For example, not only does it appear that women may have thirty per cent more neurons firing at any one time which can lead us to overthink things, but the cingulate gyrus, the brain's *worry wart* appears to be larger in women making us much better at recognizing our mistakes and ruminating about them. Add to this the generally higher levels of estrogen and lower levels of testosterone coursing through our veins, and it's no wonder we're prone to avoiding conflict and risk, even at the cost of winning.

Yes, it does seem there may be good biological reasons why we lie awake at 3 am in the morning still going over the tiny passing criticism someone made days ago and why we have a tendency to over-prepare for things. But are we really just victims of how our brains are wired when it comes to confidence?

Other researchers argue that our lack of confidence is also shaped by our social experiences. Let's face it, for most of us, school is where we were first rewarded for being good and doing things the right way. This usually involved quietly figuring things out and finding the perfect answer, whilst not making a fuss or being challenging. The result is that studies suggest women often learn early on in life to avoid taking risks, making mistakes or stirring things up, while men (for whom one study found got eight times more criticism for their conduct as boys than girls do) learn that a little scolding, failure or debate can be taken in stride.

It's not just inside the classroom that we seem to learn different messages about confidence. While girls are six times more likely to drop out of team sports as teenagers, boys keep playing. This gives boys the opportunity to learn how to own victory and survive defeat; with some studies even suggesting this experience explains a direct link between playing sports in high school and later earning a larger salary. It appears to be a vicious social cycle: as girls we lose confidence, so we quit competing, thus depriving ourselves of the development opportunities that would help us to discover that failure is an important part of learning.

Add to this the social experiences we may have encountered at home, (don't be too bossy) and at work, (don't be too nice but don't be too assertive) and it's easy to see why we start to hesitate, hold ourselves back and dim ourselves down, rather than confidently turning our thoughts into action. No wonder we wind up hoping that competence will matter more than confidence.

And then, of course there's the way we look. Researchers have found that at every age the physical appearance of women plays a disproportionate role in building our confidence. And who can blame us when studies suggest that while overweight men can be seen as powerful, savvy, competitive, and intelligent, overweight women are often deemed less organized, less competent, and lacking in self-control. Mind you we also don't make it any easier for ourselves. Not only are women far quicker to criticize our own physical appearance than men are, but only two per cent of us are actually confident enough to describe ourselves as beautiful.

Can our confidence be improved?

While it's tempting to simply shrug our shoulders and blame all of these obstacles when we don't do the things that matter most to us, it would be misguided. Yes, our genetics, our schooling, our upbringing, our looks, and our society have all been found to impact our sense of confidence, but so have our own choices.

For example, when Zach Estes at the University of Milan, asked five hundred male and female college students to solve a series of 3-D spatial puzzles, the women scored measurably worse than the men. No surprises here, after all, it's generally accepted that women aren't as good at math. But when Estes reviewed their results, he realized it was actually because many of the women hadn't even tried to answer the questions they weren't completely sure about. Rather than confidently take an educated guess, they simply left them blank.

So Estes asked the students back to complete a similar test, insisting students answer every single question. This time, the gender stereotype vanished. Both the men and women scored an average of eighty per cent, suggesting identical ability in this area of math. When the women were forced to turn their thoughts into action, they were every bit as capable as their male colleagues.

Curious about the potential for confidence to be manipulated, Estes decided to ask the students to take a further test but this time, after each question they were required to note down how confident they felt about their answer. Now the women's scores fell to an average of seventy-five per cent while the men's rose to ninety-three! One little nudge was enough to rattle our self-doubts causing us to underestimate our abilities and start performing accordingly.

Unfortunately, Estes' results aren't unique. Numerous studies across multiple industries suggest women often judge their own performance as worse than it actually is, while men judge their own performance as better than it actually is. When asked to evaluate themselves, female medical students also gave themselves lower scores than the male students, despite faculty evaluations showing that the women outperformed the men. And despite comparable credentials, potential male political candidates are sixty per cent more likely to think they're very qualified to run for political office.

Finally, Estes decided to see what would happen if confidence was boosted at the outset. Students, both men and women, regardless of their previous results were randomly selected and told how well they'd done on the other tests, and how much the researchers were looking forward to seeing their next results. This time anyone, regardless of gender, who had been primed to feel confident, improved his or her scores dramatically. This series of studies is a fascinating example of how confidence can fuel our beliefs, shape our choices, and impact our performance, for better or worse.

Should we rid ourselves of self-doubt?

Clearly if we just stopped doubting ourselves and fearing that we're imposters, then confidence would easily flow forth. Well perhaps. It's true that self-doubt can make it difficult to turn our thoughts into action, but nature has wired our brains with these uncomfortable feelings for the practical purpose of guiding our behaviors. For example, self-doubt can help motivate us to prepare and work hard to deliver our best performance. It can help us to avoid making the kind of mistakes associated with too much self-confidence. And it helps to keep us humble and open-minded.

Feelings of self-doubt are not in themselves the problem when it comes to improving our confidence, but like any emotion it's our ability to know when to embrace it and when to move past it, that is the key to shaping our success and wellbeing. Researchers have found that self-doubt becomes unhealthy for us when we:

- Become defensively pessimistic in an effort to avoid taking on new challenges.
- Procrastinate and try to put things off.
- Sabotage ourselves so we can logically blame our failures on other factors—like "I'm so hungover no wonder my presentation was terrible"—in an effort to protect ourselves from really trying and failing.
- Drive ourselves to overachieve in an effort to prove ourselves wrong and risk burning ourselves out.
- Suffer from the imposter syndrome and feel unable to accept praise for our efforts because we don't believe we really deserve it.

Now if you're reading this list and having an "oh sh*t" moment, let us assure you once again that you're in good company. The good news is that awareness is the first step to changing any pattern.

What can we do to improve our confidence?

After interviewing leading researchers around the globe, best-selling authors Katty Kay and Claire Shipman of *The Confidence Code,* concluded that confidence is within reach for women if we choose to practice being authentic, think a little less, and regularly take action. What neuroscientists call plasticity—our brain's ability to change over time in response to new patterns of thinking and behaving—they call hope. But why would these practices make a difference?

As we observed in authentic leadership, confidence comes from playing to your distinctive strengths and values, whilst allowing for vulnerability when needed. We can listen to others opinions, without apologizing for our own. We can ask for help, without undermining our own abilities. We can be focused, and still be approachable. We can interact with confidence and presence in any setting when we get comfortable with who we really are.

We also saw earlier that the female brain is wired to overthink things. We replay our mistakes, cling on to criticism, catastrophize about small challenges, and over prepare the simplest things. Ruminating drains the confidence from us, so it's important to rewire this thinking pattern and know when it's time to draw a red-line under negative thoughts and move on. Instead of running ourselves down with stories about why we're not good enough, perhaps we need to try a little self-compassion and start talking to ourselves like we would to a friend.

And finally, it seems nothing builds confidence like taking action, especially when the action involves risk and failure. Turning our thoughts into action means stepping outside our comfort zone, opening ourselves up to learning, and discovering that sometimes failure provides our greatest lessons. Each time we choose to do one small, brave thing, the next time it gets a little easier and soon confidence begins to flow.

Discovering your strengths

One of the things that has surprised us most in our programs, is how often women feel that bringing their true selves to work would limit their careers. On the one hand, this fear is understandable; after all, most of us have either been given explicit feedback or received implicit signals that our softer sides are best left at home. But on the other hand, how do we really expect to find roles that are enjoyable and sustainable when we leave behind some of the best parts of ourselves every time we step into work.

This was a big part of how Michelle wound up so unhappy in her role in New York. Having thought being the global brand director for one of the world's largest firms would be the job of her dreams, you can imagine her disappointment when she realized that having finally climbed all the way to the top of her career, she was professionally and financially handcuffed to a role that was draining away her energy, her creativity, and her confidence. Looking for a quick win to restore some joy in her work, when Michelle first started researching the field of positive psychology she found that one of the most promising approaches was to develop our strengths—the things we're good at and actually enjoy doing. Why might this work?

It turns out that our strengths represent our patterns of thinking, feeling and behaving that when exercised excite, engage, and energize us, and help us to perform at our best. In fact, a growing body of research over the last decade is finding that when it comes to our careers developing our strengths is good for: Our wellbeing, helping us to feel happier, less stressed, more energized, and satisfied with our lives; our performance helps us to feel more confident, to experience faster growth and development, and to find more meaning in our work; and for the bottom-line with people in strengths-focused teams reporting lower turnover, increased productivity, and higher levels of customer satisfaction.

How to work with your brain

You can test this for yourself. Grab a pen and write your first and last name with your dominant hand. If you're right-handed, you'll use your right hand, and if you're left-handed, you'll use your left hand.

When you've finished, swap the pen into your non-dominant hand—the hand you don't usually write with—and write your first and last name once more.

Notice any differences?

Provided you're not ambidextrous, chances are you found writing your name with your dominant hand fairly easy. You didn't have to think too hard about it; it didn't require a lot of effort, and you were probably reasonably happy with the result. But if you think back to when you were at school and first learning to write your name, it probably wasn't quite so effortless. This is because each time you perform a behavior the cells in your brain called neurons are lighting up and talking to each other and initially they struggle to get the messages through—in this example to hold the pen and create the shapes that form the letters of your name—with everything else going on in your head.

Somewhere along the way though a teacher made you practice writing your name over and over again, causing these cells to wire together into neural pathways that made it more efficient and effective for these messages to be carried through your brain and executed. You've probably heard the phrase "neurons that fire together, wire together" and this is exactly what it means. This is why your strengths represent the way your brain is wired to perform at its best.

Of course, the same process also underlies your weaknesses. You might have noticed that when you went to write your name in your non-dominant hand that it took you a little longer, it required more concentration and effort, and you probably weren't as happy with the results. This is because you've not yet built the neural pathways to support this behavior. And while neuroscientists have discovered that your brain's natural plasticity means you can absolutely take a weakness and turn it into a strength, it's important to be realistic about the effort and commitment this might require. In another area of research still being hotly debated, some researchers suggest that it may take you as many as 8,000 to 10,000 hours of practice to really master an area of weakness. To put that number into context that would be a couple of hours, every day for about eight to ten years!

The challenge when it comes to developing your strengths, is that your brain is also wired with a negativity bias that makes you much better at spotting your weaknesses and feeling an evolutionary pull to fix them, than you are at spotting your strengths and finding ways to build upon them. This is why when you observe your successful male colleagues, instead of valuing your differences you fill yourself with stories of self-doubt about whether you're really good enough. It's why organizations and their leaders tend to give us feedback and invest their resources in trying to *fix* us, rather than capitalizing on the diversity we bring.

Some studies even suggest that in most workplaces people spend around eighty per cent of their time focused on fixing weaknesses, and only twenty per cent of their time trying to build upon strengths. But as we continue to learn more about how people and organizations are wired to perform at their best, the recommendation is that we should be trying to reverse this equation and focus far more of our energy and efforts on doing what we each do best.

Now let us be clear here: We're not for a moment suggesting that being more authentic at work gives us a license to ignore our weaknesses. Authenticity starts with knowing ourselves, the strong, the weak, and everything in between. It becomes a way of being and fuels your presence when you're able to understand how to genuinely show up in different situations to achieve the desired results. This means knowing which strengths to draw upon and how much of your strengths might be required. It also means knowing when to own your weakness and how to harness these vulnerabilities. So how do you figure this out?

How to do more of what you do best

Unfortunately, it appears that many of us are blind to our strengths. While you may have no problem listing off your weaknesses, the ability to name our top five strengths is something most of us struggle with. And we were no different. Beyond the technical talents that had gotten Michelle stuck in a job she didn't want, she had no idea what her strengths were, the first time she sat down to try and imagine what might be possible if she spent more time at work building on what she was good at and actually enjoyed doing.

Fortunately, over the last decade increasingly robust tools have been developed to help us identify our strengths. For example, if you want to better understand your talents—the *what* you do in your job—then you may want to complete Gallup's StrengthsFinder (www.gallupstrengthscenter.com). If you want to better understand your character strengths—the *how* you like to work—then you may want to complete the free VIA Survey (www.viainstitute.org). Both tools require you to complete an online survey that provides you with a ranked list of your strengths and generally researchers recommend that your top five strengths—often referred to as your signature strengths—will feel most like your authentic self and are what you should particularly focus on finding ways to develop at work.

We've found each tool can be incredibly helpful, but the one that often sheds the most light on how we can be more authentic at work, without having to immediately quit our job is the VIA Survey. This is what we use in our programs. Created by fifty-five social scientists who spent three years scouring the world's religions, philosophies, ancient history, and modern culture for universal, measurable, and buildable examples of humanity at its best. The character strengths they identified like *perseverance*, *curiosity*, *teamwork*, *bravery*, and *love* are all aligned to the values that you hold. These are the things you'll do whether anybody pays you or recognizes you for them because you believe this is how you should show up in the world. And because they're focused on the kind of experiences that engage and energize you, we've found they can be incorporated into any role, no matter what your job description says and without needing a word of permission from your boss.

But how are you going to use a strength like *love* at work without getting fired for it? The generic descriptions that come from any of the strengths assessment tools can leave you scratching your head about how the different strengths could be valued in your job. To make the results more meaningful, in our programs we ask the women to think back to the last time they were really engaged, energized, and enjoying their work. As they begin to describe what was happening, the kind of work they were doing and what they were able to achieve as a result, it starts to become easy to spot the strengths they were using and how they're being drawn upon in other parts of their work.

Fuelled with the confidence and enthusiasm this new insight brings, we find the temptation is for people to want to rush back to work and simply begin using their strengths more. After all, the research says this will finally make everything so much easier and more enjoyable. And what could go wrong if you were using more *honesty*, *humor*, or *hope* in your job? Let's just think about that for one moment. What could go wrong if you used your top five strengths—the ones that feel truly authentic—to help you do everything at work?

At this point in our programs, we ask the women to raise their hands if their strengths have ever gotten them into trouble. And very, very slowly hands go up around the room. Usually, it's those with the strengths of *honesty* who raise their hands first.

Of course! Then people with the strength of *humor* will all have a story about where they've made a joke at the wrong time. And finally people with the strengths of *kindness* and *love* feel like they're giving and giving to everybody else until there's nothing left for them.

The truth is we all overplay our strengths some times. These are the moments when you feel like everything should be coming together at work, but it's just not quite going to plan, or other people don't seem that happy with your efforts. They're the times when you're working so hard you're on the verge of burning yourself out. And in our experience, they're often what underlie most of the *weakness* feedback you've ever been given.

The first time Michelle took the VIA Survey she had a big *a-ha* moment about how she was overplaying her strengths at work. For the previous three years, three different bosses, had given her the same feedback about her performance: "You're doing a great job, but at times you're doing too much and going too fast." What? Surely everyone else just needed to get it together and speed up! In truth, she had no idea what to do with this feedback. She worried that like riding a bike too slowly, she might fall off and be unable to keep doing a "great job" which kept getting her promoted. So she did what most of us do with feedback about weaknesses we don't know how to fix, and put it in the too hard basket.

Michelle's first VIA Survey results listed *zest*—energy and vitality—as her number one strength. As she reflected on ways this strength showed up in her work, she noticed how when she was really excited about an idea this incredible surge of energy would propel her into action at a hundred miles an hour. While this had lots of advantages, it also meant that sometimes she forgot to take her team or colleagues with her and unintentionally created issues around buy-in and trust.

What if the feedback she was being given wasn't about fixing a weakness, but instead was about dialing back a strength she was overplaying? What if, in these moments, she dialed back her zest and instead used her strengths of *hope* and *gratitude* to bring people with her? Motivated and confident about finding better ways to develop her *zest* strength in different situations, not only did Michelle's colleagues heave a sigh of relief but the outcomes she was able to deliver improved dramatically.

Of course, there is also the possibility that at times you might be underplaying your strengths at work. If you ever feel yourself leaning away from opportunities, procrastinating and putting things off or dragging yourself through parts of your job, then the chances are there are strengths you're not using as intentionally as you could. We know when we're underplaying our strengths because the same task starts to show up day after day on our to-do lists.

Finally, we've found it helpful to be aware that sometimes our strengths collide with others. For example, when Michelle had to work on a project with a leader who was renowned for being a bit of a stick in the mud, her strength of creativity took a real battering as every idea was met with a swift and resounding "No!" As the relationship became more and more awkward, in desperation she started trying to find the strengths in this man (after all supposedly we all have them). It actually took no time at all for her to realize that every time this guy spoke about sticking to the timeline, balancing the budget or delivering a milestone, he lit up suggesting that *prudence* was one of his top strengths.

And suddenly everything made sense. Michelle's strength of

creativity and his strength of *prudence* were colliding repeatedly on this project. Every time she suggested a new idea, he saw it as a potential threat to keeping the project plan on track. It turned out that he wasn't actually trying to be difficult; he was just playing to his strengths. By being able to see how their strengths were colliding, Michelle found that not only was the personal sting removed from their encounters but also she could actually start to respect what he was trying to achieve. Of course, this didn't mean she loved having her ideas knocked back, but it did help her pitch them in ways that made it clear they could be accommodated without throwing the plan into disarray.

So our advice is; don't use your strengths like a blunt instrument and just try to do more of what you do best at work. If you want to feel truly confident, use them like the intelligent tools they are and start really tuning into the moments when you're using your strengths well, and when you're overplaying or underplaying what you do best. Notice how some strengths cluster together, what you can do to develop the lesser strengths that may be important to you, and how your strengths collide with others. And start making mindful choices about the strengths that will serve you best in different situations and for different outcomes. This is the kind of self-awareness that truly enables us to be authentic in our jobs.

Putting your strengths to work

Take the free VIA Survey at www.viacharacter.org and then print out the questions below from www.leadlikeawoman.net/bookplaysheets and record your answers to them.

- When you review your VIA Survey results take a moment and tune into how you feel about them.

- Do you feel satisfied with the picture your results are painting? If yes, your challenge will be finding ways to develop your strengths more consistently at work.
- Are you wondering why certain strengths are rated differently than you expected? If yes, your challenge will be finding ways to use the strengths you value but may not be developing regularly yet at work.
- Do the strengths not feel at all like you? If yes, check in with colleagues, friends, or family who know you well and ask where they would rate your strengths. Use their feedback to determine the most accurate ratings for you.

If you're unclear on what some of the strengths are download Michelle's free ebook on the VIA Strengths for more detailed descriptions on how they show up in people jobs at www.michellemcquaid.com/ssas/ebook.

- When you're ready, think back on some of your high-point moments—those times that are memorable and stand out—when you've felt really engaged, energized, and enjoying what you were doing at work. What *exactly* was happening in each of these moments? What were you doing? How did you feel? What makes this moment so memorable? And, most importantly, which of your strengths were you using (there may be more than one strength in play)?
- Then think back on those times when you missed an opportunity at work because you lacked confidence, feared failure, or procrastinated for too long. What *exactly* was happening in each of these moments? What were you working on? How did it feel to hold yourself back? What might it have cost you or your team? And, most importantly,

which of your strengths might you have been underplaying in these situations, which if dialed up could have got you a better outcome?

- Now, think back on those times when despite putting in your best efforts things seemed to keep misfiring, people didn't appreciate what you were doing, and you may have almost burned yourself out. What *exactly* was happening in each of these moments? How did it feel to be working so hard and yet still be unable to deliver the results you wanted to or be appreciated for your efforts? What did this cost you personally and professionally? And which of your strengths might you have been overplaying in these situations that, if dialed back, could have helped you get a better outcome?
- Finally, think back on those times when despite your best intentions you've really struggled to work well with someone. Who are the people that come to mind? Which strengths do you think they may have been using (for a strength spotting table visit www.leadlikeawoman.net/bookplaysheets)? How might these strengths have collided with any of your own? How might this knowledge have improved your relationship?

If you're struggling to find your strengths in these moments, ask someone who knows you well to look at your survey results and share their answers to these questions. It can also be helpful to review any development feedback—formal or informal—you've been given in the past to see if you can spot where you've used your strengths well and where they may need balancing.

What does this mean for your weaknesses?

Does being more strengths focused mean that you should just ignore your weaknesses? After all 8,000 to 10,000 hours of practice is a lot of time, energy, and effort. Should we just leave the things we don't do well in the too hard basket or tackle them head on? If you've spent most of your career trying to inch your way toward perfection, you might want to be sitting down for this next bit. It turns out that perfectionism is not the key to success. In fact, research suggests that perfectionism hampers achievement, and is correlated with depression, anxiety, addiction, life paralysis, and missed opportunities. So could it be that owning your weaknesses might actually be the very opportunity you need to get comfortable with vulnerability and all the benefits that it brings?

Rather than striving for perfection, it appears we do better when we open ourselves up to healthy growth. This means being honest with yourself about the weaknesses you possess. It means letting go of the perfectionist belief: "I am what I accomplish and how well I accomplish it." Only then will you be able to own what you don't do well and make informed choices about how to deal with it. As you get clear on what your weaknesses are you may find that you can minimize these requirements in your role, that you have a colleague who can complement what you lack, or that as a team you can start finding ways so that each of you works more to your strengths each day. And if none of these approaches are possible, and you're really willing to do the work, then by all means tackle the weakness head on to gain at least a basic level of competence. Just be realistic about the time and effort it may take to really see the results you want.

After becoming clearer on her strengths, Michelle finally felt safe enough to admit that she was naturally far more task-focused than a people-focused leader. Her strengths were generally all about getting the job done, rather than tuning into the people around her. And while this approach had been OK on her way up the management ranks, her inability to consistently bring out the best in the people around her suddenly became a real weakness in her global leadership role.

In the short-term, she decided the best approach would be to find a deputy who excelled in looking after others. Having found the ideal candidate, Michelle was open and honest about why she was keen to add these strengths to the team and for a while this strategy worked well. In the long-term though, she decided being unable to really connect with people and build good relationships wasn't what she wanted for her career. So little by little she invested in training and practice to begin building mastery in her area of weaknesses. Eight years on and in her VIA Survey the strength of *love* has moved from being ranked at number twenty to number one.

You can learn how to practice being vulnerable with your weaknesses by printing out the questions below from www.leadlikeawoman.net/bookplaysheets, sitting with them and asking others for their insights:

- What are your weaknesses when it comes to your work and the career your hoping to have? If you're struggling to identify them, the Realise2 Strengths Profiler (www.realise2.cappeu.com) is a helpful tool to point this out.
- For the situation you're in and the outcomes you want to achieve, what would be the best strategy for managing these weaknesses? Can you minimize them in your current role, find a complementary partner, and adopt a strengths approach in your team? Do you need to undertake training and gain a basic level of competence or is this something you're committed enough to mastering that you're willing to

do the hours and hours of practice?

- Would it help you to release your need for perfectionism, cynicism, numbing, or controlling if you could be honest about your weaknesses with others? How might your willingness to be vulnerable about your weaknesses help others? What's the best way for you to open up this dialogue so that you can be authentic? When will you begin?

Recognizing that we'd probably be better served by letting go of our perfectionist beliefs, openly owning our weaknesses and confessing that we're on a journey of self-development is often easier said than done. For many of us, it requires letting go of life long behaviors that we believed were protecting us and driving us forward but now realize may have been carrying a high personal and professional cost. In our experience, the leap from knowing to doing requires most women to think a little less. So how can we pull this off?

Stories of self-doubt and self-compassion

One of our favorite moments in the workshops we run, is when women realize they are neither crazy nor alone when it comes to the *mean girl* voices of self-criticism that chatter away in their heads. The truth they discover is that their brains are sense-making machines that love it when all the pieces of their world fit together. It's why we are constantly creating stories about: "Why is this happening? And what will happen next?"

What we often fail to recognize is that for better or worse, these stories shape the way we think, feel, and act. For example, when it comes to undermining our confidence, our resilience, and wellbeing, psychologists have found that there are some common patterns to the stories that we tell. Maybe you've heard one, or more, of these stories identified by Dr. Karen Rievich the director of training at the Penn Positive Psychology Center, when things aren't going so well:

- *"I'm not good enough"* causes us to feel embarrassed and makes us want to withdraw and avoid challenges or conversations.
- *"I'm letting people down"* or *"I should never have done that"* causes us to feel guilty, and makes us over correct and be far too nice.
- *"I'm in over my head"* or *"I'm an imposter"* causes us to feel anxious, and makes us panic and over-prepare.
- *"I'm going to be harmed"* or *"That's not fair"* causes us to feel angry, and makes us want to take decisive action, regardless of the consequences.
- *"I'm such a loser"* or *"It's all my fault"* causes us to feel sad, and makes us feel helpless and overwhelmed.

One of Megan's personal favorites, and one we know many women share is the story of "I'm not good enough." So when she was offered a huge and high-profile general management role at the age of thirty-four, in one of the biggest technology companies in the world, her story piped up loud and clear—in fact, it was deafening. It went something like this: "Wow. What are they thinking? Why would they give this really important job to me? I wonder how long it will take before they realize they've made a terrible mistake. This won't end well."

As you can imagine, it wasn't a great start to Megan's new role. Often in the workshops, we also hear the stories of guilt as women try to juggle motherhood and a career: "I'm a terrible mother and a bad colleague. I'm not capable of doing any of this well." And the stories of fear that cause us to strive and drive until we burn ourselves out: "If I work really hard and over-prepare, then no-one will see how much I'm struggling. If I pretend to be perfect, maybe they won't spot that I shouldn't really be here."

Studies have found that while both men and women hear these stories, women are more critical of themselves, and engage in more negative self-talk particularly around our ability to cope. Perhaps this shouldn't be a surprise given the tendency we saw earlier for the female brain to think more, worry more, and do its best to avoid conflict.

The other important difference researchers have found though when it comes to confidence is what we do with these stories. Generally, our male colleagues don't let these self-criticisms stop them from taking action nearly as often because they spend less time thinking about the possible consequences of failure. Whereas these doubts about our ability to cope seem to make women more fragile when it comes to dealing with failure, setbacks, and criticism making it difficult to confidently step forward.

Can you quieten your mean girl voice?

Having come to understand the very real cost to our confidence when we tell ourselves these stories, we find it helpful to label these our *mean girl* voices. After all, we'd never tell anybody else that they "weren't good enough" or "were a terrible mother and bad colleague" or "that they'd better work hard, or people would discover they were an imposter." In fact, most women admit that if anyone heard some of the things we say to ourselves, they'd be horrified.

The good news is we don't have to remain stuck in a loop of heeding our mean girl voice. With more than eleven million pieces of information coming at us every second, and our brains ability to only process forty bits per second, it seems reasonable that most of our stories probably aren't completely accurate and that we tend to overlook some really important bits of information.

Researchers suggest when the stories we're telling ourselves are undermining our confidence, we can constructively challenge them by simply asking: "Is this story true? Is it the only explanation?" When Megan was offered the big general management role and realized her "I'm not good enough" story had her almost running from what could be the making of her career, she paused just long enough to ask herself if there was any other explanation her mean girl voice might have overlooked. Like perhaps, "The people putting me forward for this role are well-respected business leaders, one of whom has managed me for years, so maybe they see something in me I don't see in myself." Or even, "The organization is OK that I'm going to have a learning curve in this role and are happy to support me, because of the other strengths I bring." You can imagine each of these stories caused Megan to feel and want to act very differently from the first story.

The goal in challenging our stories is not to delude ourselves with fairytales. Rather, it's to find equally plausible explanations and to note how each alternative causes us to think, feel, and act. And then to consciously choose to invest our energy in the stories that leave us feeling more genuinely confident. By challenging her story, Megan was able to take the steps she needed to move into the new role with a level of confidence that set her up for success, gain the support of her new peer group and team, and lead in a way that felt authentic.

When it comes to noticing and challenging our stories, Dr. Kristin Neff at the University of Texas, and her colleagues suggest that tapping into self-compassion can help to break our cycle of self-criticism, whilst still allowing us to be honest about our fears. After all aren't you worth the same kindness, concern, and support you'd show a good friend?

Self-compassion allows us to recognize that those mean girl voices aren't really trying to harm us, but in their own limited way are actually trying to protect us. In their misguided attempts to ensure our happiness, they're overly critical and unnecessarily harsh in an effort to get us to act. Instead of taming, shaming or blaming our mean girl voices for undermining our confidence, by recognizing their clumsy attempt to keep us safe, we're able to reduce our levels of stress and anxiety by seeing them for what they are; stories about the things that frighten us, and not the truth about who we are or what we're capable of.

This creates the space for us to start talking to ourselves in our *kind girl* voices. These voices allow us to be supportive and understanding. Less dependent on our performance, these self-compassionate kind girl voices help us to believe we are capable and worthy, making us less self-conscience, less likely to compare ourselves to others and less likely to feel insecure. When they gently help us ask "Is that story true?" the alternatives they enable us to explore contain far less fear of failure and a greater tendency to put opportunities and challenges into perspective when it comes to confidently stepping forward. And they remind us that if all doesn't go to plan, it simply means we're learning, just like the rest of the human race.

It's why studies have found that far from being self-indulgent or soft, the deliberate use of self-compassionate talk is an effective means of enhancing our confidence, our motivation, and our performance. They also seem to help us to generate more positive feelings that balance out our mean girl fears, leaving us feeling more joyous, calm, and confident. Now doesn't that sound like a huge weight off your shoulders?

You can practice getting comfortable with your kind girl voice by practising Kristin Neff's approach of softening, soothing and allowing by printing out the questions below from www.leadlikeawoman.net/bookplaysheets:

- Think of a time at work when you've hesitated, held yourself back, or dimmed yourself down. Describe the challenge you were facing as objectively as possible.
- What were you saying to yourself in the heat of this moment to justify your actions (try to be as accurate as possible, noting your inner speech verbatim)? What was your tone of voice? Can you spot any recurring themes in this story that often come up when you face a challenge or encounter difficulty? Does this voice remind you of anyone in your life, past or present, who is or has been particularly critical of you?
- What emotions did these stories create? How did these emotions shape your actions?
- If someone who really cared for you and with whom you felt safe, heard the story you were telling yourself in this moment how do you think they would have responded? How might they have acknowledged your concerns but then gently helped you explore other equally believable alternatives? What tone would they have used? How might this have altered your story to help you turn your thoughts into action? How might

you have felt and acted after this conversation?

- Was there a difference in the story you told yourself and the story a good friend may have helped you to uncover? If so, ask yourself why. What factors or fears come into play that lead you to treat yourself and others so differently? How can you remember to reach for this kind girl voice in the future?

Do you have a kind girl mantra?

Challenging our *mean girl* voices with self-compassion takes practice. For most of us these fears are so deeply wired into our brains that it can take years to automatically start reaching for our *kind girl* voices. In the heat of a mean girl tirade we've found it helpful to try and take several deep slow breaths, acknowledge what we're hearing and then ask our kind girl voice for her perspective.

Of course, if we're standing at the front of a roomful of people or sitting at a boardroom table in the middle of passionately presenting our ideas, taking the time for a little chat with ourselves (even inside our own heads) isn't always possible and in these moments we find it helpful to note the mean girl story, acknowledge that we'll need to explore this later, and do our best to just stay present in the moment rather than letting it run away with us.

When Michelle first started practicing she found it helped in the heat of the moment when she noticed her mean girl voice emerging to imagine putting it in her back pocket for a chat at the first available opportunity. Megan has developed a purposeful habit of acknowledging the mean girl comment, then placing it in a box, and putting it on a shelf to be unpacked later.

Like any new skill, as we practice it again and again—and boy did we find there were plenty of opportunities—spotting and gently challenging our stories became easier and easier. These days we can switch from our mean girl to kind girl voices in the blink of an eye. This has been helped greatly by developing little self-compassion mantras as recommended by Kristin Neff, that stop our brains from narrowing in and spiraling downward towards feelings of overwhelm, helplessness and despair, and instead enables us to spiral upward towards learning, growth, and confidence.

In Megan's business, she is often juggling between her executive coaching clients, speaking gigs, strategy and advisory work, writing and research. It's a varied portfolio, which she thrives on, but it can sometimes lead to competing priorities and tough deadlines. Her mean girl voice doesn't hesitate to pop up with stories of "told you you're not good enough," or "get ready to fail, no way you can deliver all of that." Pretty brutal. But after working with the kind girl philosophy for a decade now, she can quickly respond with a supportive and heartfelt "you've got this" and "it will get done, it always does." Challenging the negative stories that used to derail her, Megan can now confidently move through these moments, be mindful, and get back to business.

Rather than simply being a positive affirmation, a self-compassion mantra is a reminder in the heat of the moment to be kind to ourselves. It makes it easier for us to soften, soothe and allow so that instead of our negative emotions hijacking our confidence, we can remain present, engaged, and authentic as we navigate our way through what's unfolding.

You can create your own self-compassion mantra by printing out the steps below from www.leadlikeawoman.net/bookplaysheets:

- Imagine talking with someone who really cared for you and with whom you felt safe. What would they say were your best qualities when you're under pressure or dealing with challenges, set backs or failures? Write these down as a stream of consciousness. *Don't over think them. Don't judge them. Don't feel embarrassed by them. Just write them down exactly as this good friend might describe them. Try to have at least seven positive qualities on your page before you stop.
- Putting your humility aside for one moment, as you look at this list can you see the truth in these statements? What evidence—small or large—do you have to explain why your good friend believes these positive qualities exist within you? Note down examples next to each one of when, where or how you've demonstrated these strengths.
- Looking at this list, and accepting that when you're at your best, these statements are true of the person you are capable of being, if there was one reminder in any moment of self-doubt that your good friend wished they could whisper in your ear, what would it be? Write down the first things that come to your mind. *Again don't judge them, just write them down. You may find there is one very clear message, or several phrases appearing.
- If you were to phrase this message in your kind girl voice so it feels authentic and easy to access for you, what would your self-compassion mantra be? How can you remind yourself of this going forward? If you find it needs adjusting as you go, then do so until you have a self-compassion mantra that genuinely brings you comfort and hope in the moments when your mean girl voice is going to town.

*If you have trouble accessing the thoughts of your good

friend sometimes it can help to write in your non-dominant hand (even if it's messy!) to access this part of your subconscious.

We find that for many women, being able to think less at times is the key to helping us get out of our own way, to start seeing what we're really capable of and to holding life just a little more lightly. It's not a change that happens overnight, but it is a change worth practicing as it makes feeling authentically confident much easier.

Unleashing your growth mindset

More than anything else when it comes to improving our confidence, research suggests that taking action is the most important step. And yet it's often at this point in the workshops, when we see the women's faces go a little pale as stomachs start to churn and heartbeats speed up. Even with our strengths and kind girl voices in hand, the idea of truly stepping outside our comfort zone— getting comfortably uncomfortable—each and every day is enough to slow most women down.

It's the kind of feeling you might experience as you stand on the edge of a trapeze platform waiting to leap. Harnessed up and with a net waiting to catch you, you realize that you're meters above the ground with people watching your every move. And while the trapeze bar feels solid and reassuring in your hands, now that the moment is finally here to leap, all you want to do is climb back down that ladder, scurry back to the safety of your home and never, ever talk about this again.

We understand. No matter how prepared we feel, sometimes actually taking the leap into action is still completely terrifying. For example, as she stood backstage waiting to be announced,

Michelle would have done anything to avoid walking out and giving a Pecha Kucha talk to 2,000 people at a recent conference hosted by the Dali Lama. For most of us the idea of delivering a presentation to a group that large would be enough to have us running home. But it wasn't the size of the crowd that Michelle found terrifying, it was the fact that in a Pecha Kucha presentation you have twenty slides, each one automatically timed to be on screen for twenty seconds while you talk, with no way of stopping them. No clicker in hand. No technician to nod at. Once the clock starts, you just have to surrender in front of 2,000 people and trust the process.

Listening to the audience applauding the conference host's introduction of her name, Michelle knew there was only one way out. Despite her white knuckles, it was time to leap. To turn her thoughts into action and walk out on to that stage, put in the best effort she had and accept that whatever happened—good, bad or anything in between—it would be the learning opportunity that she and everyone else in that auditorium needed that day.

When you watch the video of Michelle presenting this talk, her words are perfectly timed to the slides which automatically click forward every twenty seconds. Wanting to make the story she was sharing inspirational for others, she'd had the slides all hand-drawn by an artist and as the slides begin appearing cameras pop up across the audience as people try to capture them. Michelle will tell you that although she was completely absorbed in the moment, her delivery wasn't as playful as she likes to be when she usually teaches.

Would she have loved her presentation to be fabulous on every front? Of course! But did she go home replaying all the words she slightly muddled and berating herself for being too nervous to loosen up and have more fun with it? Surprisingly (even to her), she did not. Although that would have been her instinct in the past, Michelle has discovered that success isn't actually about delivering a perfect result; instead it's about the willingness to show up, to do your best, and to learn from what unfolds.

While that may sound very evolved, Michelle's approach to this isn't really a reflection of her maturity or spiritual growth. Instead, she owes it to the discovery of Professor Carol Dweck at Stanford University, whose research has found that for many of us the key to confidently taking action and ensuring we achieve what we're capable of professionally and personally, is to actually let go of holding the outcomes too tightly.

Do you have a fixed mindset?

We appreciate that at first glance that probably feels completely counter-intuitive. How could focusing less on the outcomes you want to achieve, possibly make you more successful? It might even feel like you're being asked to swing from that trapeze with no net at all. Because if you're not striving, driving, and achieving great results at work, just who would you be? And why would you be valued? We encourage you to take a moment and really be honest with yourself as you sit with this question: "Who would you be and why would you be valued if you weren't achieving great results?"

If trying to answer this makes you feel slightly anxious, unsettled, or even a little annoyed that we clearly don't appreciate that delivering outcomes is what a successful corporate career is built upon, then we'd like to introduce you to what researchers describe as a *fixed mindset.* Underpinned by the belief that we each come into this world with a certain amount of intelligence, talent or ability and there's not a lot we can do to improve it, this mindset causes us to judge ourselves—and others, by the outcomes we achieve.

But when we believe outcomes are the true measure of what we're worth, it has some interesting consequences in the way we go about our jobs. Studies have found that generally: We're less willing to take on new challenges for fear it might expose our weaknesses; that negative feedback and criticism is painful to hear because we don't really think we can do any better; and that failure feels fatal so when we have the misfortune to make a mistake we to try to rush past it, sweep it under the rug or blame something or someone else. And of course in order to do all we can to ensure the desired results, we prefer to keep as much as possible within our control. So if you've ever heard yourself saying, "It's quicker to do it myself," you can say hello to your fixed mindset.

If you're reading this list and having another "oh sh*t" moment like so many of the women in our workshops, let us assure you that a fixed mindset is nothing to be ashamed about and nor does it mean that your career is over. We both spent most of our careers in a fixed mindset, and neither of us did too badly. But at some point for each of us—and perhaps this is where you can feel yourself headed right now—the constant stress and anxiety of trying to keep up with our own success became exhausting and overwhelming. We looked like ducks gliding across a pond, calm and serene on top and underneath each day, it felt like we were paddling for our lives.

The problem with fixed mindsets is they are grounded in fear. They feed the mean girl stories that we're not really good enough. They leave us constantly afraid that if we don't constantly strive and drive, and over-prepare that we'll be discovered as the imposters we secretly know ourselves to be. They can also create unhealthy levels of stress that may impair our brains ability to learn and develop, causing us to plateau and achieve less than we're really capable of.

Would a growth mindset make it easier to act?

So what's the alternative? Well Dweck has also found that some of us have what she refers to as a *growth mindset*. Underpinned by the belief that we each come into this world with a certain amount of intelligence, talent or ability but that with learning and practice we can always improve, this mindset results in us judging ourselves—and others—by the effort we make and the growth we achieve. And neurologically we now know that this belief is completely accurate.

When we believe that effort and growth are the true measure of what we're worth, it also has some interesting consequences in the way we go about our jobs. Studies have found that generally: We're more willing to take on new challenges in the hope they'll provide opportunities for growth; while perhaps not loving negative feedback and criticism we see it as valuable for our development; and that failure is simply a teachable moment (Edison has to be the poster child for this mindset with his famous quote: "I didn't fail I just found 10,000 ways the light bulb didn't work.") So in order to do all they can to grow, they focus on putting in the best effort they can and being open and willing to learn as they go.

You can imagine that not only does this mindset leave us feeling more confident, it makes it easier to set ourselves stretch goals, to ask for help as we go and to feel motivated to achieve the things that matter to us most. It sparks hope by helping us feel like we have nothing to lose and everything to gain—if we step outside our comfort zone. It appears to help us move beyond our present limitations and to achieve our true potential. Here we'd like to pause and offer you one other tip: if you're reading this list thinking, "I've got this growth mindset completely covered," we're going to respectfully suggest that's not a very growth mindset.

The truth is, just like our gender mindsets, most of us are not entirely one mindset or the other. Instead, we find our mindsets seem to exist along a continuum and sometimes different challenges or people, can send us hurtling from *fixed* to *growth*. For example, Megan is pure growth mindset when it comes to her creative process, but can be more fixed mindset on the topic of managing her business taxation process. And Michelle has no problems sitting in her growth mindset when a client is giving her feedback, but can become very fixed mindset when it's her mother.

The goal here, once again, is to start becoming more aware of which mindset we're sitting in and how it's shaping the way we think, feel, and act. When we find ourselves drifting towards a fixed mindset, that's fearfully telling us we're only worth the outcomes we achieve, then we need to know that we have a choice when this belief is undermining our confidence. Our intelligence, talent, and abilities are not defined by what we have or haven't accomplished, they are ultimately determined by the effort we're willing to make and our openness to learning and development.

Of course, this doesn't mean that our friend Cathy, at little over five feet tall, is likely to one day be the Michael Jordon of women's basketball. Again, challenging these beliefs is not about deluding ourselves with fairytales. Instead, it's about recognizing that when it comes to our success more important than believing in our abilities, is the belief that we can improve our abilities. Could Cathy even though she's not the most natural sports person, get better and better at basketball if she was willing to put in the effort and be open to the learning? Absolutely. And who knows what opportunities all that practice might open up for her. Remember, it is the willingness to try and the opportunity for growth, not the outcomes, that a growth mindset values the most.

Can you cultivate a growth mindset?

Fixed mindsets are often cultivated early in our lives. They are shaped by what we're taught by our parents, and then our schools, and later our workplaces to value. Unfortunately, particularly in Western cultures, too often the praise, recognition, and rewards we receive are all focused on the outcomes we achieve, rather than the effort we make. We're told how clever we are when we get something right, but rarely acknowledged for the learning we've gained by taking the risk to make a mistake. In a world that seems designed to only celebrate achievement, it's little wonder we come to believe that this is the true measure of a person.

If our fixed mindset is holding us back, we can gently challenge it by using our kind girl voice once more to acknowledge that achieving this outcome may be a stretch for us and that it's perfectly natural to feel afraid when we can't guarantee our success. And then we need to ask, even if we couldn't deliver the perfect result would this experience allow us to grow? Would it give us the chance to practice and improve? Would it help us to learn? Would this be a valuable experience, regardless of the result?

We've discovered that no matter how far an opportunity may

stretch us outside our comfort zone, it's hard to back out when our kind girl voice gently probes us for these answers. Before we leap, though, it's also vital that we let our kind girl voice ensure we're prepared for this learning opportunity. Do we have a plan made up of small, concrete steps to guide us? Based on our plan when, where and how do we need to focus our efforts? Who can we ask for support and feedback? What can we do to maintain our motivation and commitment for growth? How can we celebrate what we're learning?

Then with our growth mindset in place, we leap. Sometimes we soar and discover that we're capable of far more than we expected. Sometimes we fall and realize that as uncomfortable as it might be, failure is a great teacher. And most of the time—like Michelle's talk—we land somewhere in between and it's the willingness to try and the openness to learn that really makes an experience successful or wasted.

As we talked about in the last chapter mindset change is not about picking up a few tips here or there. It's about genuinely seeing things in a new way. In this case, it's what allows you to move from a judge-and-judged view of achievement to a learn-and-help-learn view of success. It's about not letting other people's definition of success, be it the sale targets your company sets or the pressure you feel from friends or family, define what matters most to you. It's about being honest enough to celebrate your screw-ups and what they taught you, as readily as you're willing to celebrate your triumphs. It's about being kind enough in the midst of a mistake, a setback or flat out failure to gently acknowledge that you're "not there, *yet.*" It's what allowed Michelle to walk on to that stage, and then off it, accepting that whatever unfolded—good, bad or anything in between—it would be worth the learning and growth opportunity.

You can gently challenge your mindsets by printing out the questions below from www.leadlikeawoman.net/bookplaysheets and sitting with these next time you're struggling to take action.

- Imagine once again that you're talking with someone who really cared for you and with whom you felt safe. How could they help you recognize that any fear you're feeling right now about this opportunity is completely natural? If they asked you to put the risk of delivering the outcome to one side just for the moment, what possibilities might you spot for learning and growth from this experience? What might it give you the chance to practice and improve? Why might this be a valuable experience, regardless of the result? Write down your responses in a stream of consciousness. Don't over think them. Don't judge them. Don't feel embarrassed by them. Just write them down.
- Now assuming, just for a moment, that you were to go ahead, see if you can outline a plan to share with this good friend of the small concrete steps you might take to really maximize this learning opportunity. Based on your plan tell her when, where and how you're going to focus your efforts. Share with her who you think you could ask for support and feedback. Let her know what you'll do to maintain your motivation and commitment for growth and how you'll celebrate what you're learning. Again write this all down in a stream of consciousness.
- When you read back both pieces of writing, how does this leave you feeling about the opportunity in front of you? Although it may still feel a little nerve-wracking is it worth turning your thoughts into action and giving it your best shot

for the learning and growth that you'll gain regardless of the result? Is it possible to just take the first step on your plan and see what happens? And then regardless of the result, learn from what worked and what didn't (remember it might be that you're "not there, *yet*"), and take the next step? And then the next one after that. And so on.

Can you channel your inner-superhero?

Eleanor Roosevelt wisely challenged us to do one thing each day that scares us. As it turns out, confidence isn't just about believing we can achieve anything; it's the willingness to try, to learn and to keep stretching forward. It's feeling fully engaged in life, connected with what matters and worthy of the opportunities in front of us. It's the willingness to turn our thoughts into action.

There is one last interesting piece of research we like to close this part of our workshops with, just in case the women find themselves quickly needing a shot of confidence and a way to bring their strengths, their kind girl stories and their growth mindsets all together in a single moment of presence. It's more of the research of Associate Professor Amy Cuddy from Harvard, that suggests striking a two minute power pose (much like Wonder Woman) can increase our levels of testosterone, which decreases our fear and increases our tolerance for risk and desire to compete—and lowers our levels of cortisol—which decreases our anxiety. By holding power postures for just two minutes before entering a high-stress situation, she found both men and women can increase their testosterone levels by about twenty per cent and lower their cortisol levels by about twenty-five per cent—a pretty significant difference. She also found that power posing increased people's tolerance for risk and pain, and their ability to think abstractly.

If this sounds too good to be true, then keep reading. Cuddy explains that hundreds of studies have examined the body-mind connection, using many different methods, from breathing, to yoga, to lowering vocal pitch, to having people imagine themselves holding an expansive pose, to simply getting people to sit up straight. Whether the body-mind effect is operating through our vagal tone, our blood pressure, our hormones, or some other mechanism, is yet to be fully understood. But what is clear is that expanding our bodies changes the way we feel about ourselves, helping many of us to feel more confident, less anxious and self-absorbed, and generally more positive.

Unfortunately, women generally have been found to show more submissive, contractive nonverbal behavior, talk less (yes, it's true), interrupt less often, and are interrupted more often. And when it comes to walking, gender differences are enormous with women appearing far more restricted in their arm movements, head movements, and length of stride. Researchers suggest this lack of naturally expanded body language is actually less about biology and is instead grounded in perceptions of power.

Now bear with us here. We've worked with enough women to know that just the word *power* can be enough to turn many of us off. But it's our heartfelt belief that you will never achieve what you're capable of if you don't at least understand how feeling powerful shapes your levels of confidence.

Social psychologist Dacher Keltner and his colleagues, propose that power activates a psychological and behavioral approach system that allows us to feel safe, in control, and optimistic helping us to see opportunities and leaving us largely unrestricted by social pressures. It helps us to see the potential benefits of taking action and enables us to show up as our authentic selves. On the other hand, powerlessness seems to activate an inhibition system that makes us anxious, pessimistic, more attuned to threats, and susceptible to social pressures. It focuses on the potential costs of taking action and causes us to behave in ways not representative of our authentic selves. Power helps us approach. Powerlessness makes us avoid.

It turns out that power affects our thoughts, feelings, behaviors, and even physiology in fundamental ways. For example, Cuddy explains while a lack of power has been found to impair our cognitive function, feelings of power seem to enhance it, improving our ability to make good decisions under complex conditions. While a lack of power makes us more anxious, self-focused, and prone to rumination, feelings of power seem to thicken our skin against judgment, rejection, stress, and even physical pain. And while a lack of power can cause us to adapt our behavior to fit in with others, feelings of power have been found to make us fearless, independent, and less susceptible to outside pressures and expectations, allowing us to be more creative.

And in case this helps you feel more comfortable, it turns out that personal power is not the desire to have control; it's the effortless feeling of being in control—lucid, calm, and not dependent on the behavior of others. In our experience, most of us would welcome consistently feeling more like this in our jobs. We believe it's important to understand that the way you carry yourself is a source of personal power, the kind of power that Cuddy has found is the key to presence. It doesn't give you skills or talents you don't have, but it does help you share the ones you do have. It doesn't make you smarter, but it does help you to be more open and resilient. It doesn't change who you are, but it does unlock the authentic leader you were born to be.

The good news—as you try to imagine standing in your next board meeting and striking a wonder woman pose before confidently asking your questions—is that this isn't about what your body language is communicating to others; it's about what your body is communicating to you. Generally, we recommend power posing is done somewhere private and uninterrupted (a bathroom stall seems to be the most popular choice) so that you can give your body language the space it needs to change your mind, so you can change your behavior and confidently turn your thoughts into action which, as we've seen throughout this chapter, changes your outcomes.

You can use the instructions below or download a recorded version of the two minute Wonder Woman guided meditation from www.leadlikeawoman.net/bookplaysheets if you're needing a quick boost of confidence:

> Plant your feet hip-width apart and when you're ready close your eyes. Then place your hands on your hips and take a deep, slow breath in through your nose and out through your mouth. Then take another deep, slow breath. And another deep, slow breath.
>
> Feel your feet really grounded into the floor providing a nice, firm base to support you. Feel the energy moving up through your calves and into your knees, and without locking your knees, push them back just slightly. Feel the energy moving up through your thighs and into your hips. Feel it running around the back of your hips and into your spine. Then imagine it moving up vertebrae by vertebrae, all the way to the top of your neck, and like a thin thread coming out the top of your head, use it to just gently lift your chin up a little

higher. And take another nice deep, slow breath.

Imagine that there is light running back down your neck now and into your shoulders. Draw your shoulders back a little more and really open up your chest. Imagine the light running down through your arms to your elbows; pull these back a little further as well. And then see the light running into your hands and give them a little jiggle so that they are really firmly planted on your hips. And inhale another nice deep, slow breath.

Keep breathing nice and slowly and as you do remember the strengths that you've discovered and the ways you're already authentically using them at work. Think about that kind girl self-compassion mantra you've created and hear her whispering it right now in your ear to remind you that you are good enough. Think about how your commitment to learning and growth will ultimately determine your success. And inhale another nice deep, slow breath.

You can turn your thoughts into action. You have everything you need to be authentic, to think less, and to take action. You just have to be willing to show up and give it your best shot. Now take one last deep, slow breath.

Let your hands drop to your sides. Give your body a little shake—when you're ready give your eyes a blink and a blink and a blink again, and confidently step forward—into whatever you need to do now.

Even with the research laid out, we understand it may still sound ridiculous that doing two minutes of anything; even a power pose can improve your confidence. So we ask the women in our workshops after immediately completing this exercise, to once again introduce themselves to as many people in the room as they can.

This time, there is neither the frenzied *work the room* backslaps, nor the tentative *trying to be nice* conversations; instead there are women calmly, purposefully, comfortably moving through the room genuinely getting to know each other. "I didn't care anymore what people thought of me," said one recent participant. "I got out of my own head and felt like I could be interested and present with the person in front of me." "It felt like I could just be myself, and that was enough," said another participant.

Cuddy suggests you can also start the day by power posing when you first get out of bed, in a meeting you can wrap your arms around the back of your chair or clasp your hands together so it forces you to open your shoulders and chest, organize your spaces to facilitate good posture, and even combine it with daily routines like brushing your teeth with one hand on your hip. Also, try to notice what happens in the moments when you begin to contract, collapse, or disappear. What are the situations or people that cause you to shrink? What makes you feel powerless? This awareness alone might help you resist the urge next time you find yourself in a similar situation.

Whether it's developing your strengths, gently challenging your stories, practicing your growth mindset or standing in a power pose, there are tested, practical ways you can improve your confidence. The trick as we've seen throughout this chapter, is to simply start trying. So how will you begin to turn what you've learnt into action?

The key ideas

- Confidence is the ability to turn our thoughts into action. Success, it turns out, correlates just as closely with confidence as it does with competence.
- Compared with men, women don't consider themselves as ready for promotions, they predict they'll do worse on tests, and they generally underestimate their abilities. This disparity stems from factors ranging from upbringing to biology. It is also shaped by our choices, in particular, being authentic, thinking less, and taking action.
- One of the most effective ways we can be more authentic at work is to develop our strengths—the things we're good at and actually enjoy doing. This means knowing what our strengths are, how we're overplaying and underplaying them, where they're colliding with others and how we can do more of what we do best each day.
- Women's self-talk is more negative than our male colleagues, and we take our stories of self-doubt far more seriously. By recognizing our stories, asking ourselves "is this true" and speaking to ourselves in more self-compassionate, kind and supportive ways we learn to gently challenge the things we tell ourselves so that we can feel more confident.
- More important than believing in our intelligence, talent and abilities and what we can achieve, is the belief that we can improve them. By no longer judging ourselves and others only on the outcomes achieved, we can loosen the grip that the fear of new challenges, criticism, and failure bring and embrace the opportunities offered for learning, development and growth that have been found to ultimately determine

our success - professionally and personally.

Leading you

- How confident are you really? Take the free survey at www.theconfidencecode.com to find out.
- Can you name your top five strengths? Do you find small ways to develop them each day at work? Take the free survey at www.viacharacter.org and grab this free ebook at www.michellemcquaid.com/strengthsebook for more than seventy different ways to put your strengths to work.
- What are your stories of self-doubt? Use the questions at www.leadlikeawoman.net/bookplaysheets to identify your stories and begin to gently challenge them. Create a self-compassion mantra to start dialing up your kind girl voice.
- As you approach new challenges or deal with criticism, setbacks, and failure, are you in a fixed or growth mindset? Use the questions at www.leadlikeawoman.net/bookplaysheets to gently challenge your mindsets when they're undermining your confidence so you can remind yourself of the learning and growth that ultimately determines your success.
- If you need a confidence boost to quickly take action, use the guided wonder woman meditation at www.leadlikeawoman.net/bookplaysheets to put these steps seamlessly together in just two minutes.

Leading others

- Do you know the strengths of people in your team? Do

you provide resources, shape their development and give them feedback around their strengths? Ask your team to take the free survey at www.viacharacter.org and visit www.leadlikeawomen.net/bookplaysheets for tips on having a meaningful strengths conversation with your team.

- What stories of self-doubt do your hear among your team, individually or collectively? Next time you hear these stories being shared gently ask: "Is that true? Is that the only explanation we can find?" Help them look for equally believable, confidence building alternatives. Ask how each story makes them feel and want to act and therefore where they want to invest their attention and energy.
- Does your team have a fixed or growth mindset? What messages do you send about what is valued—effort, outcomes or both? What can you do to role model growth mindset ways for the team to deal with new challenges, feedback, and failures?

Reflection questions

- In the past at work when you've felt genuinely confident and able to turn your thoughts into action, what was happening? What were you working on? How were you able to use your strengths to feel authentic? What were the stories you were telling yourself? What did you focus on to move past the fear of criticism or failure?
- If you were able to have more genuinely confident moments like these at work in the months ahead what might be possible? How could you develop your strengths each day? What could you do to be more mindful and self-compassionate about your

self-criticism stories? How could you focus on the learning and growth opportunities you have? How would it feel to come to work? What would you be proudest of achieving? What might your boss, colleagues, or clients notice about you? Describe these possibilities as vividly as possible.

- If there was one small step you'd be willing to take in the next one to two days to make this dream of genuine confidence a reality, what are you willing to try?

3

Building Your Personal Brand

If a colleague introduced you to someone, how would they describe you? If a client were to refer you to a potential prospect, what would they say about you? And if one of your team members had to brief an incoming peer on your leadership style, what words would they use? Right there, in those answers, lays your personal brand.

Now if you're having a mild anxiety attack thinking you haven't got the faintest clue what a personal brand is, or what yours looks like, don't panic! When first asked to define our personal brand, most of us stammer, fumble, and stare at the floor. It's an ambiguous concept, but it doesn't have to be hard or scary. Just like a company's brand or a celebrity's brand, your personal brand helps to define for the world who you are, what you do, the value you create, and why you are relevant. It helps to differentiate you from your peers, stand out in your space, and be known for what matters to you most in your career.

Regardless of which point you're at in your career—at the start, ready to progress quickly and step up a level, in an executive role or looking to reinvent yourself altogether—you want to build a career that is based on your unique strengths, and that enables you to be a confident, authentic leader, as we have discussed in earlier chapters. But there is another important part of this equation that is critical to your career success, because the days of just showing up, working hard and hoping someone will notice you, are long, long gone. It takes more than being good at your job to get the career you want, one where you can truly shine, achieve your goals, and lead like you want to. And a critical part of this equation is how you represent yourself when you show up, who pays attention, and how you leverage that to do your purposeful work.

It's important to realize that we shape our personal brand, but it's also shaped by people's perceptions of us. Marketing guru Seth Godin suggests that if you want to know what your personal brand is, go and ask fifty people what they think of you and what your superpowers are: He says you'll pretty quickly realize what you're famous for (and those answers may delight or horrify you). Whether you know what it currently is or not, it's important to examine whether you have intentionally defined and crafted your brand for yourself, or whether other people are doing it for you.

It's also necessary to know where you want your personal brand to take you, which is why the first part of our work is getting clear on the vision you want for your life, what gives you purpose and how this can shape your career. And importantly, we will not only give you the tools to build your brand, but a plan to put it into action.

Creating the life you really want

We start building our authentic personal brand by asking the question, who are you really, at your core, when no one is looking? And who do you want to be? For our brand to be truly authentic, we can't build it in isolation of our lives. To answer these questions, you need to get crystal clear on the ideal vision you have, for the life you want to create.

Since Megan wrote her best-selling book, *Getting Real About Having It All*, which included one of the opening chapters, *Creating Your Life Vision*, she has had endless conversations with women on this topic. When asking women the seemingly simple question of "what do you want for your life," there are typically three reactions that she witnesses.

The first is a bit of a stunned reaction, quizzical with a response of "Hunh?!" like no one has ever asked them this before (and they are usually right, no one has). The second is often a defensive response, and it goes something like, "Are you ****** kidding me (add expletive to keep it real). Between the kids, the house, the job, my boss, my endless to-do list, the dog, and that bloody cat, how on earth would I have time to think about my freakin' life vision?" Yep, we feel you. And the third reaction is often one of sadness. It can come with a look of defeat, a sense of longing and a deeply unmet need to create something better for themselves if only they could find the space, time, and permission to really hope for it.

So where might you start? It's not enough for us just to say, "go and create a vision for your life." It's a pretty ambiguous ask, and with no further direction, you could ruminate on that question indefinitely. You want to create a vision for your life that is compelling, inspiring, and aspirational so that it guides what you do each day with positive intent and excitement. To do that, and before you begin to actually envisage it, there are two important guiding rules we want you to follow.

Firstly, there are no *shoulds* in the process of creating your life vision. This is not about what you should do or what anyone else wants you to do. It's all about you; your wants, your needs, your dreams, and your desires. Keep this as a guiding thought and it will help you dive deep into what you truly want. It can be really helpful as you start to do this work that you keep a list of *shoulds* that come up for you, so you can address them later on. For now, just capture them.

The second principle is that you don't need to know how you will get there. You just have to be willing to dream the dream. It's not, at this stage, about the pragmatics of doing. If you sit in that headspace, it becomes almost impossible to get to the heart of what you really want.

When Megan was working up to eighty hours a week as a director of marketing for one of the world's biggest technology companies, raising her young son as a single parent and doing her first Masters degree, she dreamed of living a balanced life with more family time, being more on purpose, and feeling well, not crazed, anxious, and stressed. What she dreamed of most was just space to breathe. At the time, she couldn't even imagine how she could create that life for herself—she was about as far away from that picture as you could get—but she stuck with the vision, built the pieces, and slowly, slowly over the next few years, that dream came to life.

When Michelle was on the verge of leaving the United States to move back to Australia and decided she wanted to study positive psychology with Professor Martin Seligman in Philadelphia, it seemed completely impossible. Only by daring to be honest about what she really wanted for her life, was she able to put the pieces together, and get her boss, and her family to agree that for one year she would fly back and forth every three weeks for class.

So at this stage, it's not about the how. Give yourself permission to suspend your judgment and your thoughts of "there's no way on earth *that* could happen" and stay in the element and question of "what could be possible?" instead.

With those fundamentals laid down, let's walk through the following exercise. In our programs, this is one of the most revealing parts of the entire journey. You will find below four deceptively simple steps. We say deceptively because although the process looks simple, you really need to give it your love and attention, and ample time and space to ensure you are going deep enough to get to the heart of what you want to create. There is no timeline here; you can sit in each section for as long as you need to, and revisit, revise, and build on it whenever you need. Let the journey be whatever it will be. You may have tears, there may be heartfelt joy, and you may tap into feelings and longings you haven't experienced in a very long time. Let it unfold, be honest with yourself and trust your subconscious to show you want it is you truly want. You can print this entire exercise out as a worksheet at www.leadlikeawoman.net/bookplaysheets to help you really journal through the process.

Part one: write your heart out

Start with this question: What do you really want? If you could have anything in your life, unlimited by money, time, energy, or permission, what would you include? To help you figure this out, we have recorded a beautiful life vision meditation that you can download at www.leadlikeawoman.net/bookplaysheets. As you work through this process, you might like to use the meditation as an additional support to get into the zone of what you would truly love to create for your life. We suggest you listen to it as a tool to support your journaling process.

When we talk about a life vision, we're talking about having a clear view of how everything in your life fits together in your ideal picture. It's about what your dream existence looks like. It's your aspirational life. And it includes every part of it, including things like:

- Purposeful work
- Community
- Friends
- Lifestyle
- Where and how you live
- Hobbies
- Romantic relationship
- Spiritual life
- Personal growth
- Education or further study
- Family life
- Your finance
- Health and wellbeing
- Charitable pursuits
- Your bucket list
- Fun and recreation
- Your creative life
- And more . . .

Sit with this list and start writing. In a paper journal

and with a good old-fashioned pen or pencil, write. You can write long flowing sentences or dot point lists. You can draw pictures, doodle, and daydream as you do it. Think of things you want to do, experiences you want to have, people you want to meet, places you want to visit, jobs or vocations you want to try, hobbies you want to revisit, passions you want to pick up, your spiritual life, family life, creativity, travel, parenting, home life, and anything else that comes to mind.

You are getting to the vision of what your best possible life could look like. Write down the small things and the big things, the seemingly insignificant, and the major mega dreams you may long have buried in the deepest darkest recesses of your mind. This is your time and space to get it all out of your head and heart, and down on paper.

You may need to dig a little. It's pretty common when women start this exercise, that they often draw a blank. That's OK. You may have to sit with this for a while, meditate on it, and work out how to dream again if it's been a while since you've tried. If you are stuck, write this question on a post-it note and stick it in your journal, your day planner, on your computer or your bedside table, "What does my best possible life look like?" By asking a question, we start to engage the part of our brain that is constantly on the look out for answers, scanning all the possibilities available to address the question we have posed. Carry a little notebook with you, and when you think about something you would like in your life, write it down. This is a good place to start, and will lead to deeper journaling when the time is right.

Don't put pressure on yourself. Whilst this can be a confronting exercise, it's not meant to be stressful. Use a mindset of curiosity and see what unfolds. There is no time limit, no one to show your responses, no deadline to meet, and no outcome to get to. There are no ridiculous ideas. Just your heartfelt hopes. Rest in the knowledge that you have begun and that you are bold and brave enough to dream about a better life for yourself. And for this part of the process, let that be enough.

Part two: emotionally fuel your vision

Now that you've written down a whole lot of things you would like to have in your life, how do you actually feel about each aspect? Take some time and look at each item. How psyched do you feel about each area? If you had to narrow it down, which ones would be on the top of your *must have in my life* list? Circle ten things that are most important to you.

Now we want you to really sit with one of your items. It could be that you want more time and space for wellbeing practices so you can create balance in your life. This is a very common one, for us included. Think about how you would feel if you brought this vision to life. Feel into your body. We want you to charge this aspect of your vision with as much positive emotion as you can. It might be a sense of vitality, bursting energy, radiance, and happiness from feeling so alive and well. It might be a sense of peace and contentment that you are finally making wellness a priority. Really feel into this. Visualize what you would look like, the actions you would be taking, what your day looks like with this new, healthier and more balanced you in it. The more you can embed and enliven this sense of emotional charge into your vision, the more you can feel it and not just think it, the easier it will be for you to bring it to life. And the more committed you be will each and every day to realizing it.

Work through each element on your vision list, and do the same process. Then, go through the emotions you have laid out, and see if there are common threads. Coming up with your *Core Desired Feelings* as defined by Danielle LaPorte in her book *The Desire Map*, will further focus your attention on how you want to feel each day when you are working to create this ideal life, as well as keep you in check when you are off course.

Part three: visually create it

Now it's time to get visually creative. We invite you to create a vision board (our favorite part of the process). The science of positive psychology and neuroscience suggests that positive images pull us forward. You may have heard stories from people who have said that they had things on their vision board that were brought to life. Or you may have read how athletes use positive visualization to accelerate their skills and development or support their healing and recovery process after an injury.

Megan has three large vision boards above her desk in her home office. There is one with inspiring women she admires surrounding an outline of her Ph.D. thesis, and on the bottom half, dream houses (all with a beach view and pool, a girl can dream). The middle one is for current and future creative and business projects; books waiting to be written, products in the pipeline, and quotes and images that remind her of her purpose and keep her focused on the big picture. The third board is filled with images of inspiration; yoga poses, fortune cookie wisdom, peonies, more quotes and things that bring her joy and happiness. Together, they are as much about art as they are about vision, and they inspire her every day as she works, writes, and creates.

Michelle has her vision board in her bedroom right next to her closet; so every day as she gets ready she can be reminded of the life she's choosing to create. Created the first week of each year, her board has images of favorite words (like passion, play, and courage), people who are important to her (family, friends, mentors, teachers, team members, and global inspirations) and ideas that represent the life she wants to be living (a woman running along the beach, the New York skyline, and a house she dreams of buying).

There are a hundred different ways you can build your vision out. You could use a big notebook or art journal and fill it up with different sections of your dream list. Use an online tool like Pinterest to create a virtual option. You can build physical boards like we have. Start a scrapbook if you want to carry it with you, or if you live in a shared space and need privacy. Or just use a wall of your house. You can get inspirational images from magazines, Pinterest, the internet, and your own photos. Cut them out, print them, pin them. Use quotes, greeting cards you find inspiring or funny, write things down on post-it notes and you can hang mementos as well. Megan has a piece of antique Chinese jade she bought at a flea market in New York, and a necklace with a pendant of Goddess Durga from Byron Bay hanging on hers. There really are no limits to what you can use or what you can create. Go crazy. And most importantly, enjoy the life you're dreaming about.

Part four: look for opportunities to start

Once you have spent time journaling about your life vision and creating your vision board or journal, it's time to start bringing it to life. As you work through the rest of this book, you will have opportunities to bring this dream into reality. We will teach you how to plan your career, develop your wellbeing hope map, and build a grit goal hierarchy so you can actually achieve what you are visioning here.

For now, all we want you to do is start opening your eyes to the opportunities you have to bring your vision to life, in the life you already have. Marianne, a participant in one of our workshops, recently told us that one of the best parts of figuring out her life vision was how much easier it made seeing the opportunities that were right in front of her for the taking. See what you can bring into your life, right from where you are today.

You deserve to live a life that you love. Not one that you can just get by in, or one that is just OK, but a life that is full of radiance, that is vibrant, that is bursting with meaning and joy. It's in your power to create that life for yourself, to work with purpose and live each day like it matters. It may take some time, and it most certainly will take some work. But it's worth every step of the journey so that you can show up each and every day, and live a life that matters.

An integral part of creating a life vision that is compelling and inspiring, and that supports the personal brand that you want to create, is doing purposeful work in the world. So now, let's look at how you find your purpose, bring your brand to life, and create meaning in your career.

For the sake of what?

Now that you have spent some time visioning your ideal life, how did it feel? It may have felt amazing, and given you clarity on how you can bring your work, personal brand, and life together in a way that makes perfect sense. Or perhaps, like many women we work with, it may have felt good to dream the dream, but it was still fairly directionless when it comes to your brand and career. Which brings us to the next part of building your personal brand; defining what you are called to do, and for the sake of what are you willing to bring your ideal life vision into reality.

This is a pretty big question so you might want to strap yourself in: What is your purpose? Or asked another way: Why are you here? Or another: Why do you get up and do what you do every day? For most of us, these questions are not easily answered. We go about our work and life most days without pondering these profound questions, because let's face it, it's daunting and overwhelming and to be perfectly frank, for some of us it feels like it could blow our minds if we sat with it for too long.

We long to be more than the sum of the tasks we perform, and yet finding meaningful work feels like something we just can't afford to think about let alone pursue. When a sense of meaning is found in our jobs, a growing body of evidence suggests we're happier, more motivated, more committed, and more satisfied, which enables us to perform better. The fact is we have a universal need to feel like what we do matters, and that our hard work isn't wasted.

And importantly, when it comes to our personal brand, as we will discover soon, people don't buy what we do they buy why we do it. So getting to the heart of our why is where it's at if we want to build a brand that matters, and have a purposeful career that we love.

So let's break this down for you like we have done with thousands of other women in our programs, so this question becomes more manageable, and you can navigate the path to finding your answer.

Why purpose matters in your career

When you think about the work you most want to do in the world, what lights you up? What would feel meaningful for you? It may be a stretch from where you sit now, but if you're really honest, what is the work you would do even if nobody paid you to do it, or recognized you when you did? As courage coach, Margie Warrell asks: "For the sake of what are you willing to get out of your comfort zone, to risk failure, to put your ego aside and truly show up?"

Studies have found that women who develop a sense of purpose in their work by pursuing goals that align with their personal values and advance the collective good are able to look beyond the status quo to what's possible and find compelling reasons to take action despite their personal fears and insecurities. Purpose helps us to leave our ego at the door and take up activities that are critical for our success such as networking, negotiating, and making sure that we're heard. It helps us to focus our attention more on shared goals, on learning and growth, not just for us, but the teams that we're in.

Purpose also fuels effective leadership. When you have a more purpose-driven goal as a leader, it helps connect other people to what you're trying to achieve and to model the kind of behaviors that are acceptable in that team. Reflecting back to chapter one on authentic leadership, following purpose goals elicits our feminine traits, taking us from a drive and strive masculine mentality, to a more supportive and collaborative feminine one that inspires commitment, boosts resolve, and helps colleagues also find deeper meaning in their work.

What's driving you?

One of the reasons it can be challenging to uncover our true purpose is because we have it drummed into us from an early age what success looks like. How we were raised, our family values, what we were taught in school (and who we were taught by), the friends we grew up with, who we married and what we habitually focus on, all impact what our particular flavor of success looks like to us now.

If academic parents raised you, then it's probable that getting a good education, including a college degree, would be a marker of success. If your family had little money to spare when you were young, and you grew up listening to stories about hardship and scarcity, then it's understandable that your definition of success may involve financial security over pursuing passion.

But in order to experience a sense of purpose, it's vital the goals you set for yourself are intrinsically meaningful. They must be personally significant and in accordance with your own values and passions rather than dictated by your family, friends, workplaces, society, or even your boss.

For example, in one study, researchers found when we use other people's expectations to motivate us we tend toward career goals that focus on how much money we'll earn, how powerful our job titles sound and how impressed others will be by what we're doing. However, even when we achieve these *profit goals* they found we generally feel no more confident, or satisfied, but what does change are our levels of stress, anxiety, and other negative wellbeing indicators.

Michelle certainly experienced this in her career. As a young graduate, she dreamed of running a public relations company. A fancy job title, plenty of money, a chance to impress her family and work that was interesting, what more could she want? By the age of twenty-six, she was the general manager of a boutique PR company for one of Australia's largest advertising firms. But once the glow of her promotion wore off, she realized the role wasn't very fulfilling. Clearly she was going to need a bigger job.

Over the next decade, she kept climbing and climbing. Each new job title and pay rise filled her with excitement at first, but as the months passed she'd find herself increasingly disillusioned and strung out. Unfortunately her story is not unique. The career treadmill of bigger and bigger jobs is one many of us find ourselves stuck on at some point because we're not taught about the likely consequences or the potential alternatives.

The same study found however that when we honor what's intrinsically meaningful to us, our career goals are more likely to be focused on opportunities for growth, connection with others, and making a positive contribution in the world. When people achieved these *purpose goals* they reported feeling more confident or satisfied and enjoyed less stress and better wellbeing indicators.

When Michelle finally stepped off the career treadmill of power, money, and popularity and started choosing her roles for the growth, connection, and contribution they could bring, it was both a leap of faith and a pivotal moment in her career. She asked her employer at the time to create a new role for her that would give her the chance to be a subject matter expert in positive psychology for the firm. It was a sideways move for her career, but what she longed to do. And although the title was less impressive and the earning potential limited, she'd never been happier at work. Ironically six months later, without even asking she was promoted to the highest level she could go in the firm, and paid a lot more money as they saw the value of what she was capable of, when she was truly motivated and living on purpose. And in the process, it allowed her to completely transform her personal brand.

The good news is studies show meaning can be found in any job. Take the tale of three men crushing stones. When asked what they're doing the first replies "breaking big rocks into little rocks," the second says, "feeding my family," and the third explains, "building a cathedral." A sense of meaning fuels our sense of self-worth and gives us a sense of control over our fate at work.

Yet often when we link a sense of purpose to our work, we assume that we have to be engaged in some great and noble endeavor. But it's important not to ignore the small daily differences you can make which, over time, add up to much bigger ones. No matter what your job, you can draw meaning from it. Consider the following example from a study by Yale psychologist Amy Wrzesniewski who found that hospital janitors—whose responsibilities were to sweep the floors, dust, and empty the wastebaskets—were equally likely to describe their work as a job that paid their bills, a career that would lead them to other opportunities, a *calling* which helped people to recover from illnesses by ridding the hospital of dangerous germs. And those who saw their job as a calling found their work far more engaging and enjoyable.

When you really start to observe why you are doing what you're doing each day in your career and life, you may be surprised by the answers. And being the observer is a great place to start in uncovering your true purpose, the compass that guides you on the long and winding road to where, and who, you ultimately want to be.

Are you waiting to be struck by purpose?

Of course *find your purpose* or *follow your dream* are popular themes of advice often passed on from notable business leaders in college commencement speeches. It sounds simple enough, but even when we have a sense of our life vision, the reality is that finding a way to connect what we want to goals that are bigger than ourselves can be a big ask. So we wait, willing ourselves to one day be struck by a bolt of inspiration, which clearly lays out our purpose in front of us.

We hate to break it to you, but researchers have found that this is rarely the case. Instead, our purpose usually unfolds bit-by-bit. It often starts with the discovery of our interests, followed by a lot of development, and then a lifetime of deepening. Steve Jobs wasn't struck with the idea of creating personal computers and changing what was possible for people. He tinkered with electronics as a kid, dropped in and out of creative classes at University, worked at Atari and finally, after joining a computing club, got inspired to build computers with great graphical interfaces.

Likewise, Michelle didn't wake up one day realizing she wanted to use positive psychology and neuroscience to bring out the best in people at work. She spent a decade working in organizations around the world that despite their best intentions seemed to bring out the worst in people. Feeling stuck in her own job, she stumbled across the growing research on human flourishing, started reading everything she could find and then went on to study her Masters degree. Then she convinced her employer to let her start teaching and applying these ideas for others.

So if your purpose still feels a little fuzzy try printing out the following questions from www.leadlikeawoman.net/bookplaysheets and without overthinking them, but as honestly as you can, play with what comes to mind. In our experience we all have a sense of our purpose, it's just a matter of getting still enough to hear it calling.

- *Discover your interests* - What do you like to think about? Where does your mind wander? What do you really care about? What matters most to you? If money wasn't an issue what would you choose to do and why? How might this help others? What do you love doing, are good at and get lost in? And, in contrast, what do you find absolutely unbearable? If you find answering these questions hard, think back to your teen years, the stage of life when vocational interests commonly sprout.
- *Know why your goals matter* - Look back at the ten priorities you circled for your life vision. Take them one at a time and for each ask: "Why does this matter?" Keep asking this question for each one until you reach the answer: "Just because." Note

this down. Once you've done this for all ten, see if you can find a pattern or common themes to your *just because* answers. How do they align to your interests? How might they help others? What might this suggest about the purpose drawing you forward?

- *Play around* - As soon as you have even a small direction in mind, give yourself permission to explore it. Go out into the world and do something small with it and notice what happens and how you feel about it. Remember interests must be triggered again and again so find ways to make this happen. Keep asking questions, and let the answers lead you to more questions. Continue to dig. Seek out other people who share a similar purpose. And have patience. Give it time to allow your curiosity, knowledge, expertise, confidence, and curiosity to carry you forward.

Owning your why

Simon Sinek is the author of *Start With Why: How Great Leaders Inspire Everyone to Take Action*, and the New York Times best-seller, *Leaders Eat Last: Why Some Teams Pull Together and Others Don't*. Fascinated by the leaders and companies that make the greatest impact, his concept of *start with why* took the world by storm with his May 2010 TED talk. The thinking is simple: Sinek says that "people don't buy what you do they buy why you do it".

When you bring this into personal context, the question to ask yourself is: Why do you do what you do? On Sinek's website, he has his team photo's and roles, including things like Chief of Simon, Architect of Solutions, Head of Partnerships and Chief Revel Officer. Certainly quirky and kind-of-cool. But the thing that really stands out is what is written below each photo and title. It's their *why* statement.

Kim, the Chief Revel Officer: "My Why is *to* support and encourage people so that they revel in who they are."

Monique, Chief of Simon: "My Why is *to* figure it out and make it happen *so that* others have a perfect experience."

David, Chief of What's Next: "My Why is *to* propel positive change *so that* people can more meaningfully touch the lives of others."

And Farah, Designer: "My Why is *to* connect the dots for others *so that* we better understand each other."

Megan's Why Statement is "*To* change the conversation on women, leadership and work so that we can create a better world."

Michelle's Why statement is "*To* bring out the best in herself and others, *so that* more people can consistently flourish at work and in life."

When it comes to your work, what would your sentence be? Print out the following questions from www.leadlikeawoman.net/bookplaysheets and see if you can capture your why in a way that could be clear and compelling for others. Don't worry if it doesn't emerge perfectly the first time. In our experience, this is a good challenge to have in your journal, or on your desk, so you can move words in and out of the statement until you land on the answer that feels true to who you are.

- Complete your statement: My why is to ________________, so that ________________________.
- When you've found your answer, try sharing it with friends or colleagues you trust and ask them if the sentence resonates with who they know you to be. Have you missed anything

they think is important? If they were working for you, what sense of meaning and purpose might this help them to feel about their own jobs?

- Keep playing and seeking feedback until you feel confident you have a statement that really captures the meaning of your work. Try to start weaving this into conversations, where appropriate, with your boss, your team, and your clients so they understand your purpose and feel connected with your dream. Note how this is key to building and conveying the essence of your personal brand.

For us, everything we do in our careers is driven by our purpose, and that's underpinned by our passion for what we do and the difference we want to make. It guides our decisions, the clients we work with, the boundaries we set, and how we manage our lives. It keeps us connected to meaning, and ensures that whilst profit is absolutely important (we are entrepreneurs raising families, so of course), our goals are first-and-foremost driven by purpose, and our life satisfaction and wellbeing is directly correlated to how we stay true to those goals.

Creating a career you love

Now that you have context of what a personal brand is and why you need to build it, as well as enhanced clarity on your life vision and purpose, the question becomes, what does that mean for your career?

For many women, their career is an afterthought, a treadmill they habitually run on every day, or a battle they have to will themselves through. We also know that for a large percentage of women, there is no plan or even a vision guiding them forward, and it's down to sheer luck where they end up and how they get there.

We don't want this for you. We don't want you to be one of the seventy per cent of women Megan found in her American research study *Getting Real About Women and Work*, who don't have a career plan that is working for them or one of the forty-eight per cent of women who are literally winging it when it comes to their careers. There is so much more available to you if you take the time to be intentional about where your career choices are taking you.

Creating your career plan

Think back to the last career development discussion you had with your manager, your coach, or mentor. It might have gone something like this: here's where you're at, here are your performance gaps, and here are the next roles that make sense for your career based on where you are likely to be most successful (or more often, where we need you to be).

Now think about this: What if you let your life vision and your purpose drive your career plan to build the kind of personal brand you dream of? What if, instead of just winging it, being on the treadmill, or suffering through your days, you made decisions based on what was most meaningful for you, what felt right, where you could make the most difference and what you wanted to be known for? What if you developed a career plan that was actually a purpose plan, and that was built on your strengths, was infused with your passions, and felt authentic to who you are? Imagine waking up to that life every day? What would it feel like? What would you do? And what would be your very next step?

It's important as you go through this process to not just think about the next linear step that makes immediate sense to you. When Megan works with her executive coaching clients on career strategy, she encourages them to see beyond traditional career paths, not just look at the next rung in the ladder, but to seek opportunities sideways as well. When Isabelle came in for her first coaching session having worked for fifteen years in senior human resources (HR) roles, she thought her next role was naturally going to be as a HR director of a large company. This is what she thought she *should* do, and what career advisors and recruiters had told her was her next logical step.

But as we started to explore what she was most passionate about, what felt purposeful, and what work would be a good fit with her new life vision, she realized that what she actually wanted to do was pursue strategy consulting work in the HR space. It was very different to her initial assessment, but it became radically clear as we worked together, and answered questions about her brand and what she really wanted to be known for. Your career is often more like a lattice than a ladder, so think creatively about all of the potential options available to you, no matter how out of your initial comfort zone they may be.

As you think about building a brand and career based on your life vision and purpose consider the following questions, which you can download at www.leadlikeawoman.net/bookplaysheets:

- When you think about your life vision and what purposeful work could look like, how would you assess your career options? Write a list of all the potential options you could explore, with up to twenty items on the list. Often we can come up with the first three to five items, but the really creative ideas often come when we push through the easily thought of to the really left of center.

- What is the next career goal you want to set for yourself? It could be a linear step from where you are now, or it could be something you have uncovered through your life vision or purpose work that will take you in an entirely new direction. Think about the goal you want to set for the next twelve months, and then if you are so inspired, perhaps envisage what a longer-term goal of three to five years might look like as well.
- Based on that goal, what skills, experience, and knowledge do you need? Identify any gaps in expertise that may need filling. That could mean undertaking a new role, working on your leadership skills, building your political capital or studying on your own time to become a subject matter expert. Make a list of gaps and actions you'll need to take to fill them.

What do you want to be known for?

Now that you have a sense of where you want to take your life and your career it's worth stepping back for a moment and checking if your personal brand is taking you to the places you want to go. Is being known as the *problem solver*, *the organizer* or *the deal maker* actually serving you well? One of the most important questions you can ask when building your personal brand and looking at what's next for your career, is *what do you want to be known for*?

Personal branding expert, William Arruda explains that your personal brand is not your job title. If you're relying on your job title to position you to others, then you'll wind up being a commodity and blend into the crowd of thousands of people who do the same thing that you do. Instead, he suggests people with strong brands know the value they create, who they're creating it for and the outcomes that people expect.

Your personal brand is not just what you do; it's how you do it, for whom you do it, and why you do it. It's about the difference that only you can make for others because of the unique value your purpose, strengths, expertise, and experience brings to others. People with strong personal brands get noticed because they share their passion for what they do in a way that is relevant to the people they want to serve.

Take this example, as Arruda outlines in his book *Ditch. Dare. Do! 3D Branding for Executive Success:* what if at your next networking event you met Sarah, who introduced herself to you as "a biologist and senior researcher of Bio Research at ABC Pharmaceuticals." Would her personal brand grab your attention? Probably not. But what if Sarah said, "I manage a team of scientists who design drugs for very rare diseases and make a difference in people's lives. It's a great reason to go to work every day." That sounds a little more interesting and memorable. Or how about if Sarah said, "I battle bugs every day, the kind of bugs that cause rare diseases and make people really sick. My team and I won't rest until we've squashed them." Now you have a chance to see the passion, dedication, intelligence, and irreverence that is authentic and unique to Sarah. This is her personal brand, and it won't easily be forgotten.

Of course your personal brand has to be believable, it isn't a case of just wishing to be someone you're not, but it can be about growing into the person (and brand) you want to be. When we first met Lyrene in our workshop, she was an operations manager in a financial services company. She was incredibly capable and had built a strong personal brand in the role she was in, but her heart just wasn't in it. Passionate about people and creating positive change, she wanted to be in a role that helped unlock human potential in her workplace. But she had no requirement in her current role, or any brand permission, to play in that space. She couldn't just walk into the office and declare she was moving on her from her personal brand of *operations guru* and would now be a *people expert.* She needed to lay out a path of brand evolution and give people time to evolve their understanding of the unique value she was capable of bringing.

After attending our program, Lyrene went back to work and spoke with her manager about the additional value she felt she could bring by leveraging her strengths and sense of purpose. This was the first step in shifting her brand, and enabled her to start picking up additional development opportunities and involvement in HR programs and special projects whilst still doing her current job. Then as time went on and Lyrene consistently talked about and sought out ways to act upon the personal brand she wanted to be building, she began to be recognized more and more for the people expert she was becoming. In fact, this enhancement of her personal brand recently helped Lyrene land a key promotion, and elevate her career to an entire new level.

If you've started to realize that your brand is a long way from where you need it to be in order to realize your life vision and your purpose, Dorie Clark in her best-selling book, *Reinventing You: Define Your Brand, Imagine Your Future,* suggests it's worth thinking about how you can start telling the story of where you've been, how your past relates to your future and where you're going now.

For example, when Megan was head of strategy for a global technology company, she loved her work driving the business strategy for a five billion dollar business. But the parts she loved the most were her adjacent roles leading gender diversity, and organizational culture and change. These remits supplemented the strategy role perfectly, and over the seven years she led these parts of the business, her brand evolved from purely business strategist to also include gender and leadership expert. Through demonstrating to the business the criticality of diversity, culture change and positive leadership to the growth strategy she was responsible for, her CEO and general management peers began to see her as the key thought leader and advocate for these areas in the business. Over time, Megan successfully repositioned herself to become one of the most sought after experts in the space she had strategically grown her brand in to, and helped her make the transition to running her own business in these fields.

So how do you want to be remembered by others? Play with the following questions, which, you can download at www.leadlikeawoman.net/bookplaysheets:

- Imagine it's one year from today and you've achieved the career goal that you set for yourself above and are honoring your life vision and your purpose. How would the value you create, who you create it for, and the expected outcome be described by a:
  - Customer recommending you to one of their friends.
  - A peer explaining your role to a new colleague.
  - Your boss recommending you for promotion.
- Based on this, write one or two sentences that could be used in an email to introduce and position yourself to a client, a colleague or at a networking event. Try to capture the value you create, who you create it for and the expected outcome of working with you. For example, Michelle's might read: I use my curiosity and creativity for how our brains work to teach people in workplaces how to consistently flourish and perform

at their best. Megan's might read: known for my passion and expertise in women, leadership and work, I help women step into their power and create positive change for organizations.

Below are some suggested personal brand templates that might help you (just pick one of these to complete) and remember to convey your warmth and strength:

- I use my __________ and __________ for __________.
- Known for __________, I __________.
- Using __________ (key strength), I __________, by providing __________.
- Through my __________, I __________, when I serve __________.

  Or feel free to create one that feels authentic to you. Think about Sarah the bug squasher!

- How believable do you think this brand statement would be to the people you work with today? If it feels like a stretch, think about how you can start telling the story of where you've been, how your past relates to your future and where you're going now. What are the steps you'll need to start taking to make this brand evolution believable to others?

Building the right relationships

When it comes to making your life vision, your purpose, and your career plan a reality so that you can build the personal brand you want to be known for, managing your relationships is a critical component to success. Mentors, sponsors, and networks can play a pivotal role in supporting you, helping you navigate your career, and can also provide an opportunity for you to learn, collaborate, and give back. It is so important for you to trust your own inner voice and guidance, as we believe that deep down you always know what's right for you. But that doesn't discount the immense benefit of key relationships and how they can help you unlock your potential, tap into your wisdom, and fast track your success. With that, let's look at the first core relationship, mentors.

Finding the right mentors

We think mentoring has been getting a bad rap over the past few years. As the battle to get and keep more women in leadership positions rages on, and endless versions of the same strategies and programs are tried with mixed results, mentoring seems to have been labeled as an old school strategy and no longer something that will contribute to cracking that proverbial glass above our heads (we desperately think it's time for a new metaphor, how about an entire new paradigm?).

When Sylvia Ann Hewlett published her book, *Forget a Mentor, Find a Sponsor,* the mentoring train seemed to have well and truly left the station. And when Sheryl Sandberg wrote in, *Lean In: Women, Work and the Will to Lead*, that "searching for a mentor has become the professional equivalent of searching for Prince Charming," the train kind of came off the tracks right there.

Now, to be fair, neither Sandberg nor Hewlett were saying you should forget about mentoring altogether, but they were certainly sending a message that it's not a critical strategy for your career success. But the truth of it is that mentoring works. Whether it's through an informal one-on-one relationship or a formal organizational program, mentoring consistently gets results for both the mentor and the mentee—when set up with the right intention and managed with the right level of structure and accountability.

And yet so few women, it seems, actually have a mentor. According to trend research report *Women as Mentors: Does She or Doesn't She? A Global Study of Businesswomen and Mentoring*, sixty-three per cent of women have never had a mentoring relationship, even though sixty-seven per cent of the same women rate mentorship as highly important to advancing and growing their careers. Even more staggering is research from career networking website Levo League that reports a massive ninety-five per cent of millennial women have never sought out a mentor at work. So why the gap?

In many cases, women who work in organizations without formal mentoring programs have less access to mentors and enjoy fewer benefits from the relationship when they do have one, as reported by non-profit organization Catalyst in *Making Mentoring Work*, and this is a frequent barrier to advancement. So if you are working in a business that does have a formal program, get engaged in it and make the most of the opportunities it can provide.

However, we also know that one of the main reasons women aren't engaging in mentoring relationships is that they are simply not asking. As one woman, an executive in a pharmaceutical company reported in the previously mentioned *Women as Mentors* study: "It's like walking up to someone and asking them to be your friend, and no one does that." And yet ironically, seventy-one per cent of women in the study reported that they always accept invitations to be formal mentors in their workplace.

It's important to note that asking the right person is of critical importance. Walking up to a complete stranger who you don't know and asking them to mentor you in a completely vague way, as Sandberg and even Oprah Winfrey report happens to them all too frequently, is not a great strategy. This is entirely different from making a well thought out request to someone you know, as we will cover shortly.

Why should you bother seeking a mentor?

We know you're busy. So you may be reading this thinking that getting a mentor is just another thing to add to your endless to-do list. You may also still be thinking that if you just keep your head down, work hard, and produce results, that the work will take care of itself and that you really don't need to waste time on these extra and perhaps nice to have relationships.

But we're sorry to say that you'd be wrong for making these assumptions. The *Women and Men in U.S. Corporate Leadership: Same Workplace, Different Realities* report found that having an influential mentor was among the top career advancement strategies for senior women executives, and numerous research studies state it as critical in the early stages of your career. We also know from our own experience of having mentors and from the endless stories we hear from women who have nurtured and navigated successful mentoring relationships, that they can be powerful beyond measure—when you get the secret sauce right.

So what will you get out of it? Mentoring relationships are highly valuable to help you learn, navigate, grow, and obtain or hone your skill sets. They can significantly fast track your career in many areas; learning how to manage the politics of your workplace, understanding how to advocate for yourself and negotiate a pay rise, working out how to get the right balance in your work and life, asking for professional development opportunities, or just understanding how to ask, period. Working with the right mentor, or mentors as you may have more than one, can be an essential element in your career progression, your understanding of self, as well as your IQ and EQ when it comes to your office dynamics.

How can you ensure mentoring success?

A question we are often asked is how do you actually make a mentoring relationship work? There are some guiding principles we recommend you follow when requesting, setting up, and managing your ongoing mentoring relationship. Here is your checklist to enable mentoring success.

- *Work out specifically why you want a mentor* – as you think about your personal brand, career trajectory and what you are grappling with in the short to medium term, get honest with yourself about what you really need. Political navigation, negotiation skills, confidence tips, work-life balance, reality checking—get clear on your why—so you can ensure you ask the right person to support you.
- *Set your intention* – it's important you are clear on your intention for the relationship and what you would like to gain from it. So many engagements fail because the mentee is too ambiguous on why they are there in the first place. By getting clarity for yourself, you will not only maximize your gains, but you will ensure you don't waste the time and energy of your mentor.
- *Find the right person to ask* – typically you would seek out a mentoring relationship with someone you want to learn from. Take a look around inside and outside your current organization, and think about who has knowledge or experience that you

could benefit from. Your future mentor could be a senior manager in your business who has a particular skill set you want to obtain, or a management style you want to emulate; an industry leader you admire for their thought leadership in an area you wish to develop; a peer who has a particular skill that would help you become more well rounded; or even a team member, particularly if they are from a different generation, who can reverse mentor you on certain things.

- *Decide what your ask is* – what exactly are you asking for? Receiving a request to be my mentor with no parameters or specificity is a huge frustration by anyone who has ever been approached, ourselves included. Get clear whether you are asking for a monthly formal meeting, a thirty-minute coffee catch up once a quarter, or a more informal call, as you need them. We prefer sending an email with a clear request outlined, rather than a phone call or face-to-face request where the person is on the spot and has to respond instantly. Be clear about what you're seeking, why you are asking them specifically, and how you envisage the relationship would work. Remember to not be greedy in your initial request, and be very respectful of the person's time, energy, and schedule.
- *Manage the logistics* – You need to be the driver of the actual meetings. Whether that means speaking with the mentors assistant to give them the necessary details of the meeting, to booking the meeting room, or initiating the phone call, take charge and make it as easy for your mentor as possible so that all they have to focus on is giving you the best advice possible. You should also go into every mentoring session with an agenda. This could be a simple list of dot points you would like to discuss or a specific question you want to focus your entire session on. In some sessions, it's fine to chat and see

what comes up for you, but in most instances, have an agenda to make the most of the opportunity in front of you.

- *Follow up* – Most mentors like to be kept apprised of your progress as you work together over time. Whether that's sending your mentor an email after a job interview, giving them feedback after a big presentation you sought their advice on, or sharing the result from a pay rise negotiation, keep them in the loop and provide feedback on how their advice and guidance impacted your performance and outcomes.
- *Give thanks* – Gratitude is a really powerful tool in any relationship, but especially in a mentoring one where the mentor is giving up their time and hard-won advice, for free. From a simple thank you email, to a phone call or hand written note, ensure you are expressing your gratitude for their support in a way that is meaningful and heartfelt.
- *Don't over stay your welcome* – The last tip here is not to drag out the relationship. It's a good strategy to set a time frame at the start of the mentoring agreement. Margaret is a senior executive in a large bank who takes on five new mentees at the start of each year for a strict twelve-month relationship. Regardless of what happens during that time, she concludes the mentoring at the end of the year. She also sets clear goals with the mentees and holds them accountable throughout the time they work together. Your relationship with your mentor may go for three, six or twelve months, but stay tuned in to when it has run its course for either or both of you, and exit graciously.

As with any relationship, getting the magic right between mentor and mentee can be a hard ask, but it's a critical part of any successful mentoring partnership. Keep your mind and options open, and be willing to give the relationship time to click into place.

Getting the sponsors you need

In our workshops one of the most frequently asked questions is, "What's the difference between a mentor and a sponsor?" A mentor is a person who will advise you and share their knowledge, whereas a sponsor is someone who will advocate for you on your behalf, using their influence and power to do so. Whilst anyone in an organization can act as your mentor, a sponsor must be in a position of power or highly placed in the business, or they won't have the clout to pull you through the hierarchy or lobby for your visibility and success.

As Hewlett stated in a recent *Forbes* article, "If mentors help define the dream, sponsors are the dream-enablers. Sponsors deliver: They make you visible to leaders within the company—and to top people outside as well. They connect you to career opportunities and provide air cover when you encounter trouble. When it comes to opening doors, they don't stop with one promotion: They'll see you to the threshold of power."

When it comes to women in business, a 2010 study by Catalyst found that men tend to find mentors in powerful positions who also sponsor them, making the relationships much more valuable, whereas women are most frequently advised through mentoring but not advocated for. Rather than only advising you or providing advice, a sponsor is someone who goes into bat for you, this could mean advocating for you to get assigned to a hot project or land a promotion, helping you with visibility and political currency, ensuring you are on the succession bench for career making roles—or speaking positively about you when you're not in the room.

Whilst sponsors can play a pivotal role in helping you advance, a common misconception we find with the women we work with is that they think that is all sponsors are relevant for. But there are many other aspects of your brand and career that the right sponsor can advocate for. It could be helping you negotiate work flexibility, advocating for study opportunities, sponsoring a sideways move, or navigating a move back into the workforce with a secure reentry point. Sponsors can help you progress in ways that are meaningful to you, they actively support and promote your personal brand, give you additional credibility, and have skin in the game for your career success.

A sponsor takes an interest in your career not out of altruism, but as an important investment in their own career, organization or vision. A sponsor will often look at their sponsee like a protégée, and will be deeply invested in their success as it holds career or political currency for them. Your role is to earn their investment in you by delivering outstanding results, building their brand or legacy and generally making them look good. Sponsorship is a strategic alliance, a long-range quid pro-quo.

If you speak with any senior professional, male or female, they will tell you stories of how a particular person sponsored them into a senior role, supported them through a career making (or breaking) situation, or advocated on their behalf. What you may not hear, however, is their use of the sponsor language, as many people, especially women, don't make the link between a senior person's support and advocacy and sponsorship.

Why does this matter? It matters because there are a number of different types of sponsors, the two most important being those that you already have, even unknown to you, and those that you actively cultivate.

Who is currently sponsoring you?

Think about your career. Who has played a pivotal role in supporting you to get to your current position? If you take a good look, you will notice that there may have been one or more people who have been instrumental. That may have been through helping you on a particular project, advocating for a promotion, championing a pay rise, or instilling just the right amount of confidence.

When Megan looks back on her corporate career, there were three key leaders who were critical in her progression and success. The first was her female boss at GE when she was a young, up and coming marketing leader; she put Megan in her first management role, championed her pioneering work across Asia, and backed her as a future leader in the business. The second was her managing partner in a global professional services firm. He sponsored her into the business, into her first director role, followed by key global projects and high profile assignments. Then, after an acquisition saw them become part of a global technology company, he sponsored her into the key marketing roles that would shape the next part of her career, including becoming the director of marketing for a multibillion dollar company. And then there was the CEO, who used a significant amount of his own political capital by creating a new executive role for Megan when she was at a career and life turning point.

Some of these sponsor interactions were known to Megan at the time, and some were not. The point is that you may already have active sponsors who are helping you in unseen ways. It will help you to identify who your current sponsors are, both inside and outside your organization, and how you can further develop that relationship and support them in return. Your current sponsor could be your immediate boss, a former manager, a peer you worked with who has moved to another part of the business or outside the company, a current or former client, or a more senior leader who sees political or brand capital in supporting or being aligned to you.

Leveraging your current sponsors is a great place to start in building your career and amplifying your brand currency. Once you have identified them, ensure that they know what your career aspirations are, how they can support you, and what you can do for them in return. For each of Megan's sponsors noted here, she delivered (and over delivered as her tendency was) to ensure that their faith in her, and their backing, was always rewarded and worth their time, energy, effort, and political capital. Remember, a sponsorship relationship is always a two-way street, and this is critical to keep in mind for longevity.

Cultivating new sponsors

Just like going up to someone and asking "Will you be my mentor?" flat out asking someone to be your sponsor can make for an awkward, unfruitful, and potentially embarrassing conversation. You typically don't just ask for sponsorship, you earn it, but there are ways to cultivate a new sponsor relationship if you think strategically and intentionally about it.

Start by identifying senior leaders who are already aware of your skills and strengths, stand to benefit from your help, and have the clout to move you toward your goal. Consider not whom you report to, but whom your boss reports to. You will spot potential sponsors by their ability to act in favor of your career, which could include connecting you to key people, giving you stretch assignments, offering critical feedback, and promoting your visibility within their networks.

Looking at your career path and what your next step might be, who are the senior people whose support would be a game changer for you? Once you have identified them, work out ways to build a relationship and demonstrate both your capability and your value. In her book *Forget a Mentor, Find a Sponsor,* Sylvia Ann Hewlett has these suggestions for navigating a potential sponsor relationship:

- Find ways to get in front of your potential sponsor by asking a supportive manager for stretch assignments in your target sponsor's line of sight.
- Request a meeting for career development advice.
- Attend networking events or informal gatherings where you may have a chance to introduce yourself.
- Suggest collaborating on a project of interest for your sponsor.
- Become part of an internal network.
- Join a non-profit board or committee that your sponsor is part of.

Once you have the opportunity to connect, show them what makes you worth sponsoring or describe what you can bring to a potential sponsors goals or team. When the opportunity presents itself (or you create it), help them see why you would be a good investment of their time and political capital, what you're willing to do for them and what help you'd like in return. Spell out the mutual benefits clearly and concisely. If they decline, ask if they can direct you towards a more appropriate leader. This may feel bold, and it is, but by remembering that it is a win-win relationship and that you have value to add and support to provide, it can help infuse you with the courage you need to progress this relationship.

It's also important to remember that unlike mentors, sponsors don't need to be leaders you relate to or one's you aspire to emulate. What's important in sponsorship is trust and mutual benefit, not affinity to a particular leadership style.

Deliver on your promise

Nothing makes you easier to sponsor than outstanding results. What sponsors are looking for is someone who will deliver standout performance and be loyal and reliable. Help your sponsor understand how you're contributing towards their goals and the results you're achieving. Be willing to go the extra mile. Do you have skills or knowledge your sponsor may lack that can be shared in reverse mentoring? Perhaps you're a subject matter expert in an area that your sponsor is not that could be highly useful and valuable on a current project. Do you have access to information, formal or informal, that would be valuable or provide capital and currency for them? Learn about what they value and keep your eyes and ears open for ideas, research, and contacts that may assist them. And remember to ask for help when you need it. Ask clearly and have a win-win plan in place.

When thinking about your mentor and sponsor relationships, come back to these questions, which you can download in the playsheet from www.leadlikeawoman.net/bookplaysheets.

On mentors:

- For where you are in your career right now, what could you use help with? Is it navigating the politics in your business, developing leadership skills, or creating some balance for yourself? Think about the context and where a mentor could help you most.

- Who could possibly mentor you? Once you have decided what you need support and guidance on, work out who the right person is. Look inside and outside your workplace; ask friends, colleagues, or your manager, to help identify the right person (or people).
- Once you have your mentor in place, ensure you are taking the lead and effectively managing the relationship, keeping your mentor up to date, and giving thanks for their support and knowledge sharing.
- Most importantly, make sure you are tuned into your own inner wisdom and knowing. If you struggle to tap into that source, start a meditation practice and refer to chapter four on Mindfully Maintaining Wellbeing to help you do that. Nothing external to you can ever super cede what you know to be true. The key is getting to that truth, and trusting yourself to follow your own internal guidance.

On sponsors:

- Remember the difference between a mentor and sponsor so that you are seeking out the right support from a sponsor who will advocate for you, not just give you advice.
- Think about who may have sponsored you in the past, and who could currently be sponsoring you, with or without your knowledge. Look for those senior people who you know have your back, speak about you when you're not in the room and help you get career making opportunities.

- Who are the sponsors you may need to cultivate to achieve your career goal identified earlier in the chapter? Look for opportunities to be introduced, work on a project in their business area, or connect with them and make yourself both known and valuable.

How to network your way to success

Now what we have covered off mentors and sponsors, let's look at your expanded network and how it enables your career plan and builds your personal brand. If the very idea of networking makes you want to groan, you're not alone. For many women, the idea of having to build a network remains challenging. Anxious that it requires us to push our own agendas, brag about our accomplishments or use people to advance our own interests, most women would rather stay home. But does networking your way to success always have to be driven purely by goals that are self-serving? What if the purpose was actually about genuinely connecting with people and discovering how you can be of service to others?

Whether you're an introvert or an extrovert, your relationships with others have been found to impact your levels of wellbeing and performance. Each time you genuinely connect with someone else the pleasure inducing hormone oxytocin is released into your blood stream. In addition to helping you to connect with others, oxytocin has been found to help lower your levels of cortisol (your stress hormone) and improve your concentration and focus.

In addition, extensive research shows that people with rich networks achieve higher performance ratings, get promoted faster, and earn more money. This is because your networks can give you access to invaluable knowledge, expertise, and influence that you won't have alone. Every significant opportunity we were ever given in our corporate careers—be it a new job opportunity, an overseas posting, flexible hours, further study—came through our networks. So how can you make networking an authentic, joyful, and enriching experience?

Professor Adam Grant at Wharton Business School recently challenged some of the conventional stories we tell in organizations about what it takes to climb to the top of the success ladder. While many workplaces create a culture where employees are pitted against each other for limited resources and opportunities and encouraged to be takers who put their own interests first, or matchers who try to evenly exchange favors, his research suggests that neither approach predicts long-term success. Instead, he found that it's the employees who approach their relationships as givers—who strive to be generous in sharing their time, energy, knowledge, skills, ideas, and connections with others—that consistently rise to the top of the success ladders.

How can this be? Takers, matchers, and givers all can and do achieve success. But when takers succeed it usually comes at the cost of others and as a result people tend to look for ways to knock them down. Matchers are usually so busy exchanging favors no one really benefits. What sets givers apart over time is that when they succeed it creates a ripple effect, enhancing the success of people around them and building a slow and steady upward spiral of goodwill and trust that enhances their personal brand and propels their careers forward. As a result, givers build formal and informal teams that are cohesive and coordinated and establish environments in which customers and suppliers feel that their needs are the organization's top priority, helping them to achieve higher levels of profitability, productivity, and customer satisfaction, along with lower costs and turnover rates. Being a giver is probably not good for the quick win, but it pays significant benefits over the long-term.

The reality is that each time you connect with someone you have a choice to make: Do you try to get as much as you can to advance your own cause, or to contribute as much as you can without worrying about what you receive in return? Grant's research suggests that the choice you make ultimately plays as much of a role in your success as hard work, talent, and luck.

But before you rush out to start helping everyone today who crosses your path, there's an important twist in this research you need to be aware of. Some givers wound up at the bottom of corporate success ladders because they were simply too caring, too trusting and too kind to protect their own interests, get their own work done and avoid being exploited. There is even some evidence to suggest that when compared with takers, on average, givers earn fourteen per cent less money, and are judged as twenty-two per cent less powerful and dominant by their colleagues.

In contrast, givers who are successful capitalize on the strengths of giving whilst avoiding the pitfalls, so they don't end up becoming exhausted and unproductive. They do this by coupling their concern for others, with a healthy dose of concern for themselves. They give more than they receive, but they keep their own interests in sight, and use them as a guide to choose when, where, how, and to whom they give. They do good, and they do well by giving wisely and mindfully, willfully collaborating, powerlessly communicating, advocating for others, and for themselves, and asking for help. Let's look at each of these in turn.

Giving wisely and mindfully

Successful givers don't just give because someone asked. Instead, they hold themselves accountable by constantly asking: "How can I be of the most service to others?" Then they use their answer as a daily guiding star to capitalize on their strengths, build their personal brand, maintain their wellbeing, and connect their networks in ways that are aligned with their purpose. This helps them to place boundaries around how they offer their advice, assistance, and resources so they can maximize the benefits for others and feel like they are making a positive difference, without burning themselves out.

For example, Michelle is often asked for advice about studying positive psychology. At first she tried to answer every email, take every call or make time for every coffee, but she soon found this came at the expense of the work she felt could be of the most service in the world doing. While she's committed to encouraging people to study the science of human flourishing, Michelle realized she'd need to create some boundaries around these particular requests. So she made each Wednesday night her time to pay it forward and have a coffee, jump on the phone or return an email of someone who wanted to know more about positive psychology programs.

Fortune Magazine discovered that the best-connected networker on LinkedIn, a shy software geek called Adam Rifkin used a similar approach. His giving is governed by a simple approach: You should be willing to do anything for anybody that takes fives minute or less. It might be making an introduction, sharing some knowledge, giving some feedback, or making a recommendation for them. Then when people offer to do something in return to thank them, he encourages them instead to pay it forward and do a five minute favor for someone else. By instilling the value of giving in his network Rifkin grows the opportunities and value for everybody and this has been his secret to authentically building an incredible network.

Willfully collaborating

Successful givers recognize that if they can contribute effectively to a group— rather than being a lone star—everyone is better off. From sales teams to paper mill crews to restaurants the more giving group members do, the higher the quantity and quality of their group's products and services. When you put the group's goals and mission first, show the same amount of concern for others as you do for yourself, and are willing to give away credit to the group, studies have found that the group will reward your individual sacrifice.

Megan found this to be true when she was part of the inaugural team for the Male Champions of Change initiative in Australia. Lead by the former Australian Sex Discrimination Commissioner Elizabeth Broderick who was frustrated with the stagnant numbers of women in leadership within corporates and government, she brought together twenty-five of the countries most powerful CEOs to collaborate on how to create real change in gender diversity. The groups mission was to gain significant breakthroughs by putting competitive business issues aside, leaving ego's at the door, sharing what was and wasn't working and navigating how to create positive change. Through this willful collaboration and open giving of the CEOs and the implementation leaders, together with Elizabeth and her team, progress was and still is being made that would not have been possible had everyone continued on their own solitary path.

Powerlessly communicating

Instead of trying to gain dominance by communicating powerfully, speaking forcefully, raising their voice to project authority, promoting their accomplishments, and selling with conviction and pride, successful givers influence others by showing respect and admiration for others. Having established their competence, they tend to talk in ways that signal vulnerability, reveal their weaknesses, make use of disclaimers, hedges, and hesitations, and ask for advice rather than imposing their views on others. They use questions to influence people's intentions and actions, they show openness to other's ideas, and they seek advice when they lack authority. They are authentic and mindful about how they choose to speak in an effort to build trusted relationships.

As the youngest and often only female leader in boardrooms led by powerful men, Michelle was amazed to discover the power of asking questions. After spending most of her career advocating and telling, she was shocked to learn that every action we take is actually preceded by a question and that this is where the real power of changing people's ideas and behaviors lay. As she began asking more questions, she also found that even in a very deficit-focused organization, it was the questions that looked for the true, the good, and the possible that built the most value. By shaping her business cases and presentations around appreciative questions, making space for conversations and recognizing that behind every cynic was an unexpressed hope, Michelle finally had strategies green-lighted, and budgets approved that had been previously stuck for years.

Advocating for others and for themselves

Rather than falling into the empathy trap that can turn givers into doormats who are easily exploited, successful givers shift their focus from people's emotions and feelings to their thoughts and interests so they can make decisions and cut deals that create win-win outcomes. By looking for opportunities to benefit others as well as themselves, givers think in more complex ways that increase the value for everyone involved.

For example, studies have found that over the course of a thirty-five-year career a woman loses an average of more than one million dollars partly because we negotiate lower salaries than our male colleagues. A huge factor in this gap is our unwillingness to ask for more money for ourselves because we don't want to put our bosses or employers out. But the moment you ask a woman to imagine they are negotiating on behalf of someone they mentor, they out negotiate most men by fourteen per cent. So what might be possible the next time you go in to negotiate your salary if you imagined you were doing so on behalf of all the women coming behind you who deserve to be fairly paid for their roles? If we each started advocating for others, and for ourselves, perhaps we could finally close the gender pay gap.

Asking for help

Finally, instead of being embarrassed or feeling like they are a burden, successful givers will ask for help when they need it. Having built a broad network through their generosity, successful givers create a lot of goodwill in the relationships they build. And while strong ties are an easy place to turn to when you need help, givers have the added advantage of being able to ask dormant ties (people you've known in the past but not spoken to or seen in a while) that can provide novel information, ideas and contacts because they move in different circles to you.

In one study, researchers asked hundreds of executives to seek advice on a major work project from two dormant ties. When they compared the value of these conversations to the advice from current contacts, the dormant ties were actually more useful. The executives received more valuable solutions, referrals, and problem-solving assistance from people they used to know than from their current friends, colleagues, and acquaintances.

Can you be a successful giver?

When we first met Amy in the program, she was an ambitious young marketing manager working in a large professional services firm and struggling to navigate the pace and politics to create the career she wanted. A natural introvert, Amy had come to realize that simply sitting at her desk each day, doing her best work and hoping someone would notice was derailing, instead of fast tracking, her professional opportunities.

Even though she described herself as allergic to the big-noting, self-aggrandizing, elbows-out form of networking she saw across the firm, as she looked at the research on relationships, Amy came to understand that it would be at least worth playing with ways to make networking more authentic for her. When she thought about how she could use her strengths to best be of service to others, she decided to start looking for ways to make navigating social media easier for people across the firm.

She began slowly by sharing an easy-to-apply LinkedIn or Twitter article with one new colleague each day. Based on the positive responses she gained, next Amy started to offer her time to guide teams working on key white papers in the firm that could be shared through social media and willingly crediting them with any success they achieved. As the momentum for social media across the firm began to grow, she decided to invite some of the early adopters to join her in hosting a monthly lunch-and-learn session for others who wanted more hands-on guidance. And when corporate risk management policies made it difficult for people to capitalize on the opportunities of social media, she sought the advice of her new network on how they could make a business case together to overturn these limits.

It took less than three months for Amy's network of contacts across the firm to grow from forty-two to 503 people. Her willingness to go beyond what was expected in her job and to help people in an area where they were really struggling, quickly built her personal brand as an expert in this space and connected her with people at all levels and across every part of the firm. Not only did Amy start to enjoy her work more because of the value she was providing, but when she asked for help, these relationships became instrumental in opening up new advancement opportunities, championing her for promotions, and continuing to build her reputation and network inside and outside the business. It turned out that when she networked in a way that was authentic to her, she wasn't allergic to it at all.

Just as we hold beliefs about what successful leadership traits look like, the beliefs many women hold on what is required to network successfully, are just stories that need to be respectfully challenged. Networking doesn't require you to talk endlessly about yourself, work a room for the best contact, or try to take advantage of others. Instead, the best way to network your way to long-term success is to genuinely and mindfully be of service to others.

You can test the beliefs you're taking into your relationships at work and see if your dominant style is to be more of a taker, matcher, or giver in your networks currently by completing the free five minute survey at www.giveandtake.com. Then print out the questions below from www.leadlikeawoman.net/bookplaysheets and start to find small ways you can begin networking more authentically and effectively to improve your wellbeing and your performance at work.

- When you look at your purpose, the personal brand you want to build, and the strengths that you have, how can you be of the most service to others at work? If you were wisely and mindfully supporting others what would you give, when would you give it, how would you give and whom would you give to? How can you place boundaries around the advice, assistance, and resources you're giving to maximize the benefits for others and feel like you're making a positive difference without burning yourself out?
- What percentage of your work is currently spent actively collaborating with others or being a lone star? Is there one project you can focus on in the coming weeks to allow you to explore the strength givers find in interdependence? How could you ensure you're putting the group's goals and mission first, showing the same amount of concern for others as you do for yourself, and give away credit to the group? How can you note the benefits of this experience?
- Think back over the last time you presented an idea or attended a meeting where decisions were being made: How many questions did you ask and how many statements did you make? Do you generally try to dominate others by using more powerful communication (speaking forcefully, projecting

authority, promoting your accomplishments and selling with conviction and pride) or are you trying to influence others by using more powerless communication (being open about vulnerability and weaknesses, using disclaimers and hedges, asking for advice)? Remembering that every action is preceded by a question, try preparing for your next presentation or meeting by identifying and asking the questions that would help the group look for the true, the good and the possible in the situations you're reviewing.

- When you're negotiating with others is your focus primarily on their emotions and feelings or their thoughts and interests? Is your empathy for others creating win-lose outcomes for you? How can you remind yourself in these moments that by advocating for others and for yourself (think about the women negotiating pay rises) you can create win-win outcomes that increase the value for everyone involved.
- When was the last time you asked someone in your network for help? Did you ask someone who was a strong tie or a dormant tie? What might be possible if you tried once a week, for the next month to genuinely ask one person in your network for help with the things you are working on or the career plan you've mapped? What help do you need? Who might you ask? How could you monitor this experiment?

Maintaining your brand momentum

So, now that you're on the path to building your personal brand, getting clear on your life vision, working on purpose and using that to direct the way you think about your career and your relationships, what now? We have some final actions for you to think about that will help propel you forward, maintain your momentum, and get you unstuck if you are still a little quizzical with what comes next. Reflect on these actions, and print off the personal brand checklist and worksheet at www.leadlikeawoman.net/bookplaysheets.

Getting a handle on your current brand status

If you haven't already done so, make sure you get a clear picture on your current personal brand. The best way to find out what people think is to ask. Email ten or more of your friends, peers, past and present managers, clients, and business partners and ask them to answer the following questions:

- Which five words would you use to describe me?
- What are my greatest strengths?
- What are my weaknesses or derailment factors?
- What are my superpowers, those things that I do better than anyone else you know?
- What do you think my career sweet spot is or could be?

When you get this information back, take a deep breath, and look for common themes, surprising comments, and how this collective view of your brand sits with your current personal view. Is the external perception close to where you want to be, or a long way away? Were there strengths and superpowers highlighted that you weren't aware of, or that you can really use to your advantage? Think back to the content in this chapter on career goals, brand gaps, and skills development, and factor this information into your plan to achieve your goals.

While you are getting a handle on your external perception,

take a good look online to see what is visible about you, and how you are showing up. This means doing a Google search on your name, looking at your social media presence on platforms like LinkedIn, Twitter, and Facebook, and taking a good honest look at how you could be perceived through the information that you have put out there, or that someone else has. Get all the information available to help prepare you for what comes next, getting yourself to market.

Taking your brand to market

Once you are really clear on all we have covered, it's time to look at how you build your brand in the market. Now don't panic; that doesn't mean you have to be out doing speaking engagements, writing articles for magazines, splashing yourself all over the internet or profiling yourself across town. They may be strategies you want to investigate, but that's not all taking your brand to market means.

Let's start small with these immediate steps:

- *Check your LinkedIn profile* – with your fresh take on your personal brand and career goals, are you portraying yourself in the best possible light, highlighting your most relevant experience and covering the skills, knowledge and information that supports your brand and aspirations? Update your profile as needed to ensure you are using this powerful platform to your best advantage.
- *Check other social media* – are you being consistent with your brand across any other social media platforms you are using? Do a search and make sure you are, from your descriptive details to the posts you are making.

- *Where is your CV stored?* – Often in organizations your CV is kept on file in human resources, performance management databases, or high potential women files. Try and identify where old versions of your CV might be stored and see if you can update them to reflect your current career and brand status. Also think about any recruiters, agencies, or industry bodies that may have an old version of your CV or profile and reach out to get it updated.
- *Promoting your brand within your company* – look for opportunities within your current business to build social proof for your brand, and edge you toward the career goal you specified. Are their meetings you can attend, presentations you can give, brown bag lunches you can host, content you can write, and special projects you can put your hand up for? Ask your mentor and sponsor the most effective channels to promote yourself, and be of service.
- *Building your brand in the market* – if you do have a goal to become more visible outside your company, then start to look for ways to promote yourself and your work. This could be starting a blog, hosting events or workshops, taking a leadership role with your industry association, publishing your thought leadership in industry magazines or websites, through to speaking engagements at events in your specialized area. Think small, but also dream big. What would be the most courageous goal you could imagine to build your brand in your market? What would a dream engagement look like? What could it mean for your career aspirations? Small is a good place to start, but don't limit yourself to staying there if you want to play bigger.

This chapter has been quite a journey. Building your personal brand is an exciting opportunity. Doing this in the context of creating your life vision, defining your purpose and creating a career you love, is even more thrilling. Nothing you have or will create here is stagnant, and it will continue to evolve, develop, and grow as you do. Keep coming back to the exercises and your journaling over time to keep your vision, purpose, career, and brand alive, energized, and aligned, and it will keep you grounded in, and inspired by all that is possible.

The key ideas

- Your personal brand helps to define for the world who you are, what you do, the value you create, and why you are relevant. It helps to differentiate you from your peers, stand out in your space, and be known for what matters most to you. It's important to identify what your authentic personal brand looks like, as it will help you clearly navigate your life, your career, and how you lead.
- You have the power to create the life you want to live, and you can start by giving yourself permission to dream about what that life could look like. Thinking about the elements you want in your life, how they come together, and how you want to feel each day are inspiring pathways to create a life that fills you with excitement and energy.
- Getting to your *why* is a critical part of building your personal brand and showing up each day in a way that is authentic and meaningful. For the sake of what are you creating this life vision? What work feels meaningful for you in the world? Building your why statement will help you create clarity on why you do what you do each day.
- The best career plan is one that is driven out of purpose and meaning, that is grounded in your why, and that supports your version of what success looks like. Core planning elements include how you will assess your career options broadly and creatively, set a clear current goal, fill any gaps, and build your brand statement to help you achieve your aspirations.
- Your relationships, particularly mentors and sponsors, can be an essential part of building and supporting your brand, and your career. Understanding the difference between these roles, who is best placed to perform them, and how to

cultivate them, are important aspects to be managed with intention and gratitude.

- Networking can be a fulfilling experience, both personally and for your career. Reframing networking by looking at where you are a giver, taker or matcher, and pivoting your behavior to be a healthy giver, is a powerful way of growing your network, building your career, and serving your relationships.

Leading you

- Use the tools we have outlined in this chapter to get crystal clear on the core elements of your personal brand. Who are you when you show up as your most authentic self and who do you want to be? What five words best describe your brand, and how do you best live it in the world?
- Are you creating the life you really want to live? Get clear on the vision you want for your life. Journal about the core elements, create a vision board, and start infusing your vision with positive emotions and small actions to bring it to life.
- Don't wait to be struck by purpose. Define and own your why and write down your personal statement to keep you moving forward on your purposeful path. Watch Simon Sinek's TED talk at www.ted.com to further fuel your thinking about getting to your why.
- Assess your career options by viewing your career as a play gym not a ladder. Are you looking broadly enough at what is possible for you? Reflect on your list, your immediate goal, any gaps that need filling, what your personal brand statement could be, and how it will move you toward the purposeful work you are seeking.

- Create your list of current and potential mentors and sponsors and build an action plan to connect with existing relationships, create pathways to build new ones, and do both with a sense of gratitude for the opportunities these relationships provide.
- Go through the exercises on being a giver, matcher, or taker, and determine how you can bring more healthy giving behavior into your work. Remember to download the playsheets at www.leadlikeawoman.net/bookplaysheets to support your journey.

Leading others

- What is your personal brand as a leader? Reflect on your own journey, core brand elements and how you bring this to life in your career. Once you have done that, think about how you can support your team in doing this for themselves. Facilitate a dialogue with your team members around the core elements required to build an effective personal brand, and support them to work through this checking back with you on their progress. Provide them with the personal brand playsheets from www.leadlikeawoman.net/bookplaysheets to support their inquiry.
- Think about each individual woman that you lead: Are you aware of what their vision is for their life and what meaningful work looks like for them? Set up a development conversation where you can get to know them on this level and build a supportive platform to lead and enable them to reach their holistic goals, they will be more engaged, productive, and loyal as a result of your efforts. Print out the life vision worksheet at www.leadlikeawoman.net/bookplaysheets to help you navigate this conversation.

- Do the women in your team have a career plan? Have they assessed their options widely and objectively? Are you clear as their leader what the potential next steps are that are in line with their personal brand and goals? Print off the personal brand checklist on our website to ensure you are discussing each area and helping them build out a well thought through plan.
- Do each of your team members have the mentors and sponsors they need to help develop their career effectively? Again, have a discussion with each woman you lead (and the guys too) to see where they are at and what connections you may be able to enable them with. Also look at who you are mentoring and sponsoring, and who is doing that for you. It's important to walk your talk authentically, so take the personal steps you need as well.
- As a leader, are you a giver, taker, or matcher? Test your own beliefs with the survey at www.giveandtake.com so that you can see where you personally sit and what your dominant style is. Then observe your team. How do they network effectively, if at all? Where might they be overplaying their giving, or negatively impacting relationships through being a taker? Help each team member work through what this means for them, where they sit, and how they can be more effective.

Reflection questions

- In the past when you've felt like your career and life were moving in exactly the direction you most wanted, what was happening? It might have only been for a small moment or for an extended period of time but when you've felt like you were living on purpose, that you were being recognized for what you do best, that you were being supported by others, how did this feel? What were you able to achieve? What made this moment possible?

- If you were able to have more moments like this and build an authentic personal brand to support the career you really want in the months and years ahead, what might be possible? What would you be known for? How could you stay connected to your life vision? What could you do to start really honoring your sense of purpose? How would this shape your career? Who are the mentors or sponsors that could you help you make this happen? How would you start reaching out to your network? What could you do to really live your brand at each day at work? Describe these possibilities as vividly as possible.
- If there was one small step you'd be willing to take in the next one to two days to start making this dream of building an authentic brand a reality, what are you willing to try?

4

Mindfully Maintaining Wellbeing

At our core, we all want to be well. We're searching for radiant, vibrant wellbeing. And even if we struggle to articulate exactly what that means, we know it when we see it. It's why we stare longingly at glossy pictures of healthy people in magazines, and get waves of envy from being around that friend who just oozes wellness out of her every pore. It's all perfectly natural.

The problem is that the word *wellbeing* gets thrown around a lot. In fact, from Buddha to the explosion of the self-help movement, history is paved with thousands of suggestions on how to create and maintain this ambiguous concept. But just what *is* wellbeing and why might you want to *mindfully* maintain it?

In its simplest form, wellbeing is our ability to feel good and function effectively. It gives us the resources to navigate the highs and lows we all experience in our work and lives, whilst enabling us to flourish. As a result studies are finding that people who have higher levels of wellbeing reap all sorts of benefits. Not only are they more resilient, have more energy, are healthier and happier, but they are also more charitable, better liked by others, are more creative and productive at work, and earn more money. It turns out that wellbeing is what makes it possible for us to be well and do well.

We know that sounds simple enough. And yet the reality is that perhaps like us, you've discovered that maintaining your wellbeing is a lot harder than it looks. In fact, a recent study shows that when it comes to our wellbeing, seventy per cent of us report that we actually spend most of our time somewhere between *functioning* and *flailing*. In other words, most of us are *just* getting by.

But surely that's just life right? After all, by now we all know that we *should* move regularly, eat wisely and sleep deeply, but the daily demands of life, increasing workloads, and even our own beliefs about our sense of worth, mean that many of us wind up making choices every day that undermine our wellbeing. Let's be completely honest: Despite our best intentions, finding the time and energy to look after ourselves is challenging. But what if it didn't have to be?

The foundational tools of wellbeing

At the point in our workshops when we start talking about wellness, the women are on the edge of their seats hoping there's some magical pill we can offer that will help them create this glowing picture of health. And while what we've discovered isn't quite as quick and simple as swallowing a tablet, we're happy to tell you that researchers are finding there are a lot of small, every day actions you can take to create the kind of vibrant wellbeing you've been dreaming about. It starts by understanding the importance of the foundational tools of wellbeing: sleep, eat, move, and restore.

Sleeping deeply

Much has been written recently on the importance of sleep, not least being Arianna Huffington's story of waking up in a pool of blood after hitting her head on the corner of her desk, when she passed out from exhaustion. Researchers suggest ninety-five per cent of us need somewhere between seven and nine hours of sleep per night. Unfortunately, roughly two-thirds of us report we don't get enough sleep and as a result studies have found we're damaging our health, our mood, our cognitive capacity, and our productivity.

We found that when it came to sleeping deeply, there was a common mistake we and the women we met, were often making: The assumption that one less hour of sleep to finish off that report or to catch up with friends, wouldn't make that much difference to how we felt the next morning. Instead, it seems the exact opposite occurs. For example, one study found that losing ninety minutes of sleep reduces our daytime alertness by nearly one-third. And according to another researcher, four hours of sleep loss produces as much impairment as heading into work having just drunk a six-pack of beer.

Yet somehow we seem to continue to sacrifice sleep because study after study shows we are lousy judges of how a lack of sleep impacts our performance and our health. "Like a drunk," the Harvard sleep expert Charles Czeisler wrote, "a person who is sleep deprived has no idea how functionally impaired he or she truly is. Most of us have forgotten what it really feels like to be awake."

This seems to be particularly true of working mums who report being the most fatigued of all those suffering sleep deprivation. Our bodies run best on a 24-hour circadian rhythm that regulates our sleeping and waking cycles. But if we lose access to our normal time cues (like daylight and darkness) it appears our bodies drift into 25.4-hour days, throwing off our sleep cycle by up to ten hours a week. This disruption of our natural rhythm has been found to contribute to a host of issues from weight gain to heart problems and depression.

Here are three small changes researchers have found can help you get your sleep back on track:

- *Maintain a consistent schedule of sleeping and waking, even on the weekend.* Resist the urge to sleep in until noon, and instead, treat yourself instead to a one hour or less afternoon nana nap. At night, set an alarm to tell you it's time to get ready for bed. Keep in mind that your body has a tendency to push later and later if given the chance, so you need to get to bed before you hit your second wind.
- *Create a bedtime routine.* Give yourself at least forty-five minutes to wind down before bed with clear nighttime cues to help your body relax. Dim the lights. Lower the temperature by two to four degrees. Turn off electronics (smart phones, iPads, computers, and TVs or anything with blue LED light as it impacts your sleep hormones). Write down what's on your mind—especially unfinished to-do's or issues. Try some restorative yoga or meditate. Read a non-stimulating but enjoyable book.
- *Don't worry if you wake in the middle of the night.* It appears that waking in the middle night is perfectly natural, given we've evolved to have what researchers call segregated sleeping, a *first sleep* and a *second sleep* with a short waking period in between. Rather than lying there anxiously watching the

minutes tick by, try some slow breathing or meditation. If you need to sit up for twenty minutes, keep the lights low and read or listen to some relaxing music before heading back to bed. Studies have found this time can be the most relaxing time of your day, provided you're not worried about sleeping!

The most effective way Megan found to move from an all-night workaholic insomniac to the land of dreamtime, was creating a bedtime routine. Her ritual goes something like this: once the house is quiet for the night with her son in bed and the last of the work done, she pads her way down to the kitchen, takes her evening vitamins and makes herself a cup of relaxing tea (a night time blend or chamomile is great).

She turns off all the lights and heads upstairs to do some gentle restorative yoga, before getting into bed with a book or a magazine. Now this is key—her bedtime reading has to be light, or her mind will be buzzing all night with new ideas, so no gender studies or psychology reading at bedtime! Instead, she reads a chapter of a spiritual book, or flicks through a health magazine and drinks her tea. Then she puts a few drops of lavender oil on her temples, does ten or so minutes of meditation while lying in bed, and then it's off to dreamland for her. Having done it for a long time, for Megan this is a ritual she looks forward to and finds calming for its sheer sense of repetition. Grounding her at the end of the day, and bringing a sense of peace, she also finds it's an easy and busy proof practice she can do even whilst traveling.

Eating well

While there's a lot of conflicting advice about what we should and shouldn't be eating and drinking, it would be safe to say that no one is advocating you should intentionally consume more refined sugars, fried foods or alcohol. This alone can be a challenging starting place for most of us, ourselves included. So how can we manage to eat well, whilst still living in the real world, maintaining our sense of joy for food, and not driving ourselves crazy?

We found it helpful to start thinking about food not as calories, but as energy. You see scientists have found that just about everything we eat is converted by our body into glucose, which provides the energy our bodies and brains need to stay alert and productive. When we're running low on glucose, we have a tough time staying focused, our attentions drifts and our bodies become sluggish. This helps explain why it's hard to do anything very productive on an empty stomach.

But as Social Psychologist Ron Friedman explains, the part we rarely consider is that our bodies don't process all foods at the same rate. For example, foods like pasta, bread, cereal, and soda release their glucose quickly, leading to a burst of energy followed by a slump. Other food, like high-fat meals (think cheeseburgers), can provide more sustained energy, but require our digestive system to work harder, reducing oxygen levels in the brain and making us groggy.

Most us know this intuitively, so why do we often fail to make good decisions about what we eat? Unfortunately, we're often at our lowest point in both energy and self-control by the time we try to decide what to eat, making a chocolate brownie or a bag of fries hard to resist. Unhealthy food options can also seem easier and quicker to grab, causing us to think we're saving time without appreciating the impact on our performance half an hour later. It can be hard to manage our food choices as we attend poorly catered workshops or meetings, or when the healthy salmon dish we ordered at the restaurant arrives with a high-sugar sauce smothered on top of it. And if we're completely honest, sometimes no matter how bad we know particular food or drinks may be for us, the taste is so good, or the shared experience with friends is so enjoyable, we just don't care what we're putting into our bodies.

Fortunately, the trick to eating right is not learning to resist temptation. It's making healthy eating the easiest possible option. Here are three approaches researchers suggest trying:

- *Make your eating decisions before you get hungry.* Studies show we're a lot better at resisting salt, calories, and unhealthy fats in the future than we are in the present. Think about the meals and snacks that will be within your control this week. What can you have on hand to make good eating choices easier? Try to set your sights on foods that are good for your near-term energy and long-term health. For example, Michelle carries in her bag an insulated flask with her homemade green smoothie and several protein balls so that during the day she has everything she needs to maintain her energy. And Megan likes to carry small bags of nuts, filtered water, and protein bars to keep her going.
- *Eat small and frequently.* Spikes and drops in blood sugar are bad for your productivity, your brain, and your body. Smaller, more frequent meals maintain your glucose at a more consistent level than relying on a midday feast or big evening meal. Start your day right with a high-protein breakfast, then note where your natural energy slumps occur during the day (for many of us it's around 10 am, 1 pm, 4 pm and 7 pm) and at these times stop to eat something nourishing and check

in on your water consumption (often we mistake thirst for hunger).

- *Track how you're going and adjust accordingly.* There are a few good and bad ingredients in most meals. No matter how hard you try, you will eat some foods that are not ideal. So do a little accounting in your head. Ask yourself if what you are about to eat is a net gain or a net loss for your energy, based on what you know about all the ingredients. Look for foods with less fat, fewer carbohydrates, and as little added sugar as possible. Then keep servings small and indulgences rare (pick the moments you can afford the energy slumps), and you're likely to have less guilt, more enjoyment, and better health. By developing the habit of asking this question, you will make better decisions in the moment and be aware of how you're tracking across the day.

Other small tips from researcher Tom Rath that have helped us gradually improve upon what we were eating include:

- Buy use it or lose it food to avoid things that are too processed.
- Lean towards produce with dark and vibrant colors; fruit and vegetables that are green, red or blue are good nutritional sources and help foster the production of dopamine, which plays a key role in the experience of curiosity, motivation and engagement.
- Study nutritional labels and look for packaged products with less than 10g of sugar in a single serving.
- Replace chips, crackers, and snack bars with nuts, seeds, apples, celery, and carrots.
- Try to eliminate one form of red or processed meat from

your diet for good.

- Replace all juice, soda, and sugary beverages with water, tea, coffee, or other unsweetened drinks.
- Set a goal for eating foods that have a ratio of one gram of carbs for every one gram of protein (most nutritional labels will tell you this). Try to avoid foods with more than five to one carbs to protein.

Born with a fast metabolism, Michelle was able to spend most of her life eating mindlessly until she turned thirty and everything started to slow down. Challenged for the first time in her life to notice what she was consuming she quickly realized there were a lot of stories she was invested that made it hard to eat well.

For example, "my stomach doesn't wake up before lunch," turned out not to be true and she found she had far more energy and was more alert after two scrambled eggs for breakfast. Then there was "I don't like the taste of wholemeal," but it turned out that when the quality of the product is a good seed-based bread can be every bit as delicious as a white loaf. And how about "I need sugar and fried foods for comfort," when low and behold a bowl of fresh cherries, or a handful of strawberries will also work.

As Michelle began to slowly challenge her stories about food, she came to understand that what she put in her mouth had a profound impact on her levels of energy. So now when it comes to eating she considers what she has to do in the hours ahead and tries to have quick, delicious and good food in reach like protein balls, nuts, green smoothies, fresh fruit and vegetables, eggs, seeded bread, and organic soups. It doesn't mean she doesn't still indulge in the odd glass of wine, spaghetti carbonara, or chocolate soufflé; it's just that she tries to do so mindfully (and in small portions) at times when she doesn't need to rely heavily on her energy.

Being mindful of what she eats also helps Michelle to notice the foods that feel good for her, and the ones that don't serve her so well. Increasingly, researchers are finding that each of us is unique in the way we absorb and metabolize nutrients based on factors such as genetic makeup, gut bacteria, body type, and chemical exposure. This means the same dietary advice can't be good for everyone. And while personalized nutrition services are growing in popularity, scientists caution that there is still much to be learnt before this approach is reliable. So in the meantime, be mindful of how the foods you eat impact your energy levels so that little by little, meal by meal, you can make small adjustments that improve the way you eat.

Moving regularly

We thought exercising three times a week would have us covered when it came to moving regularly, only to discover that this probably isn't enough to counter all the hours we spend sitting in our jobs. Declared the most underrated health threat of our time, it turns out that on average most of us sit for around nine hours a day—yes, we spend more time sitting than sleeping. Just take a moment now to add it up: you probably sat down as you had breakfast, traveled into work, attended a few meetings, sent some emails, had your lunch, made a few phone calls, completed key tasks, traveled home, ate your dinner, and watched some TV, or caught up with some friends. It all adds up.

Frighteningly researchers have found that inactivity is now killing more people than smoking, with more than six hours of sitting a day greatly increasing our risk of an early death. In fact, every hour we spend on our rear ends saps our energy and ruins our health. We had no idea. It turns out that the problem with sitting is that it takes an immediate toll on our health. As soon as our bottoms find a comfortable place to land, the electrical activity in our leg muscles shut down, the number of calories we're burning, the enzymes that help break down fat and our good cholesterol all drop considerably. And just to add insult to injury, the act of sitting for long periods literally makes our backsides bigger, with long periods of pressure on our cells found to make our fat tissue expand.

Yet for most of us sitting for several hours a day is an inevitable part of our jobs. The key to countering this seems to be increasing our activity as much as possible by getting up and moving around throughout the day. Walk across the office to talk to a colleague rather than sending an email. Take the stairs instead of the elevator. Stretch whenever you can. Every extra opportunity you have to move counts.

One of the easiest and most popular ways to increase our daily activity is to strap on a pedometer and start counting our steps. Researchers suggest this is a simple and effective way to keep track of just how much we're moving, the goal being to reach 10,000 steps a day. Whether it's a FitBit, a Jawbone, a smart watch, your smart phone or an old-fashioned pedometer, there are plenty of ways you can count your steps. The good news is that while 5,500 steps a day is considered sedentary, every step you take above this as you build up the amount of movement in your day helps to improve your wellbeing. Of course you can also trade off other activities for steps with ten minutes of moderately intense activity (anything that increases your breathing and heart rate) thought to be worth 1,000 steps and ten minutes of highly intense activity (anything that causes you to puff) thought to be worth 2,000 steps.

Of course, your steps should be complemented with regular exercise. Researchers suggest thirty minutes of physical activity—anything that makes you move your body and burns calories—five times a week, or 150 minutes in total seems to be a good guide for most of us, even if you need to do ten or fifteen minutes a couple of times a day to reach this goal. More important though than what researchers recommend works for some of us, some of the time is finding out what works best for you. This means checking in with a doctor or health expert on what the ideal amount of exercise is for your body. It also means figuring out what kind of exercise you enjoy doing and are most likely to stick with. A little bit of exercise you want to show up for is better than no exercise at all.

Three ways researchers suggest you can make moving regularly more effective include:

- *Every twenty minutes move for two minutes* – When you have no choice but to sit for several hours a day, at least break it up. Even two minutes of leisurely walking every twenty minutes is enough to stabilize your blood sugar levels and taking regular breaks has been found to improve your creativity, and productivity.
- *Exercise early* – Just twenty minutes of moderate activity could significantly improve your mood for the next twelve hours. So, while working out in the evening is better than no activity at all, you essentially sleep through and miss most of the boost in your mood. Exercising before you eat breakfast, instead of after, could also burn additional fat and improve your glucose tolerance.
- *Measure your 10,000 steps* – When people are assigned to wear a pedometer as part of randomized controlled trials, overall

activity levels go up by twenty-seven per cent. Take a walking meeting, catch up with friends as you move, try a walking desk while you're writing, and get on the stepper while you watch TV. There are plenty of small ways to increase your daily movement.

Michelle spent most of her life swearing the words fun and run did not belong in the same sentence. In fact, she swore black and blue to one personal trainer that her body just couldn't run because she couldn't get enough air through her nose! Oh, the stories we tell. It wasn't until Michelle saw the research on the impact high-intensity exercise like running has on the brain's ability to learn and grow that she was willing to rethink this long-held story. Completing her Masters of Positive Psychology at the time and needing every advantage she could get, she finally strapped on a pair of sneakers to put the research to the test.

You'll never believe it but not only was she able to breathe when she ran but when she stopped telling herself how much she hated every minute of it, running could be almost enjoyable. And even though she'd spent most of life telling anyone who would listen that she wasn't a morning person, it turned out that running along the beach as the sun rises was no trouble at all once she realized how well this prepared her up for the day ahead. Last year she even completed a fun run with her ten-year-old son, and later confessed that when you run for the right reason and with people you love—it can indeed be kind of fun.

Gently restore

As difficult as we may find it to make time to sleep deeply, eat well, and move regularly, we find that for most women, gently restoring themselves is the most challenging of all the wellbeing steps. It's not that what's required is hard—these activities have the potential to be pure bliss—it's that we simply don't believe we are worthy of being looked after, even by ourselves. And even if we do believe it, creating the space to put ourselves on the top of our to-do list, when there is so much else going on, often feels like an impossible task. Check this for yourself right now: Just for a moment pause and ask yourself, "What have I done in the past week to slow down and nurture myself?" If you're like a lot of the women we meet, it's probably a pretty short list.

So why is this so hard for us? Like most of the challenges when it comes to mindfully maintaining our wellbeing, the main protagonist is our story of "We're so busy!" Not only are we trying to keep up at work, but also we're usually flat out looking after everybody else. Let's be honest: While getting enough sleep, eating reasonably well and fitting in the odd exercise class might make the cut because they're the hygiene factors of human functioning, how could we possibly justify taking the time to nurture ourselves? Imagine finding an hour for a relaxing massage, just because you deserve it. Or how about an unhurried daily meditation practice, just because it made your soul sing with pleasure. Maybe even an uninterrupted, candle-scented bubble bath . . . just because you can.

Gently restoring ourselves is about balancing our do-everything, please-everyone, keep-all-the-balls-in-the-air energy, which left unchecked eventually burn us out. It means doing things that leave us feeling well, rested, and cared for like enjoying nature, savoring a good cup of tea, reading for pleasure, practicing some restorative yoga or taking a nap. We know that these things might seem like indulgences you simply can't afford, but let us assure you that making time for restoration is essential for your wellbeing and that you are worth every moment.

It's important to mention here, without getting all doom and gloom about it, what the alternative looks like. While we find that the majority of women we work with are firmly planted in the functioning part of the wellbeing scale—getting by, but by no means feeling vibrantly well—many of the women we work with are also dangerously close to burn out. And trust us, as Megan will attest to from her own personal journey, it's a long road back from that place.

When we consistently neglect what our body and soul needs to thrive, in the mistaken attempt to just keep running on the never-ending treadmill of work and life, we start to wither. That withering could look like a small and intermittent zapping of your energy, to a complete loss of your sparkle and enthusiasm. It's just not worth the journey to exhaustion when there are so many small, busy-proof ways to fuel your spark, restore your energy, and nurture yourself.

One of our favorite ways is to meditate. Now before you dump this idea in the too hard basket, let us share how we've made this a joyful and restorative practice that can be done anywhere in as little as two minutes. We often find that while the idea of quieting our minds can be appealing, the reality of trying to think about nothing for extended periods of time and failing miserably with our busy monkey minds quickly puts many of us off the idea of ever meditating again.

So you can imagine our relief when we found that actually being aware of our wandering minds and then gently choosing to bring them back to stillness, was actually the whole point of mediation. The more we got it wrong, the more practice we got at restoring our sense of peace and calm. It turns out that in its very best form meditation is simply a way to train your brain's ability to pay attention so you can focus your mind on the things that actually matter. Think of it as a very gentle mental workout, without any sweating. Yes, it's called a practice for a reason!

Chade-Meng Tan, Google's master of mindfulness suggests we try to mindfully mediate like this: Sit quietly and set an intention for your meditation—it might be to improve your wellbeing, to restore yourself, or to practice training your mind—and once you're clear on why you're sitting in stillness, simply bring your attention gently to your breath. You may find yourself in a state where your mind is calm and concentrated and this may last for a long time, or for many of us, just for a few seconds.

If you find yourself getting distracted and realize your attention has wandered, rather than beating yourself up, just note that this is a wonderful moment to practice bringing your wandering attention back to focus on your breath. This is not failure. It's simply a chance to build your mental muscles. Acknowledge that you're learning, remind yourself of your intention and this time try to stay focused a little longer on your breath.

Meng suggests starting your meditation practice the easy way by just sitting for two minutes. Then as your ability to focus your attention improves see if you can keep extending the time a little longer to ten minutes, and later if you can even sit for thirty minutes, or an hour. With enough practice he notes you may even be able to bring your mind to this state on demand and stay in it for a prolonged periods of time to bring yourself more calmness, clarity, and happiness. And if that feels like a pipedream right now, don't worry. Even two to five minutes of meditation, twice a day, can lead to profound changes in your mindset, your levels of calm, and your restoration. Start small, and stay small for as long as you need.

Of course, there are many kinds of meditation. If sitting isn't for you, then you might like to try a walking meditation out in nature or just from your office to the printer. Or if paying attention to your breath feels tedious then you might like to try a guided meditation focusing on loving kindness or self-compassion. Alternatively, you may enjoy coloring in mandalas, listening to a beautiful piece of music, or simply breathing slowly as you stretch your body. The point of meditation isn't the method; it's giving your brain the space to restore by shifting from doing to being just for a little while.

Megan developed a toolkit of restorative practices not long after her burn out. From aromatherapy oils to bubble baths, herbal tea, painting and reading breaks, she has her kit of things she can use in as little as two minutes, to recharge and restore her throughout her days. One of the core parts of her practice is the way she anchors her mornings. Most days, Megan spends an hour or more at the beach, fairly early but not insanely so, walking, swimming, and just being. Not only does she get her exercise for the day, as well as her meditation practice (which is typically only five or ten minutes), but also her spirit is full, and she leaves feeling grounded and invigorated for the day ahead.

Whatever methods you choose, please make time and space to create your own toolkit of gentle restorative practices, and feel the way they nurture you, in all aspects of your being. To start moving towards consistent, vibrant wellbeing it's important to understand how you're currently doing and what's working well so that you can continue to build on it. Print out the questions below from www.leadlikeawoman.net/bookplaysheets and spend a little time getting really honest about where you're at and where you want to be heading.

- Over the last six months would you describe yourself as languishing (struggling to get out of bed in the morning), functioning (you're getting by, but it doesn't feel like there is much energy to spare) or flourishing (you feel fully engaged in life)? If you were to think of this as a scale with zero representing completely languishing and ten representing consistently flourishing, where have you been sitting when it comes to your wellbeing? This is just for your own information so please be as honest as you can.
- Looking at your chosen number, what's been working well when it comes to mindfully maintain your wellbeing? What's making it possible for you to sleep, even if you'd like more of it? What are the good eating choices you're making, even if they're not consistent? What movement are you getting, even if you're worried it's not enough? How are you gently restoring yourself, even if these moments are small and infrequent? What are the bright spots of your wellbeing? What wellbeing strengths do you have to build upon (you will definitely have some, so try to really look for them even if they are tiny glimmers right now)?
- If you were to consistently build upon the wellbeing strengths you already have, where do you think your wellbeing would be on the scale six months from now? What might this make possible? Why does this matter to you? What would you need to do to move towards this number?

Why hope lights the path

So by this point in the chapter, you may be feeling that this is all very compelling, but understand the reality that maintaining your wellbeing can still be so hard. The fact is that eighty-nine per cent of us believe that tomorrow will be better than today, but only fifty per cent of us believe that we can make so. Scientists explain this as the difference between wishing and hoping. When we simply *wish* that our wellbeing could improve, we take a more passive approach expecting that sheer willpower will enable us to pull off these changes. But when we *hope* to improve our wellbeing, we feel compelled to act whilst being realistic about the obstacles we may face.

Hopeful people understand that moving from where your wellbeing is today to where you want it to be is rarely a straight line that can be powered by the sheer force of willpower and self-control. Social psychologists have discovered that most of us have a limited supply of willpower that makes this approach difficult to sustain. Self-control works like a muscle that gets fatigued and worn down by the stress that comes with regulating your thoughts, feelings, and actions. So don't feel bad if you started your week saying you won't touch a glass of wine, but by Tuesday after a long day you guzzled two glasses with dinner. You're not a terrible or weak person; your self-control muscle just got exhausted.

The good news is that just like any other muscle, getting enough sleep, eating well and exercising can build up your willpower. Health psychologist Kelly McGonigal explains that this is because the need for willpower sets off a coordinated set of changes in your brain and body called the *pause-and-plan response* that puts you in a calmer state so you can resist temptation and override self-destructive urges. Requiring extra energy in your brain's prefrontal cortex—the thinking part of your brain—this response is more likely when your brain is well rested, nourished by a more plant-based, less-processed diet and supported by additional gray matter which can be achieved from exercise and meditation.

That also sounds simple enough, but can you spot the wellbeing challenge? In order to have the willpower to sleep deeply, eat well, move regularly, and gently restore yourself, you need to already be sleeping deeply, eating well, exercising, and restoring. This is why, despite our best intentions, so many of us quickly tire and run out of self-control when it comes to improving our wellbeing. We're wishing that we had enough willpower to keep us moving towards the change we want, but when it comes to consistently acting on our good intentions our brains aren't yet equipped to pull it off. It's enough to make you reach for yet another glass of wine.

So what do hopeful people do differently? Researchers have discovered that hope occurs when your rational self meets your emotional self in three simple steps:

- *Want-to goals* – rather than *have-to*, *should-do*, or *expected-of-me* goals that are clear, meaningful, and excite you about the future.
- *Multiple pathways* – forward that allow you to anticipate difficulties and potential setbacks, so you're resilient enough to reach your goal.
- *Agency* – to shape your life and take responsibility for making things happen.

Each of these steps forms a continuous feedback cycle that enhances your hope. In the sweet spot of this cycle, you're able to focus on your long-term goals to make better short-term choices and regulate your behaviors. You begin to believe in your ability to create the changes you want, while at the same time recognizing the limits of your control. You devote time and effort to mindfully maintaining your wellbeing and understand the difference between helpful critiques and challenges (which you can use as learning tools) and the messages that create doubt and sap your energy.

Shane Lopez one of the world's leading researchers on hope, describes it like this: "Hope is created moment by moment through our deliberate choices. It happens when we use our thoughts and feelings to temper our aversion to loss and actively pursue what is possible. When we choose hope, we define what matters to us most." Studies have found that hope seems to give you the energy to make this happen by helping you to be more productive, feel more satisfied and boost your wellbeing.

In our programs, we teach women to use hope to light their path forward when it comes to mindfully maintaining their wellbeing by creating a hope map. You can download the template for your map at www.leadlikeawoman.net/bookplaysheets and use it to complete the following steps:

- In the goal column, write down one *want-to* goal for the next three months when it comes to improving your wellbeing. Remember it's not a *have-to*, *should-do* or *expected-of-me* goal, but something that you genuinely want for yourself. Something that feels meaningful and is aligned to your life vision. Something you've been longing to have the confidence to make happen.

  Good goals are like looking through a pair of binoculars, they make fuzzy distant objects much clearer. When it comes to setting your goals we find it can help to imagine a ladder with steps numbered from zero at the bottom to ten at the top. The top of the ladder represents the life vision you imagined in the last chapter. The bottom of the ladder represents the life furthest away from these hopes. On which step of the ladder are you currently standing? On which step would you be excited to stand three months from now? What clear, specific, positive goal does this suggest you should set yourself?

- In the pathways column, write down three joyful pathways to help you reach this goal. The aim is to shrink your goal into smaller, more manageable, concrete steps that enable small victories to fuel your confidence, enthusiasm, and energy to trigger an upward spiral of positive behaviors.

  Try to be as specific as possible about the *where*, *when*, and *how* of these steps so you know exactly what you need to be doing. They might include steps you can take to help you sleep deeply like creating a bedtime routine, eating well by finding good, high energy food you can have on hand, moving more by getting a Fitbit, and counting your steps or practicing meditation. Try to choose pathways you'll genuinely look forward to doing. They should feel like small gifts to yourself.

- In the obstacle column, identify the obstacles that might disrupt each of these pathways. What will make them hard to pull off? It might be having enough time, sticking to it regularly, or finding the energy to get started. What's likely to get in your way?

  Studies have found that you're much more likely to achieve your goals when you plan for the obstacles up front. So be realistic and honest about the potential difficulties and setbacks that may bring you unstuck.

- Finally around the edge of the page, write down what you can do to maintain your energy and willpower to follow through on your pathways. Who can support and encourage you? How will you track your progress? What can you do to celebrate the small milestones along the way?

  If you want a little extra accountability try apps like www.stickK.com to make your goals public and binding. Created by Yale economists, on this website, you'll select your goal, set your stakes (you place a bet, risking either your money or your good name), pick a referee (who monitors your commitment and progress), and build a support team to cheer you on.

- Then put your hope map somewhere you can see it each day. We find the fridge, a mirror you use regularly, or your vision board are favorite spots for many of the women we work with. Just be sure not to use this as another thing to beat yourself up about, and instead use it as a gentle daily nudge towards mindfully looking after yourself. Note what's working for you and what's not and update or adjust your pathways as you go.

When Kelly joined one of our workshops she described herself as "exhausted from just trying to keep up with the life she had created." A partner in a large law firm, with two kids under the age of five, a good marriage, and lovely friends, Kelly had discovered that living the dream was far more than a full-time job. While she was generally in good health, there's nothing like children in day care to help you catch every little cold, and she was running low on energy, and struggling to keep up with everything.

Kelly's life vision entailed finding more purpose in her work by helping others and shaking up the very entrenched practices of a traditional law firm. She wanted to have the time and energy to play and enjoy her young family and she longed to start doing more traveling with them. It seemed the simplest of dreams, but she couldn't imagine how she could possibly fit in one more thing.

Kelly new she *should be* doing more to maintain her wellbeing. She managed to walk quite bit and tried to get to the gym a couple of times a week—some weeks were better than others. She tried to eat reasonably well, grabbing a piece of fruit when she could and being mindful of not consuming too many fried or fatty foods. And she did OK on sleep, except for the 4 am wake up calls most mornings when her children climbed into bed and she didn't have the heart to turn them away. She was getting by, but it would be fair to say it was closer to functioning than flourishing.

When Kelly sat down to create her hope map she realized that when it came to the kind of energy she wanted to have to realize her life vision she was probably standing on rung five, when she really wanted to be moving closer towards ten. She decided that for the next three months she'd focus on trying to move herself at least towards a seven, which helped her to set a wellbeing goal of: "Mindfully maintaining my wellbeing, so I have at least ten per cent more energy to put towards doing the things that matter most."

Committed to getting the basics of wellbeing working for her Kelly chose the following pathways and noted the obstacles that might bring her unstuck:

- Getting more sleep each night by sending the kids back to their own beds after a cuddle. The most likely obstacles would be difficulty holding this boundary and needing to remind herself that getting enough sleep was a kind act for everybody.

- Eating better by having more energy fuelling options on hand at home and at work. The most likely obstacles would be trying to find good food she liked the taste of and removing temptation from her path, particularly when she was tired.
- Really measuring how much exercise she was getting by using the Fitbit that had been sitting in her draw. The most likely obstacle was forgetting to charge it and put it on.

Then around the edge of her page Kelly noted ways she could maintain her motivation and willpower. She decided to enlist her husband's help in holding her accountable to these changes. She put a chart in her diary to give herself a score out of ten each night for each pathway, so she could correct her course the following day if needed. And she decided that each week she consistently hit seven and above, she would treat herself with a bath, a glass of wine, and a trashy movie to restore herself over the weekend.

With her hope map in hand, Kelly left the workshop determined to try to make these changes stick. When we checked in several weeks later we were amazed by the progress she was making. Not only was she getting more sleep and eating better, but she'd so gotten into the habit of walking a little first thing in the morning and a few more steps at lunch that she'd signed up for a two day hill climb in a month's time and was easily beating her target of 10,000 steps a day. Of course, there had been days it all came together, and days it unraveled a little—remembering to nudge the kids back to their own beds was hard when their bodies were snuggled in—but the best change Kelly had found during this period, was knowing how to reorient herself when things didn't go to plan and gracefully start over.

Kelly's story is one we hear again and again from the women who go through our programs. Perhaps the biggest change that takes place for them when it comes to mindfully maintaining their wellbeing isn't really any of the tips we teach on sleeping deeply, eating well, moving regularly or gently restoring themselves, but is in how they can build pathways of hope to gently carry them towards the outcomes they want.

How to build habits that stick

Hopefully now the pieces of this wellbeing puzzle are really starting to come together. You understand the small changes you can make to the way you sleep, eat, move, and restore and how you can use hope to light the path forward. But how do the Kelly's of the world really pull off mindfully maintaining their wellbeing in a busy world? After all it's one thing to have a plan and another thing entirely to find the time to execute it. We found that the women who struggled to realize their hopes all had one thing in common: They were just *too busy* to find the time to look after themselves. If this is what you're feeling, don't worry, there's no judgment here. We spent many, many years stuck in the same story.

We're not for a moment doubting how much you're already juggling. Demanding jobs, families to tend, friendships to enjoy, and lives to maintain. But here's the thing: Getting all of these things done isn't really about the amount of time you have, it's about the amount of energy you bring. When you're short on sleep, skipped breakfast and haven't exercised all week because you're too busy you make completing that next report, negotiating that deal, and being present for the people you love far harder than it needs to be. It's like setting out to hike a mountain and intentionally choosing to leave all the supplies that would make your journey easier at the bottom.

Throughout this chapter we've seen how sleeping deeply, eating well, moving regularly, and gently restoring ourselves fuels our energy, our willpower, our hope, and our productivity. From now on, the moment you hear yourself saying you're too busy to make time for these activities, you need to slow down for just a few seconds to give yourself a self-compassionate nudge in the right direction. The fact is you are never too busy to look after yourself. Yes we said it. You are never too busy to look after yourself. And this comes from two women with decades of experience juggling full-time careers, post-graduate studies, growing families, and our own needs.

As Megan likes to say: "You're busy with what you've said yes to." Try to really sit in the truth of this statement for a moment, even if it's uncomfortable. When you look at how much you have on your plate right now, who put it there? We aren't trying to be mean asking this question. Sure, there are always things that come from our boss, or responsibilities at home particularly with children that are unavoidable. But a lot of the things we have committed ourselves to were our own choosing.

You're busy with what you've said "yes" to. We realize it may not be the most thrilling observation, in fact, if you're like some of our clients it might even make you feel a little mad to hear it at first. But your life, your work, your wellbeing, are the result of your choices. That may be a scary thought because it means that you have to take responsibility for what you are saying "yes" to, what you will say "no" to, and how firm you will hold those boundaries in place. But it can be one of the most empowering thoughts available to you because all else being equal, it really is all down to you. So feel free to own it.

Of course, we appreciate that you still have to live in the real world, and just because you intentionally or accidently said "yes" to something, doesn't mean that you can suddenly find hours each day to look after yourself. So we want to meet you half way on your busy schedule and show you how you can start maintaining your wellbeing on even the craziest day, in just eleven minutes.

Researchers at Duke University estimate up to forty per cent of your actions each day are not conscious choices but mere habits. That's a little more than six hours each day you spend mindlessly doing things. No wonder William James the father of modern psychology, cautioned that: "All our life, so far as it has definite form, is but a mass of habits—practical, emotional, and intellectual— systematically organized for our weal or our woe, and bearing us irresistibly towards our destiny, whatever the latter may be."

Now we're guessing, that like us, you'd like some of these habits to be moving you towards wellbeing. Luckily, researchers at MIT have found that our habits run on a simple loop: Cue, routine, and reward. For example, take the habit you have of brushing your teeth; your cue might be getting ready for bed, your routine is to brush your teeth, spit and rinse and your reward is the clean feeling you're left with and probably your bed! This leaves you feeling rewarded for your habit, so next time your cue goes off you repeat the pattern all over again.

A good cue lowers the amount of activation energy you need to use to get your habit started. You can anchor it to habits you already have, like getting ready for bed, so one behavior flows seamlessly into the next. You can embed it in your environment, like one of our friends who slept in his running gear, so you almost fall into the habit. Or you can use a when/then statement to prime your brain—like when I go to the restaurant then I will order the healthy salad—and when you find yourself in a situation you already know what you should be doing.

A routine can be physical, mental, or emotional, and it can be incredibly complex or fantastically simple. It all depends on what you're trying to achieve. The longer you practice, the stronger your neural pathways grow, and the easier and more enjoyable your habits generally become. But more important than the duration, is showing up and trying so if you only have a few minutes then start there and see what happens.

The reward is the step we find most people miss, and yet it's what makes maintaining your habits more likely. Whether it's checking it off a list, sharing your good news, noting it in a gratitude journal or making yourself a cup of tea, rewarding your efforts releases feel-good hormones that create positive memories of your routine, so that you'll want to repeat it next time your cue gets triggered—don't short change yourself on celebrating what you've achieved.

When we started really trying to improve our wellbeing, like many of you, there were times we really struggled to squeeze everything in. As a result Michelle decided to try using her brains natural habit loop to create eleven minute habits. To be clear there was no science to the eleven minutes, it was simply busy-proof. No matter how much she had going on she could always find eleven minutes somewhere and she figured a small start was better than not starting at all.

Here's how she did it. When Michelle decided to start running she began with just eleven minutes. She created a thirty second cue by anchoring it to waking up in the morning and embedded it in her environment by putting her alarm on top of her running clothes. Not wanting to wake the kids she's developed quite an art of quickly diving on top the alarm and as she's then up and out of bed the easiest thing is to get dressed and head out the door. She'd then run for ten minutes. And when she returned home her thirty second reward was a glass of ice cold water before hitting the shower.

It might be hard to imagine that such a small dose of daily running could do anything. Physically that might be true, but mentally it built Michelle's confidence that she could get up early, she could run, and it was worth doing. Within a week, she had downloaded an app to help her work her way up to five kilometers a day and despite traveling for work, the occasional illness and even a bout of profound grief she's managed to maintain this habit consistently.

Michelle's also used this approach to create a bedtime routine of restorative yoga, a daily meditation practice, to ensure she drinks two liters of water each day and eats small regular snacks. Each time she looks for a cue to trigger off the behavior—the alarm on her smart phone gets a great work out—and with a reward she wants so much, she'll complete the routine just to get it.

Of course, every now and then despite her best efforts she'll find there's a wellbeing habit she just can't quite get started. When this happens she's learned the trick is to play around with the cue or the reward until you find something that fits. For example, when she started her bedtime routine of restorative yoga she set the alarm on her smart phone to remind her to finish up what she was doing and head to the yoga mat. And night after night she'd turn the alarm off and ignore it. So she started putting it out of reach of whatever she was doing so she'd have to get up to turn it off. And night after night she'd turn the alarm off and sit back down again. Finally, when she put the kids to bed she put the alarm on the yoga mat in front of her bed. Now she had to walk on to the yoga mat to turn it off each night and given this was a change she wanted to make it felt completely self-defeating to turn around and walk back off. Much easier just to do a few downward dogs.

If you're struggling to move forward on the pathways you've chosen for your hope map, see if you can create a little eleven minute habit to get started. All you need is a solid cue to kick you off, a clear routine you'll perform, and a reward so good you'll perform the habit just to get there (although, try to do this without alcohol or chocolate if you can). As you play with these practices remember that good habits shouldn't constrain you, they shouldn't constrict you, and they shouldn't be a burden in your life. Rather, they should liberate your energy to do more of the things you love.

Can you nudge your way forward?

If even the idea of creating a wellbeing habit right now turns you cold with dread, there is another approach you might like to try. It's the science of nudges. In reality most changes happen incrementally. It's rare that we go from zero to one hundred in a heartbeat.

Psychologist Daniel Kahneman defines nudges as "nano-sized investments" that lead to "medium-sized gains." The costs are low, and the mechanisms operate through what behavioral economists refer to as "choice architecture," contexts explicitly designed for good decision-making. Originally employed by governments in the United States, United Kingdom and Australia to try and nudge their citizens into paying fines, conserving energy, and staying in school, Professor Amy Cuddy believes the same principles can be applied to self-nudges to produce small psychological and behavioral improvements in the moment.

She suggests nudges are effective for several reasons:

- First, nudges are small and require minimal psychological and physical commitment. For example, changing the size of people's dinner plates from twelve inches to ten inches has been found to help people serve and eat twenty two per cent less.
- Second, nudges operate via psychological shortcuts. Socially it's generally considered greedy to eat more than one dinner plateful of food, so people's behavior was being nudged via normative influence (deciding how to behave based on what's socially appropriate) as opposed to informational influence (deciding how to behave based on an assessment of objective reality). We often look at what other people are doing and infer which actions are proper, especially if we identify with the people we're observing.
- Finally, although we tend to assume that our behaviors follow our attitudes, studies suggest the reverse is just as likely to be true and our attitudes will also follow our behaviors. For example, when we've eaten everything on our plate we're more likely to believe we're full.

Cuddy suggests that unlike more ambitious changes, long-term life goals, and forced self-affirmations of things we don't actually believe, self-nudges appeal to our natural, hardwired tendencies. When you give yourself a self-nudge, the gap between reality and goal is narrow; it's not daunting, which means you're less likely to give up. As a result, your behavior change is more authentic, lasting, and self-reinforcing.

We've nudged our way to wellbeing by using apps that lock our technology at a regular time each evening so we get to bed; carrying delicious, healthy snacks in our bags so when we're out and about it's easy to eat well; by booking walking meetings to make sure we get enough movement; and by putting regular girl's nights in our diaries. When you think about the wellbeing changes you'd like to start making, are there small ways you can nudge yourself forward?

If you're struggling to move forward on the pathways you've chosen for your hope map, see if you can create a little eleven minute habit to get started. Print out the questions below from www.leadlikeawoman.net/bookplaysheets and create your own busy-proof daily wellbeing habit.

- Pick one of the pathways on your hope map that you'd like to start with, or simply select a wellbeing behavior you'd like to improve.
- Reduce the time and energy it takes to get new wellbeing behaviors started by creating a cue. You can anchor it to habits you already have, so that one behavior flows seamlessly into the next. You can embed it in your environment, so you almost fall into the habit. Or you can use a when/then statement to prime your brain, so when you wake up in the morning, then you already know which wellbeing action to take.
- What's the wellbeing routine you'll practice each day? Remember even a busy-proof ten minute routine is better than not starting anything. Is it going for a walk or run

each day, completing a seven minute workout using an app, preparing some healthy snacks or a healthy meal to eat, creating a bedtime routine or practicing meditation?

- Then whether it's checking it off a list, sharing your good news, noting it in a gratitude journal or making yourself a cup of tea, be sure to reward your efforts so you release the feel-good hormones that help accelerate habit creation. Don't short change yourself on celebrating what you've done (although try to do it without alcohol or chocolate if you can!).

As you play with these practices remember that good habits shouldn't constrain you, they shouldn't constrict you, and they shouldn't be a burden in your life. Rather, they should liberate your energy to do more of the things you love.

Setting boundaries to make it all work

The final part on our wellbeing journey is learning how to define and maintain your boundaries. "Oh, why did we leave the toughest part for last, and can't we just ignore this section?" we hear you cry! Don't panic. Whilst even the thought of a boundary puts the fear of God into most women, the ability to manage them effectively is one of the most critical parts of not only maintaining your wellbeing, but also managing the other parts of your career, leadership, and life we are covering in this book. So hold on tight, get your NO muscle ready, and let's take a look.

We are the queens of boundaries. We know where to set them, are clear on our non-negotiables and aren't afraid to deal with people who push back on them or choose to flat out ignore them. Yes, we can be pretty fierce when we need to be. But it wasn't always the case, especially for Megan who has learnt the hard way more than once on what your life and wellbeing can look like if you live on a slippery boundary less slope.

As with most situations, there were many contributing factors to the burn out Megan experienced more than a decade ago, which included being a single parent, trying to do her first Masters degree whilst taking on a new executive role and working up to eighty hours a week—yes, as she can clearly see a decade after the fact, it was crazy town (obviously). But what Megan also sees reflecting on her past life, is that perhaps the biggest issue was her inability to recognize where she needed boundaries, what they should look like, and what to do to manage them effectively. And she paid a high price for this lesson, one that we don't want you to ever have to experience. When she changed her role as you learned about earlier, set firm boundaries around her work, life, and wellbeing, and mastered the art of saying no, Megan was able to create the intentional and balanced life she has today.

So where do you start?

The first thing is to recognize where you need boundaries in your work and life, and for this chapter's discussion, where you need them to support your wellbeing. If you can't think of where you would start, think about the areas of your life where you feel resentful, compromised or taken advantage of, as these are often places where an unconscious boundary has been crossed and you're not happy about it. The magic is to get clear on where these areas are for you so you can start managing your boundaries effectively.

For example, women we work with set boundaries around the time they leave work, either every day, or specific days of the week to get the kids, attend a class, go to the gym, or even have drinks with the girls. Other women have a declared time at the end of the day when they shut down their email, computer, and turn off their phone, whether that is 5 pm or 10 pm. Michelle manages her boundaries very clearly with her husband around who has responsibility for their two boys at what times, generally he does the breakfast shift and she does the evening run, so she can have time to look after herself. And for some women, it can be as simple as identifying that Thursday night is bubble bath night—don't even think about coming near me until it's done.

It doesn't matter what the boundaries are, what matters is that they are important to you, and that they protect what matters most in your life. It's also helpful to get clear within your boundaries which ones are the absolute non-negotiables, and which ones you are willing to compromise on from time to time (when you choose). Whilst Megan has a firm boundary in place around her morning beach time, she is willing to compromise on it when she has a speaking engagement for an important client that may fall in the morning. It doesn't happen every day, so it's not of great impact. However for coaching clients, she doesn't take appointments before 10 am, so she has her morning ritual and writing time before the first client of her day. This is non-negotiable, as coaching days are a regular part of her week and this would fast become something she would get resentful of if she didn't hold her boundary line.

You get the point. So that probably all sounds reasonable enough right? Sure, nothing too crazy in there. But here is where things get tricky. Once you have set your boundaries, you actually have to hold them in place. And you know what that means? It means you have to say "NO." Two small letters. Major fear inducing, panic emoting, confidence shattering letters. Why is this so hard? The bottom line is that as women, we generally don't like to say "no." We are raised to please, to support, to nurture, and to help, so saying no feels like it's almost going against our nature. But it's also why women have much higher burn out rates than men, why we can feel so resentful for carrying the burden of everyone's needs, and why we don't take good enough care of ourselves.

There is one important point we want you to leave you with here: *"No" is a complete sentence.* When you have defined your boundaries to protect what is most important in your life, you don't need to explain yourself. Sure, you might have to ask your manager if you can leave on Thursday's at 5 pm if your workplace requires it. But when you are saying "no" to a friend, that you don't want to go salsa dancing on Friday night after a fifty hour work week, or you are saying "no" to your partner that you don't want to trek the Himalayas and really just want to lie on a beach in Bali, what you want and how you feel is enough.

"No" is a complete sentence. So say it. Your no muscle, just like your self-control muscle, gets bigger and stronger the more you use it. And whilst it may be hard at first because let's face it, you're a nice person and you don't want to let anyone down, once you start to feel the freedom from owning what you really want and saying no to the rest, you will throw that word around like its glitter. Trust us, all of our clients can't be wrong.

And finally, remember that you're busy with what you said "yes" to. Think about that. Stamp it on your forehead if you need to. And as that realization sinks in, and you truly start to act on it, watch what changes.

Where do you need to set some boundaries when it comes to maintaining your wellbeing? Print out the questions below from www.leadlikeawoman.net/bookplaysheets and start firing up your *no* muscle.

- Where do you feel you need to put some boundaries in your life in order to mindfully maintain your wellbeing? If this is hard for you, think about areas in your life where your wellbeing feels most compromised. This is a clue.
- What would boundaries in these areas look like? i.e. in your workplace, at home, in your relationships etc.
- What is the cost to you of not having boundaries in place?
- What impact would having wellbeing boundaries in place have on your life? Be specific.
- What expectations do you need to set and who do you need to start nicely saying no to? You may want to try these approaches from Professor Adam Grant:
  - The Deferral: "I'm swamped right now, but feel free to follow up."
  - The Referral: "I'm not qualified to do what you're asking, but here's something else."
  - The Introduction: "This isn't in my wheelhouse, but I know someone who might be helpful."
  - The Triage: "Meet my colleague, who will set up a time to chat."
  - The Batch: "Others have posed the same question, so let's chat together."
  - The Relational Account: "If I helped you, I'd be letting others down."
  - The Learning Opportunity: "I'm sorry to disappoint. One

of my goals for this year is to improve my ability to say no—you are a tough audience. I suppose it's good practice . . ."

The key ideas

- Wellbeing is your ability to consistently feel good and function effectively.
- Sleeping deeply, eating well, moving regularly, and gently restoring yourself are the foundations upon which your wellbeing is built.
- Willpower alone is not enough to mindfully maintain your wellbeing as it is fuelled by the very changes—sleep, good nutrition, exercise, and meditation—that you're trying to create.
- A better way to improve your wellbeing, or create other changes in your work or your life is to cultivate hope by having clear *want-to* goals, multiple pathways to get there that plan for obstacles up front and ways to maintain your motivation and willpower.
- We understand that you're life is busy and that fitting in looking after yourself can be challenging, but when you start measuring what you do by energy instead of time you will find that maintaining your wellbeing is the first thing you should prioritize.
- If you're struggling to fit in your wellbeing activities, try an eleven minute daily habit by harnessing your brain's natural habit loop and creating a cue, a routine and a reward or try a gentle nudge to get you started.
- Boundaries are absolutely essential for you to effectively manage all aspects of your work and life, especially your wellbeing. Get clear on where they need to be, and stick them down like superglue.

Leading you

- How are your energy levels generally? For a more extensive test of your energy levels visit www.leadlikeawoman.net/bookplaysheets and take the energy audit.
- How are you really doing when it comes to sleeping deeply, eating well, moving regularly, and gently restoring yourself? Get a free personal wellbeing plan of the small changes you can make at www.eatmovesleep.org if you feel like you're needing some extra help.
- How hopeful are you generally? You can test your levels of hope with the free survey at www.hopemonger.com to see how this is impacting your ability to create change at work and in your life.
- Do you have habits you're struggling to create or to break to improve your wellbeing? For a great breakdown on how to use the habit loop for your wellbeing or other areas of your life visit www.charlesduhigg.com/additional-resources.
- Are you clear on what your boundaries are? Do you enforce them when people are pushing back on them or flat out ignoring them? Make a list of where you need to set some new boundaries for yourself and your strategies for saying no when you need to.

Leading others

- What have you done recently to encourage your team to look after their wellbeing? Are you mindful of meeting times and when you send emails, so you're maximizing the time they have to sleep? When you serve food for workshops or meetings do you avoid sugar and transfats to help people make better eating choices? Do you encourage walking meetings, standing desks, or fitness challenges to help people get enough movement? Do your team have permission to gently restore themselves as needed?

- Does your team rely on willpower or hope to create changes? Do they have the skills to create their own hope map if they want to make wellbeing changes? How could you share this with them?
- What small wellbeing habits do you model for the team? Could you start team meetings with a brief meditation or breathing exercise? Do your team know how to use cues, routines, and rewards to make small behavior changes happen? Are there small nudges you could put in place to help them move forward?
- Do you honor the boundaries your team members set about how, when and where they get their work done? Do you set healthy boundaries as a leader to support your team's wellbeing?

Reflection questions

- In the past when your wellbeing has been at its very best what was happening? What kind of sleep were you getting? What type of food were you eating? How much exercise were you doing? How were you gently restoring yourself? What was making these behaviors possible? How did you feel? What were you able to achieve as a result?
- If you were able to make these kinds of choices more consistently now what might mindfully maintaining your wellbeing really look like over the next twelve months? How could you sleep

deeply, eat well, move regularly, and gently restore yourself just a little bit each day? What boundaries would you hold? What would others notice about you? How would you feel about yourself? Try to describe this as vividly as possible.

- If there was one small habit or nudge you could start in the next day or two to make these hopes for your wellbeing a reality, what would you be willing to try?

5

Cultivating Grit And Grace

Now you understand that the world wants new leaders, have found ways to close the confidence gap, started to build your personal brand, and discovered how to mindfully maintain your wellbeing, life should be sorted, right? From here on all the pieces should just fall easily into place. After all, you've done the work, and you deserve a career and life you love.

Unfortunately, in our experience, it is never quite this straightforward. One of the most common reasons we've found consistently flourishing is harder than it looks is because our brains are built to adapt to most things—particularly the good things—over time. This is why the thrill of victory and the sting of defeat never seems to last quite as long as we might expect. The shine wears off our hard-won promotion too fast; a bonus disappears as quickly as it arrives and an exciting new relationship wears thin over time.

It's not that there's anything wrong with us, it's just that the creeping toll of normalcy and the constant ramping up of expectations means we've adapted to our new reality. But instead of throwing out everything that previously worked, we've discovered that by staying grateful, keeping it novel, avoiding social comparisons, and being clear on the purpose of the activities you've chosen, even if they've become a little boring, it is possible to head off adaptation.

Of course, in addition to adapting to the good things we've built, sometimes despite our best efforts, things just don't unfold the way we planned. We really meant to start using our strengths more at work but we filed those results away somewhere and now can't quite remember how to start. We made great progress on our relationships with a sponsor, but now they're moving overseas, and we're not sure we can find the energy to start over. We were doing incredibly well mindfully maintaining our wellbeing, but then the holidays came, and all our good habits got disrupted, and we just haven't been able to find the willpower to start again.

The truth is, despite our best intentions, researchers have found that when it comes to making lasting changes in the way we live our lives, enthusiasm is common, but endurance is rare. We give up as we encounter obstacles, set backs and plateaus in our progress because we've grown bored, the effort no longer seems worth it; the change isn't that important to us anymore, or we believe that we just can't do it, so we might as well stop. And while there's nothing wrong with any of these thoughts, it seems many of us quit what we start far too early and far too often. So how we can help you maintain and build on the changes you've started on this journey?

Growing Grit

Associate Professor Angela Duckworth from the University of Pennsylvania has found the most successful people in any field rarely succumb to these thoughts of giving up. Instead, when it comes to mastering new behaviors they have a ferocious determination that plays out in two ways: They're unusually resilient and hardworking, and they know in a very deep way what they want. Their combination of passion and perseverance is what that makes them high achievers. In a word, they have grit.

By approaching the journey to mastery as a marathon, rather than a sprint, people with grit work consistently toward challenges and maintain their interest and effort over years despite failures, setbacks and plateaus in their progress. And while most of us take disappointment or boredom as signals that it's time to change our approach or cut our losses, people with grit read these as signs to stick with it and truly show up.

You see while it's tempting to look at what we both have achieved in our careers and put this down to a fluke of genetics or good luck, you'd be selling all of us short. Does Megan believe that Michelle is one of the smartest people she's ever met? Yes. Does Michelle believe that Megan is one of the most talented writers she's ever read? Yes. But that's not why either of us has been able to achieve what we have. Instead, what we have come to respect and value most about each other is our willingness to show up, to put in the effort, and do the hard work. And researchers have found that because this is far more of a learned skill than a heritable trait, it's just as available to you, as it is to either of us.

The problem with talent

Unfortunately, we tend to carry a naturalness bias that's a hidden prejudice against those who've achieved what they have because they worked for it, and a hidden preference for those whom we think arrived at their place in life because they're naturally talented. As the German philosopher, Nietzsche noted: "No one can see in the work of the artist how it has become. That is its advantage, for wherever one can see the act of becoming one grows somewhat cool . . . for if we think of genius as something magical, we are not obliged to compare ourselves and find ourselves lacking."

We're drawn to stories of overnight success, and conveniently ignore all the years of unrecognized, unappreciated, hard work. We get distracted by talent and create stories that hold us back from achieving what we want most. But as Duckworth explains, this naturalness bias robs each of us of the opportunity to pivot from "This is all I can do?" to "Who knows what I can do?"

This is not to say that talent doesn't matter. It does. But your talent is simply the promise of what's possible, not the guarantee. For example, in one study of competitive swimmers, researchers found that the very best performances were not a matter of extraordinary talent, but the confluence of dozens of very ordinary skills or activities, that had been carefully drilled into habits and then synthesized into a whole. They concluded that the only thing that made these performances extraordinary was the fact that the swimmers were able to consistently and correctly complete these actions all together.

Duckworth suggests talent matters because it shapes how fast our skills improve when we invest effort. But in order to achieve great things we have to take these skills and use them. For example, while Megan is a gifted writer it's the hours of effort every week that she puts into honing her craft that has evolved her skill from writing beautiful prose to capturing the kind of words that make you want to stand up and shout "hell yeah!" And while in the past a handful of Megan's friends had been fortunate enough read what she wrote, it's been the extraordinary effort she's poured into her writing in recent years that has resulted in a best-selling book and a dedicated audience around the world.

Effort builds your skills. And effort is what makes these skills productive. Meaning that effort is the key when it comes to turning your potential, into your reality. So how can you sustain the effort you've started to make during this book, into your ongoing journey?

Know what to be gritty about

Being gritty doesn't mean never giving up. It means using your passion—the interests and purpose you identified in chapter three to guide and prioritize your efforts—so you know when to persist and when to start looking for viable alternatives. Most importantly grit is about holding the same top-level goal for a very long time. Duckworth suggests one way to understand this is to envision a goal hierarchy that might look something like this:

Top Level Goal
Your purpose and guiding compass

Mid Level Goals
Pathways to achieve top level goal

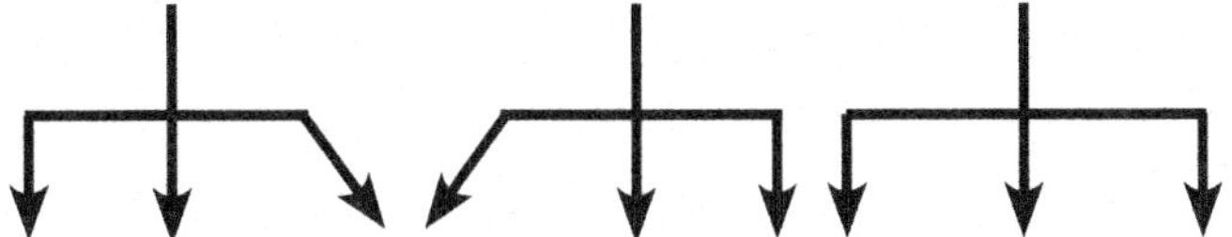

Low Level Goals
The daily activities that move you forward

At the top of your goal hierarchy would be the purpose you identified for yourself earlier in this book. This is your why. It's the compass that guides you on the long and winding road to where you ultimately want to be. It's the end, in and of itself. For Michelle this would be: "Bringing out the best in people at work."

Next, would come your mid-level goals (of which there could be several layers) that explain how this top-level goal will be achieved. These are the projects or areas of focus that are moving you forward. For Michelle this would include: "Teaching positive psychology in workplaces," "Building an online community of positive psychology workplace practitioners" and "Creating the Lead Like A Woman program."

Finally, at the bottom would be your low-level goals that detail what you're doing to make the mid-level and top-level goals possible. These are your most concrete and specific goals. The tasks you have on short-term to-do (or as we like to call them ta-dah!) lists. They are the means to the end. For Michelle right now this would include: "Finish writing the Lead Like A Woman book," "Record the Lead Like A Woman videos" and "Meet with companies to sell the Lead Like A Woman program."

Duckworth suggests that rather than a coherent goal structure, most of us struggle to be gritty because we have a bunch of mid-level goals that don't correspond to any unifying top-level goal or have competing goal hierarchies that aren't in any way connected to each other. Of course, to some extent goal conflict is a natural part of busy and full lives, for example motherhood versus career, so the idea that we would only have one top-level goal may be extreme for many of us. However, she argues that being gritty is much easier when we pare down our long lists of mid-level and low-level work goals according to how they serve just one top-level professional goal.

She also notes that giving up on lower level goals is not only forgivable but also sometimes absolutely necessary. When a lower-level goal can be swapped for another that is more feasible, efficient or fun, then by all means do so. For example, in one study researchers gave participants a math game, which was rigged so that some players always felt like they were fighting an uphill battle. They also gave the participants an offer: When things got tough, they could either drop out of the experiment and get one dollar for their troubles, or they could press on and get two dollars if they won, but nothing if they lost. Grittier people didn't solve any more math problems than their lazier counterparts, even though they felt more optimistic about the test than the others. They were, however, more likely to continue the game when they were losing, even though they risked walking away with nothing.

This was a big a-ha moment for Megan who'd often worried that she wasn't gritty enough when it came to sticking to her small goals, but has now given herself the permission to change things up when they're not working, as long as it still moves her toward her top-level goal. Being a strategist, and with strengths of curiosity, and creativity, this gives her the freedom and flexibility to find the best pathways to achieve her top-level goal in a way that works for her. The power of grit isn't to hold on to every goal no matter what the cost. The power of grit is in knowing which goals to hold on to and which ones to let go. After all, on any long journey, it's likely you'll hit a few detours.

But like most traits, Duckworth suggests the real benefits of grit lie somewhere in between the extremes of having too little and too much. After all, most of us can think of times where we stuck with an idea, job, or romantic partner longer than we should have. As best-selling author, Caroline Adams Miller cautions, *stupid grit* can see us obstinately pursuing long-term goals that present more negatives than positives because circumstances have changed. Like all of the skills we've been building on your journey, it's important to be mindful of the situation you're in and the outcomes you're hoping to achieve when it comes to being gritty.

To figure out your own goal hierarchy, print out the template and questions below from www.leadlikeawoman.net/bookplaysheets and get clear on what you need to be most gritty about as you move forward.

- Throughout this book, you've written down lots of actions you'd like to start taking to be an authentic leader, improve your confidence, build your personal brand, and mindfully maintain your wellbeing. Write them all down below into one list. Don't forget your goals around life vision, purpose, and career. Be sure you capture everything.
- As you look at this list of goals, circle the five that are most important to your career. Once you've done this, think back to the sense of purpose you were exploring earlier in this book.

  If you landed on a clear purpose, are these career goals aligned with your sense of why? Do they suggest any tweaks you might want to make to your purpose? When it comes to your career can you now write your purpose in the template provided as your top-level goal?

  If you didn't yet land on a clear purpose, do these career goals suggest a common theme that feels meaningful to you? Could this be your why? Write down your top-level career goal in the template provided—even if you need to write it in pencil for now.

Now add the five career goals you circled as mid-level goals to the template.

And then finally add any remaining low-level career goals on your original list or low-level goals you have beyond the work in this book to the bottom of the template.

- Now let's create a second goal-hierarchy for your personal life. Look back at your list of goals and circle the five that are most important to your life outside of work. Think back to the sense of purpose you were exploring earlier in this book.

  Again, if you landed on a clear purpose, are these personal goals aligned with your sense of why? Do they suggest any tweaks you might want to make to your purpose? When it comes to your personal life can you now write your purpose in the template provided as your top-level goal?

  As before, if you didn't yet land on a clear purpose, do these personal goals suggest a common theme that feels meaningful to you? Could this be your why? Write down your top-level personal goal in the template provided—even if you need to write it in pencil for now.

  Now add the five personal goals you circled as mid-level goals to the template.

  And then finally add any remaining low-level personal goals on your original list or low-level goals you have beyond the work in this book to the bottom of the template.

- Put your goal hierarchies somewhere you will see them each day to help you stay focused on the projects you are most passionate about.

The paradox of mastery

Of course, it would be great if heartfelt passion and a clear goal-hierarchy were enough to ensure our long-term success, but Duckworth suggests that to be gritty we also need to invest day after week after year in challenging practice. We need to keep looking forward to what's ahead and to want to find ways to keep growing and getting better. But don't worry; this isn't as painful as it might sound.

The opportunity of deliberate practice

As a natural introvert the decision for Michelle to build a speaking business to help teach people about the ideas and practices of positive psychology and neuroscience in workplaces, perhaps wasn't the most obvious choice when she set out. After all, her idea of hell is walking into a roomful of strangers. But although she'd had no formal training in public speaking, her informal experiences of just sharing what she'd been learning in small groups had made it clear to her that teaching others how to flourish at work was clearly her calling.

To have the impact Michelle wanted to have, however, her public speaking skills were going to need to improve, and improve dramatically. Drawing on the science of deliberate practice she sought out every speaking opportunity she could find, constantly setting herself clearly defined stretch goals for her presenting skills, doing her utmost to master these areas during her talk, and seeking immediate and informative feedback from her audience. Then she worked at honing these skills over and over until they were mastered, before setting herself the next stretch goal.

Duckworth believes that deliberate practice is one of the keys that enable gritty people to persevere towards their goals. Drawn from the research of cognitive psychologist Anders Ericsson who has spent his career studying how experts acquire world-class skills, his research suggests it takes thousands and thousands of hours of deliberate practice over years, and years, and years. In fact, as we saw in chapter two in our discussion about strengths, on average he concluded that it requires eight to ten thousand hours of deliberate practice over eight to ten years.

But what exactly is deliberate practice? Ericsson found, experts set clearly defined stretch goals that zero in on just one narrow aspect of their overall performance; then with undivided attention and great effort they strive to reach this goal (often when no one is looking); as soon as possible they hungrily seek feedback on how they did, and often much of this is negative; and finally they do it all over again, and again, and again until they've mastered what they set out to do and conscious incompetence becomes unconscious competence. Then they start all over again with a new stretch goal.

We understand that this can sound like a painful, exhausting process. After all, there's nothing very comfortable about intentionally seeking out challenges you can't yet meet, and that require you to work at the very edge of your skills. In fact, world-class performers at the peak of their careers can often only handle an hour of deliberate practice before needing a break. But while this kind of practice can be frustrating and exhausting, if you suspend in-the-moment judgments it can also be an extremely positive and joyful experience as you see yourself getting better and better over time.

Naturally, not every task easily lends itself to deliberate practice. As a result, new research suggests the impact of deliberate practice on performance varies in different settings and is best suited for building skills that can be easily broken down into discrete development goals. This led the researchers to conclude that while deliberate practice is important—and certainly worthy of exploration—it is not the only explanation for exceptional performance. For example, what about those moments when your strengths are perfectly matched to the tasks you're undertaking, and you hit that zone of flow?

The possibilities of flow

What exactly is flow? Flow is the feeling you have when time stops and you lose all self-consciousness because you're fully absorbed in what you're doing. It's a state extensively researched by renowned psychologist Mihaly Csikszentmihalyi who's studies of world-class performers suggest that flow is what allows them to perform at their highest levels because awareness and action become perfectly merged, allowing them to learn, grow, improve, and advance in ways that build their sense of confidence and satisfaction.

For example, when Michelle experiences the state of flow when she's presenting, she's not reading from her notes or reciting a perfectly rehearsed speech. Instead, she's trusting what she knows, noting people's reactions, and tailoring her message accordingly. She's fully present. Absorbed in the moment. And while afterward she couldn't tell you exactly what she said, she has a very clear sense of the impact she's had on the audience. It's these moments of flow that allow her to perform at high levels of challenge and yet feel effortless like she doesn't have to think about it—instead is able to just do it.

The good news is that these moments are available to all

of us. Flow occurs when you: Have a clear goal that balances your strengths with the complexity of the task at hand; receive regular feedback on how you're going; and when you feel a sense of autonomy and freedom in your behaviors. Although you're concentrating one hundred per cent, flow is intrinsically pleasurable because the level of challenge just meets your current level of skill. This allows you to focus on doing, rather than analyzing. It also means a lot of the feedback is telling you that you're doing things well. And as a result your confidence builds.

So when it comes to making progress towards your goals, should you focus on cultivating more moments of deliberate practice or more moments of flow? Duckworth has found that gritty people do more deliberate practice and experience more flow. Her view is that deliberate practice is for preparation and skills building and offers us the thrill of getting better at something, while flow is for performance and offers us the joy of time spent doing what we do best. While the two may never occur together, they both offer important pathways towards achieving our goals.

The challenge of mastery

But what happens when your top-level goals are reached? Frequently we encounter women, usually in their late 30s to mid-40s, who have done everything right and reached their goals only to find themselves completely stuck. They've worked hard and climbed to the top of their fields, created financial stability for themselves, do what they can to maintain good health and have people in their life to love. They look like they have everything any woman could want, but deep down in their hearts something just doesn't feel quite right.

We get it. We both had this exact same bewildering moment in our careers. We finally *had it all* and yet somehow the jobs we'd worked so hard for had reached a point where they left us feeling empty and unfulfilled. Was it just that we were working for big corporate institutions that lacked heart? Or, was there something fundamentally wrong with us and no matter what we achieved we would never really be content?

You can imagine our relief when we discovered that this feeling was a completely natural process that came with mastering our top-level goals. You see we're born creatures of progress. In fact, our survival as a species depends on it. Our brains are wired for growth which is why learning unleashes feel-good chemicals like dopamine and a lack of deep engagement in what we're doing plunges us into a depression-like state that leaves us feeling irritated, restless, tense, and tired. There was nothing wrong with us; we just needed new top-level goals—possibly ones focused more on *purpose* than *profit*—to master. It turns out that the journey to mastery is the oxygen of our souls.

As you've probably already discovered, mastery is not a straight line of steady progression. Instead studies suggest that mastery is made up of a series of smaller peaks and plateaus that can be approximated into a S-curve. Think back to the first job you had after finishing your studies and those early white-knuckle years of constantly feeling you were in over your head. Initially, progress up the mastery curve is slow, but through deliberate practice and moments of flow, you start to gain traction and enter a virtuous cycle that propels you up the steepest part of the curve and into the sweet spot of accelerating competence and confidence. Then as Ericsson's research found when you reach the eight to ten year mark you suddenly hit the upper flat portion of the mastery curve where things become far more automatic and habitual, causing many of us to experience less of the feel-good effects of learning and a heightened sense of boredom and restlessness.

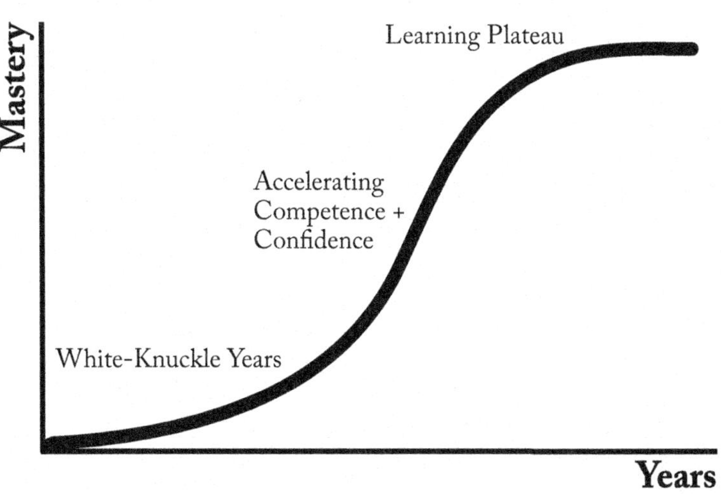

Why hadn't anybody told us? Surely this is a key piece of career planning and life advice everybody needs. Firstly, we would have been far more patient with ourselves when starting out, if we'd understood those white-knuckle moments were simply part of the learning process and with plenty of deliberate practice it was likely that we'd keep getting better. Secondly, we would have savored those middle years, mixing in moments of deliberate practice and flow and enjoying the learning and growth we were experiencing. And finally, instead of lingering at the top and becoming increasingly restless, we would have started developing new mastery curves to climb rather than plateauing and becoming stuck on our existing one.

The relief we felt at realizing we just needed new mastery curves to climb, was the same we see on the faces of the women in our program with whom we share this research. For example, when Kate joined our program she was the chief financial officer of a medium-sized investment firm. With more than fifteen years of accounting experience, she'd achieved all she'd ever dreamed of in her career and couldn't understand why the work she once loved now left her feeling completely drained. Worried that there was something seriously wrong with her, she'd signed up for the *Lead Like A Woman* program to see if there was something she was missing.

While each step of the journey made sense, it wasn't until we reached this conversation about mastery that all of the pieces came together for Kate. There wasn't anything wrong with her; she'd just reached the top of her accounting mastery curve and needed to give herself permission to jump to the next curve. During the purpose and life vision steps, Kate had felt this pull to help other women unleash their potential at work but had dismissed the idea as she lacked the knowledge, skills or opportunity to do anything like this in her career. But if she was going to spend the next decade mastering a new domain of learning perhaps this idea wasn't so far-fetched.

In the months that followed the program, Kate went back to her leadership team and gained approval for the firm's first female talent development strategy. With the help of HR she identified twenty high-potential women, implemented a sponsorship program for them and established a fortnightly coaching circle that drew on the knowledge and skills she'd learned in the *Lead*

Like A Woman program and a mix of guest speakers. She also began researching further study opportunities in coaching, leadership, and positive psychology to complement the new experiences she was gaining.

While at times she has been racked with self-doubt about what on earth she could have to offer in this new space, two years later the board has formally recognized Kate's efforts and expertise as part of their diversity strategy. She has won industry awards for the program she implemented and is sought out by other organizations wanting to learn from her success. She has continued in her finance role after finding that her new opportunities for learning and growth, put the joy and challenge back into her job without costing her the financial security or influence she'd fought so hard for. That said, she can see as her study nears completion that helping more organizations to bring out the best in their women will be the sweet spot of this new mastery curve she's climbing, so despite her nervousness, next year Kate will begin seeking out these roles. After all, like each of us—she's a creature of progress.

One of the important lessons we've learned along our journey of mastery is that it helps to have a top-level goal that is big enough to allow for decades of growth. Unfortunately, like many women, we spent far too long thinking far too small. The first decade of our careers were focused on becoming senior leaders in large organizations in the hope that we could make a positive difference in our roles. It was a good goal that took around a decade to master, but once achieved it didn't give us as many opportunities for further growth.

As we've gotten clearer on our purpose, our top-level goals—for Megan to change the conversation for women, leadership, and work and for Michelle to bring out the best in people at work—have evolved to provide us far more room for growth. Let's be honest: We could spend the rest of our lives working towards these goals and may still never reach a moment when it feels complete. This has allowed us to focus our mid-level goals on the mastery of different skills, so that when we feel ourselves plateauing we can introduce a new mid-level goal, like learning to self-publish books, creating online programs or building an accreditation program. Not only does this lower the risk of us becoming stuck at the top of our mastery curve, it also means we don't forgo all the progress we've been making towards our top-level goal. Of course, we have learned the hard way, that if you're considering climbing multiple mastery curves, it's best to tackle the white-knuckle stage one at a time if you can.

As you think about your own journey towards mastery of your own goal hierarchy print out the questions below from www.leadlikeawoman.net/bookplaysheets:

- Look at your career goal hierarchy, and consider where you are currently on your mastery curve towards your top-level goal. Is this goal big enough to allow you plenty of room to grow?

  If your answer is "absolutely" then look at your mid-level goals and think about where you are on the journey to mastering each of these as well. Will they provide you with enough challenge and growth in the years to come? Will they provide you with too much? Are there any adjustments you want to make to these goals based on your understanding now of how mastery evolves?

  If your answer is "yes, for now" then it's fine to start with this top-level goal. Recognize as you progress, however, that this goal may need to evolve into a broader purpose to continue giving you room for growth. And if you start feeling restless, remember it is likely that you've simply plateaued.

If your answer is "probably not" then now is the time to broaden your top-level goal. Revisit the section on purpose in chapter three, and give yourself more time to reflect on the positive difference you really want to make with your work. Write your top-level goal in pencil for now and work towards mastering the mid-level goals that engage you most. Then as the journey unfolds, continue looking for clarity on why these mid-level goals really matter to you. What's the end they are moving you towards?

- As you move towards mastery of your goals, think about the mix of deliberate practice and flow that serves you best. How can you be more intentional about the development of your skills?

  Would you benefit from setting a daily habit of deliberate practice? Which skills would you try to master? What stretch goals could you set? How can you seek feedback? How can you frame this as a positive learning experience?

  How can you create more opportunities for flow in your work by matching your skills to the work you're doing? What can you learn from these experiences? How can this improve your performance?

The upside of stress

While passion fuels our motivation and persistence improves our skills, ultimately grit requires us to keep putting one foot in front of the other in order to reach our goals. Let's face it: The journey towards mastery is often uncomfortable, which is why Duckworth notes that to be gritty is to fall seven times, and rise eight. She suggests that by practicing the growth mindsets we learned about in chapter two, we naturally get better at explaining obstacles, setbacks, and failures to ourselves in more optimistic ways, which helps us to persevere and seek out new challenges that ultimately make us stronger and stronger.

Megan has come to understand this all too well throughout her Ph.D. journey. Whilst the prospect of doing a Ph.D. after completing two Masters degrees seemed exciting and well aligned to her top level goal of changing the conversation for women, leadership and work, the reality has been more challenging. And the path to mastery has been uncomfortable, to say the least. While she started out with her usual zest, she quickly realized that starting a new business at the same time as beginning her Ph.D. was biting off far too much. She couldn't find the time or the energy to get her head around what was required for her dissertation outline, her topic was blurry, and after a year of continually struggling to make progress, she decided with a heavy heart that the time was just not right, and she would have to take a semester's leave of absence.

For Megan who had never had struggled with her studies in the past, it felt like utter failure. She'd let down her supervisor. She'd wasted her tuition fees. And to be perfectly honest she still wasn't really sure she had what would be required when she was due to go back. But as she tried to move from her fixed mindset that only defined success as getting the Ph.D. finished, and into a growth mindset about what this experience offered she was able to begin shifting her stories. After all, just admitting that she'd bitten off too much was a huge step forward for her wellbeing.

Maybe the time off would give her a new perspective on what she wanted to be studying. And her supervisor had been incredibly understanding and said she was happy to keep working with Megan when she was ready. By using optimistic self-talk to realize this decision wasn't permanent and wouldn't impact everything for the rest of her life, she was able to restart her Ph.D. and now, eighteen months later, is back into her research with a revitalized sense of purpose and a renewed ability to persevere to reach the outcome she is seeking.

Of course, despite all of this wisdom, there are days when trying to honor the careers and lives we want to create, can leave us feeling completely stressed out. Six months into starting her own business Michelle described the constant need for deliberate practice to improve her presentation skills, the pressure to win enough work, and the responsibility for everything from spell-checking the website to balancing the checkbook like "sitting on the spike of a cactus." Nothing felt easy or comfortable and even though she was trying to hold onto her growth mindset, Michelle had never felt so overwhelmed or stressed.

What's your stress response?

With media headlines like *Stress Kills* or *Science Proves Stress Makes You Depressed* you can understand why Michelle felt concerned that she'd taken on far more than she could handle, and was seriously considering giving up on her struggling new business and heading back to her dull comfortable corporate life. So when Megan suggested that instead of quitting, Michelle imagine what it would be like to wriggle around on the spike of that cactus for a while, you can imagine her surprise.

But here's the thing: Despite the overwhelmingly accepted

idea that stress is harmful for us, increasingly studies about stress tells a very different story. As health psychologist, Kelly McGonigal summarizes in her best-selling book, *The Upside of Stress: Why Stress is Good For You and How to Get Good At It,* "Stress increases the risk of health problems, except when people regularly give back to their communities. Stress increases the risk of dying, except when people have a sense of purpose. Stress increases the risk of depression, except when people see a benefit in their struggles. Stress is paralyzing, except when people perceive themselves as capable. Stress is debilitating, except when it helps you perform. Stress makes people selfish, except when it makes them altruistic."

How can this possibly work? Most of us believe the body's stress response is uniformly harmful and stress hormones, like cortisol, are seen as toxins we need to eliminate from our lives. Every time we feel our heart racing, our breath shorten, or our stomach twist into knots, we think our number one priority should be to shut down this stress response. When we believe stress should be avoided, each time something we care about is at stake, our fight-or-flight response is triggered creating a rush of fearful energy and motivation that primes us for self-defense, and makes us vigilant for signs that things are going poorly. This can create a vicious cycle where our heightened attention to what's going wrong fills us with self-doubt and leaves us with higher levels of cortisol, which can be associated with impaired immune function and depression.

But it turns out that our bodies don't just have one response to stressful situations. What if your pounding heart or quickened breath was your body's way of giving you more energy and strength? What if the butterflies in your stomach were a sign that you're close to something you want? What if your body was providing you with all the resources you need to rise to a challenge?

When we believe stress should be embraced, we're able to acknowledge that what's at stake is meaningful to us triggering our challenge response and fuelling us with feelings of confidence, power, and a willingness to learn. By embracing our anxiety so that we feel safe, we're able to harness the powerful mix of endorphins, adrenaline, testosterone, and dopamine that can come with any stress response, so we can take action and rise to the challenge. It also leaves us with higher levels of dehydroepiandrosterone (DHEA), a neurosteroid which helps us to recover and learn from stress and has been linked to a reduced risk of anxiety, depression, heart disease, neurodegeneration and other diseases we typically think of as stress-related.

As a result, McGonigal reports that during business negotiations, a challenge response leads to more effective sharing and withholding of information, as well as smarter decision-making. Students with a challenge response score higher on exams, and athletes perform better in competitions. Surgeons show better focus and fine motor skills. When faced with engine failure during a flight simulation, pilots make better use of plane data and have safer landings.

Finally, your stress response doesn't just give you energy, in many situations it's what motivates you to protect the people and communities you care about and importantly gives you the courage to do so. Our instinct for social connection is every bit as strong as our instinct for survival, so while it's true that a fight-or-flight stress response may make us more aggressive or withdrawn, it's also true that a tend-and-befriend stress response can make us more caring. When we care for others in moments of stress, McGonigal explains that it changes our biochemistry by: Increasing our levels of oxytocin to inhibit the fear centers of our brain and improve our feelings of empathy, trust, and connection; releasing dopamine which helps us to feel more motivated and optimistic about our ability to do something meaningful; and activating the neurotransmitter serotonin which enhances our perception, intuition and self-control to ensure our actions have the biggest positive impact.

In short, helping others when we feel stressed can transform fear into bravery, and powerlessness into optimism. It also helps to head off our defeat response to stress that causes us to withdraw, lose motivation and any desire to connect with others when we feel repeatedly victimized, beaten by our circumstances or rejected by people who matter to us. When we believe that stress is an opportunity to connect with others, rather than to escape life, it fuels us with hope and seems to protect us against the harmful effects of stress on our physical health.

For example, McGonigal notes people who volunteer after a natural disaster report feeling more optimistic and energized and less overwhelmed by the stress in their life. Taking care of others after the death of a spouse has been found to reduce depression. Becoming a peer counselor appears to help relieve pain, disability, and depression among people living with chronic pain. And after enduring a life-threatening health crisis, people who volunteer experience more hope, less depression and a great sense of purpose.

While instinctively Michelle had known that a little bit of stress wasn't going to kill her, she had no idea how many benefits may come from opening herself us to different stress responses if she persisted and stayed true to the purpose and goals she'd set herself. Megan's suggestion of wriggling around on that cactus spike so that she could learn to be comfortably uncomfortable as her journey required, opened up new depths of grit that have enabled Michelle to keep moving forward.

Getting comfortably uncomfortable

So how can you harness stress to support your resilience and grit? Rather than debating if stress is good or bad for us, McGonigal suggests the question we should be asking ourselves is: "Do I believe I have the capacity to transform stress into something good?" Try to take a moment right now and think about a significant turning point in your life that helped you to make positive changes, gave you a newly found sense of purpose, or led to important personal growth. Would you describe this period as stressful?

You see stress—the feeling that something we care about is at stake—in itself appears neither good nor bad. And while our genes and life histories can influence our stress response, it seems that it's our beliefs about stress that most shape the actions we're willing to take and the outcomes we're most likely to get. So what if instead of trying to get rid of stress, we experimented with embracing it?

McGonigal argues that when we believe that stress is harmful and something to avoid we generally feel that what's unfolding is utterly meaningless and against our will, that we're inadequate to respond and have a tendency to isolate and protect ourselves from others. We're left feeling afraid, full of self-doubt, and incredibly lonely. But when we believe that stress is best accepted and embraced, we feel that what's unfolding offers opportunities for meaningful growth, that we have the resources to respond and are more likely to reach out to others. We're left feeling courageous, confident, and connected.

The good news McGonigal points out, is that because stress is a biological state designed to help you learn from experience, your stress response is extremely receptive to the effects of deliberate practice. So if you want to be able to be comfortably uncomfortably and face challenges confidently, stand up for yourself, seek social support instead of withdrawing and find meaning in your suffering, there is no better way to change your habits than to practice this new response during stress. Every moment of stress is an opportunity to transform your stress responses.

Instead of trying to rid ourselves of stress, McGonigal suggests trying these three simple steps:

- Acknowledge stress when you experience it. Simply allow yourself to notice the stress, including how it affects your body.
- Welcome the stress by recognizing that it's a response to something you care about. Can you connect to the positive motivation behind the stress? What is at stake here, and why does it matter to you? Which part of the stress response do you need most right now? Do you need to fight, escape, engage, connect, find meaning, or grow? Even if it feels like your stress response is pushing you in one direction, focusing on how you want to respond can shift your biology to support you. If there is a side of the stress response you would like to develop, consider what it would look like in any stressful situation you are dealing with now.

- Then try to make use of the energy that stress gives you, instead of wasting that energy trying to manage your stress. What can you do right now that reflects your values and your goals? What strengths can you draw upon to respond in the way you want?

Her research has also found that it may help to set stress goals that are difficult and meaningful to give you plenty of practice, have open and honest conversations about your struggles so that you feel less alone in your suffering and to go out of your way help others so that you can access the biology of hope and courage.

Let us also be clear, the research on stress doesn't suggest that the most helpful beliefs are a naïve insistence that everything bad will turn into something good. Rather, it's the ability to notice the opportunities for learning and growth as you try to cope with things that are difficult and challenging. For example, people who report both negative and positive changes after a terrorist attack have been found to be more likely to sustain post-traumatic growth compared to those who initially report only positive changes. Think of it as an exercise in being able to hold opposite perspectives at once—the *and* rather than the *either/or*—instead of an exercise in positive thinking.

To help you become more comfortably uncomfortable, print out the questions below from www.leadlikeawoman.net/bookplaysheets and spend ten minutes writing about your values and how these can help you navigate the stress you may experience on your *Lead Like A Woman* journey.

- Look back to your VIA Survey results (www.viacharacter.org) from chapter two. Remember these character strengths are closely aligned to the values that you hold. Pick one of your top five strengths that feels the most important to the way you consistently show up in the world.

- Spend ten minutes writing about how this value might guide you forward on your *Lead Like A Woman* journey. How can it help you achieve your career goal hierarchy? How can it help you relate to the stress and discomfort you may experience?

  It turns out that writing about your values is one of the most effective psychological interventions ever studied. In the short term, writing about personal values makes people feel more powerful, in control, proud, and strong. It also makes them feel more loving, connected, and empathetic toward others. It increases pain tolerance, enhances self-control, and transforms how you think about stressful experiences and your ability to cope with them. In the long term, writing about values has been shown to improve mental health, help people persevere in the face of discrimination and reduces self-handicapping. People who write about their values once, for ten minutes, show benefits months or even years later. So really let yourself savor this exercise.

- You may want to repeat this exercise for other strengths you feel are key to the values you hold or for your life goal hierarchy. Alternatively revisit this exercise when you are feeling especially overwhelmed by stress.

The power of grace

The final challenge we find as you put all of these steps together is not to run too hard or too fast at making these changes in your work and your life. It's not to be gritty or stressed no matter what the cost. Instead, it's finding the path of grace and ease to set the pace that allows time for play and nurturing, to hold gently both your failures and your successes and to savor the magical mess and predictable rhythm that is life.

Don't expect yourself to be some kind of machine, that having downloaded a new operating system you will now seamlessly execute each step and achieve a perfect outcome. Hard work alone will not make these changes happen; in fact, it may be the very thing that ultimately undermines the career and life you want. Remember as we've seen for the other skills you've been developing on this journey, thinking about the situation you're in and the outcomes you want will be the key to determining when to be gritty and push a little harder and when to be graceful and let go just a little bit.

Leading like a woman is not about going faster and doing more, instead it's about learning to live and work in ways that make grace and ease your natural state, no matter what's happening. You can do this by:

- *Finding your natural rhythm* – Nearly every system in our body—brain, heart, blood pressure, body temperature and hormone levels—pulses in waves when it's healthy. Unfortunately, too often we ignore these needs and override our natural physiological rhythms with caffeine, sugar and our own stress hormones—adrenalin, noradrenalin, and cortisol—all of which provide short bursts of energy, but leave us increasingly over-aroused, overwhelmed, and exhausted.

  By understanding the physiological waves that guide your ability to flourish it's easier to know when to step things up, to slow things down, to stick with things or to surrender to them. Researchers call these waves your ultradian rhythm and suggest that most of us perform at our best in ninety minute cycles followed by short periods of rest. Studies have found that by tuning into your natural rhythm you can get more done, in less time, at a higher level of engagement, and with a better and more sustainable quality of life.

- *Becoming time affluent* – Researchers have found that your attitude towards time shapes every part of your life. Unfortunately, it appears that most of us underestimate the time we need and overpromise the time we have leaving us stuck in a constant state of overwhelm. Feeling like you are in a *time famine* drives stress and dissatisfaction with your life. However, studies show that when you feel more *time affluent* it is more uplifting than material wealth, and leaves you feeling more connected, happier, and healthier.

  Start by tuning into the beliefs and stories you tell about time. If you're constantly *frantic, crazy busy* or on *deadline* is this really how you want to live your life? The reality is that every day has the same number of hours in it and we are each as busy as the choices we've made. So what if we changed our stories about time and started telling ourselves that we have the perfect amount of time to complete the things that most need to be done today? After all, isn't this actually what happens on most days? By trusting that things will be done at just the right time we've found we're more mindful about prioritizing what matters, we're more realistic about the number of hours we have and we're flexible and willing to reset expectations when things take longer than we expected.

  The most unexpected part of this process is that most things seem to get done at exactly the right moment. A deadline we agonized about pushing, allows us to achieve a better outcome because the delay meant we had important new information. A meeting we were disappointed about postponing, winds up happening at the perfect moment because a situation has changed and created a new opportunity. The more we've come to trust that we have enough time, the more self-fulfilling this prophecy has become.

- *Making a tah-dah list* – Creating a daily to-do list is one of the corner stones of good time management, but is this practice serving you well or leaving you feeling despondent? Don't get us wrong; we couldn't live without lists and the joy that comes from crossing things off them, but recently we noticed even when we got everything done the feeling of satisfaction never lasted very long as we knew tomorrow they'd be a whole new list.

  So we seized upon the suggestion of positive emotion researcher Professor Barbara Fredrickson when she recently suggested that instead of a to-do list, we should keep a tah-dah list. Now as we cross each item off we take a moment to savor the feeling of tah-dah and the imaginary applause of awe and appreciation to give us small jolts of joy as we move through our day.

- *Turning work into play* – The old-school view that play is a diversion from work is gradually being overthrown as scientists discover that playing energizes us, lifts us out of the mundane, eases our burdens, renews our optimism, and opens us up to new possibilities. It's a catalyst for exploring new behaviors, thoughts, strategies, and ways of being. It allows us to see things in a different way and stimulates our brains for learning, growth, and creativity.

  The good news is that more workplaces are coming to understand the value of play and making it easier to be playful at the office. But the even better news is that you don't need anyone's permission or special equipment to be playful. Be it conquering the newest game on your smart phone, keeping pencils and a sketch pad on hand, engaging in playful banter, or gamifying every day tasks by setting yourself time or creativity challenges there are plenty of ways to play, just for the sake of playing, at work.

- *Just being* – Take small moments in your day to just breathe and be. Megan teaches our participants the profound value of the yogic breath: to breathe in for the count of four, hold for the count of four, breathe out for the count of four and hold for the count of four. Sixteen small beats and you'll be amazed how much clearer and calmer work and life looks.

  When we first dreamed of creating the *Lead Like A Woman* program back at the writer's retreat in Carmel, California, our host took us out one morning along the coast. Walking along the rocky shoreline we reached a beautiful old tree known locally for its spiritual significance to Indian tribes. Sitting at the base of this tree, breathing slowly to the count of sixteen, this question appeared in Michelle's mind as clearly as if someone had spoken: "What if everything you dreamed was entirely possible?"

  Later over hot chocolates we turned this question over and over. No need to strive. No reason to rush. All we needed to do was just be. To trust the path of ease and grace unfolding before us and confidently step forward knowing that no matter what happened, we would find a way to live our dreams.

Being psychologically agile requires the wisdom to know when to push forward and when to sit back and let things unfold naturally. It's the confidence to trust the knowledge and skills you've been building throughout this journey to navigate the natural highs and lows you experience, to learn and grow as you go and to give what is right for others and for yourself.

After all, despite all this new knowledge and good intentions, life happens. You may fall ill, your job may become redundant, you might need to care for others and you may have to say goodbye to people you've loved. Let us be very clear, no one is meant to thrive in these moments for the weeks, months, or years that it may take to navigate the struggles, loss, or grief that often comes with these experiences.

For example, when Michelle's father passed away from melanoma cancer she found that as her grief unfolded it meant her thriving life had to be stripped back to the basics. As waves of sadness kept rolling in she realized her brain just couldn't keep up with the ways she usually worked and lived. She had to set new boundaries and let people know that her capacity mentally, physically, and socially was much lower than where it would usually be. She had to adjust her expectations of what her body could keep up with and accept that a good workout constituted a gentle jog, and some days even just a walk. With an endless flow of self-compassion, she gently challenged the stories she was telling herself about how useless she was during this period and sought the help of a psychologist to monitor her wellbeing.

Initially, Michelle gave herself three months to grieve and then get on with life. But when three months passed and she was still struggling she conceded that grief may have its own plans. So she surrendered for another three months and more gently monitored that path she was traveling. At six months Michelle found she was having occasional moments of thriving, but as quickly as they appeared, they seemed to pass. It took just over a year before Michelle felt like her brain was restored from the ravages of grief and she could slowly rebuild her sense of consistently thriving once more.

The good news is that whether it's a bit of adaptation, a lot of stress or just life unfolding you have the knowledge, tools and support you need to lead like a woman and have the grit and grace to stay on the path of creating a career and life you love. This doesn't mean that every moment will feel perfect. It does mean that you can better, and more quickly, navigate yourself towards the outcomes that serve you best in different situations. It gives you the psychological agility that makes it possible to confidently embrace life's raw, magical mess.

As you move forward on your journey, we want you to learn to trust that it will be exactly what it is meant to be. You are where you are right now for a reason. And the lessons you are learning, the challenges you face, and the opportunities in front of you are the exact ones you need for your life to unfold in all of its beautiful, imperfect glory. There are no *shoulds*. There is no timeline. There is nothing here that you can't handle. And you have everything within you to achieve all of the dreams, visions, hopes, and plans you may have thought of as you have worked through this book. It's all there waiting for you. And we invite you to show up within this journey with both the grit and the grace that will ease your path.

How might grace serve you well on your *Lead Like A Woman* journey? Take the time to work through these questions which you can print out at www.leadlikeawoman.net/bookplaysheets to find ways to bring more grace and ease into your work and your life.

- When has grace served you well at work or in life? How have you accessed these moments of grace? What opportunities have they opened up for you?

- What does your daily energy rhythm look like? Try to track this across your waking hours for a few days in a row. Note what are the times of your day that you feel most energized and what are the times of the day that you struggle. Is this pattern consistent? What might it tell you about the best ways to gracefully manage your energy and prioritize your activities over the course of a day?
- What are your beliefs about time? Are you in a time famine or are you time affluent? Which would serve you best? How can your beliefs about time bring you a little more grace as your days unfold?
- If you changed your to-do list to a tah-dah list would this bring any more grace to your day?
- How do you currently play at work? How is play viewed in your workplace? If you made time for play what might you choose to do? How might this bring more grace to your journey?
- How do you currently make space to just be during your day? How can you ensure you have some space each day to just be? How might this bring more grace to your days?

The key ideas

- When it comes to mastering new behaviors the most successful people in any field have a ferocious determination that plays out in two ways: They're unusually resilient and hardworking and they know in a very deep way what they want. Their combination of passion and perseverance is what that makes them high achievers. In a word they have grit.
- Being gritty doesn't mean never giving up. It means using your passion, your interests, and purpose, to guide and prioritize your efforts, so you know when to persist and when to start looking for viable alternatives. Most importantly grit is about holding the same top-level goal for a very long time.
- Gritty people do more deliberate practice to build their skills and experience more flow as they use these skills to perform what they do best. They also understand that the journey to mastery is made up of a series of smaller peaks and plateaus that can be approximated into an S-curve, that comprises white-knuckle moments as our skills build, a sweet spot of accelerating competence and confidence and a natural plateau that makes us restless for new challenges.
- While passion fuels our motivation and persistence improves our skills, ultimately grit requires us to keep putting one foot in front of the other in order to reach our goals. But falling down seven times, and getting up eight can be a stressful experience. And while most of us believe that stress is something to be avoided, studies have found that accepting and embracing stress can leave us feeling more courageous, confident and connected so we can keep moving towards the things that matter to us most.

- Psychological agility requires the grace of knowing when to push forward and when to sit back and let things unfold naturally. It's the confidence to trust the knowledge and skills you've been building throughout this journey to navigate the natural highs and lows we all experience, to learn and grow as you go and to give what is right for others and for yourself. It's the ability to flex the tools you now have so that in different situations you can achieve the outcomes that serve you best.

Leading you

- Do you have enough grit to achieve your long-term goals? Measure your levels of grit at https://sites.sas.upenn.edu/duckworth under research and measures.
- Do you have a clear goal hierarchy to prioritize your time and guide your choices about what to give up and what to be gritty about?
- Where are you on your mastery curve at work? How can you create a daily habit of deliberate practice and find more opportunities for flow to help you persist in achieving your goals?
- What are your beliefs about stress and how does this typically shape your responses? Are you willing and able to be comfortably uncomfortable on the journey ahead?
- If there was one thing you could do starting today to walk your journey with more grace and ease where would you start?

Leading others

- While grit exists within us, it's also shaped by the cultures we find ourselves in. How gritty is your team? Do you have the passion and perseverance required to achieve your long-term goals together? You can use Duckworth's grit survey mentioned previously to measure grit levels across your team.
- Duckworth believes that developing your personal grit depends critically on the people around you. Are you a supportive but demanding leader? Does your team have a clear sense of passion? How do you encourage and measure effort? What are the stories you tell about learning and failure?
- How does your team respond to stress? Do they understand the different stress responses and how to train their bodies to harness this motivation and energy to avoid feeling burnt out, frustrated or drained by their work?
- How can you encourage a culture of grace and ease in your team?

Reflection questions

- In the past when you've truly felt like you had the grit and grace to navigate the challenges that were unfolding at work or in your life what was happening? How was your sense of purpose and passion helping you to find meaning in these challenges? What did you do to persevere towards reaching your goals? How did you manage to keep getting up in the face of setbacks, disappointments or plateaus in your progress? What did you do to manage the stress? What were you able to achieve as a result?

- If you were able to make these kinds of choices more consistently, what might the grit and grace to consistently thrive really look like over the next twelve months? How could you use your goal hierarchy to focus on what matters? Where would you choose to invest your time to keep moving towards mastery? How can you ensure any stress you're experiencing is serving you well? What can you do to maintain a path of grace and ease as you travel forward? Try to describe this as vividly as possible.
- If there was one small habit you could start in the next one to two days to make these hopes for grit and grace a reality, what would you be willing to try?

6

Creating Positive Organizational Change

In this chapter, we are going to switch gears and move our focus from individual women to addressing structural systemic change in organizations. Why are we doing this in a book written for women about women's leadership? Because it's time to change the conversation about women, leadership, and work.

Whether you're a man or woman reading this book, a manager or an employee, someone looking to be inspired, or a person seeking out change, it's time to realize that the current conversation is stuck; stuck in the past, stuck in what's not working, stuck in all the reasons that we can't get to a place of genuine equality. And staying in this conversation is not going to get us where we need to go. Not here, not now, not ever.

With our collective passion, experience, and knowledge in this space and around what it takes to deliver lasting systemic change, this chapter could have been an entire book. Megan has been advocating and working for gender equality at the highest levels for more than a decade. She is a global thought leader in women's leadership, having led gender diversity at one of the world's largest companies as part of her role as director of strategy, building the companies first gender parity strategy, reaching aggressive targets and driving significant cultural and leadership change; she is an advisor to CEOs and Boards on gender and leadership, she was a core leader in initiatives like the Male Champions of Change, devising country wide strategy and outcomes; and she is completing her Ph.D. research on changing the conversation for women, leadership and equality. Michelle has spent the last decade leading research and application in driving systemic change in organizations, governments, and societies. She is recognized as one of the world's leaders when it comes to embedding strengths practices in workplaces; she has led the introduction of positive education approaches across schools in Australia; and she is completing her Ph.D. research in methods for enabling systemic flourishing with Professor David Cooperrider a man sought out by world leaders when it comes to creating sustainable changes (you'll hear more about him later). And with our collective work as Co-Founders and Co-CEOs of *Lead Like A Woman* and the strategy work we do with organizations and governments, we live and breathe this every day.

We are here to help change the game and positively disrupt the status quo. It's time to move forward, with a sense of urgency and hope. The new conversation starts here.

Why all the fuss?

We know that women have made giant leaps forward, and incredible female leaders are shining a light on all that is good and possible for women in the world today. Malala Yousafzai becoming the youngest ever winner of the Nobel Peace Prize; Hillary Clinton changing the face of US Presidential races; Indra Nooyi and Ginni Rometty becoming the first ever female CEOs of their respective global companies, PepsiCo and IBM; Sheryl Sandberg changing the global dialogue about women, work and leadership through the Lean In movement; and Arianna Huffington showing everyone that success can have a new definition, and it's called thriving.

We also know that both the economic and business cases for reaching gender equality are irrefutable. From an economic perspective, the McKinsey Global Institute, reports that getting to equal workplace participation could add between twelve and twenty-eight trillion dollars, or up to twenty-six per cent to annual global GDP in 2025. As McKinsey reports, that's the equivalent of combining the United States and China economies today. Pretty mind blowing.

And for business? There are a plethora of credible research reports that confirm the bottom line value of women's participation in workplaces. In a 2013 report by Catalyst outlining significant research to support the business case for gender diversity, they found that companies with more women board directors outperformed those with the least on three financial measures: return on equity (fifty-three per cent higher), return on sales (forty-two per cent higher), and return on invested capital (sixty-six per cent higher).

And yet, even in light of incredible women doing world-changing things, and staggering business, and economic data, we are still here having this same conversation, nowhere near the parity we are so desperately seeking. Even McKinsey who have spent years leading research on ways to improve gender balance for themselves and many other companies, recently acknowledged that despite their best efforts they are still not where they want to be, with women representing only thirty-nine per cent of entry-level hires, eleven per cent of senior leadership roles and only four women on their thirty member Shareholder Council. While their numbers are up, it's sobering to consider if a firm with all the insight, experiences, and resources that McKinsey brings to bear can't achieve gender equality, what hope do most organizations have?

After all the numbers don't lie. While achieving gender equity has been consistently touted over the last decade, here are just a sample of data points about women in leadership positions: Women hold 17.7 per cent of government minister positions around the world; lead four per cent of the S&P 500; 15.4 per cent of the ASX 200 in Australia; and a mere seven out of the FTSE 100 in the United Kingdom. In fact, as reported in research conducted by The Guardian, there are more men with the name John (17) than there are women leading United Kingdom companies, data that is also reflected in the United States market, but on a much greater scale.

So whilst Beyoncé sings, *Who runs the world? Girls!* and books of recent times brazenly declare, *The End of Men and Are Men Necessary?* claiming that a world with women running the show is coming, you only have to look around at those in power to realize it's not coming any time soon. And as Caryl Rivers and Rosalind Barnett show in their book *The New Soft War on Women: How the Myth of Female Ascendance is Hurting Women, Men and the Economy*, it's critical that we acknowledge where we are, and not delude ourselves into thinking that the game has been won, the war is over, and we can now finally move on to other things; it hasn't, it isn't, and we can't.

What's going wrong?

The findings of McKinsey's 2015 Women In The Workplace study of more than 30,000 employees, were reported in publications from the *Wall Street Journal*, who ran an in-depth feature with the headline trumpeting "What's holding women back?" to *Elle Magazine*, who wanted readers to know how "New data explains why you can't get that promotion." On the report's website, McKinsey summarizes the problems for women as follows: At every stage of their career women are less eager than men to become a top executive; women experience an uneven playing field due to gender bias; most employees do not believe gender diversity is a leadership priority; while development and flexibility programs are abundant most employees fear they will be penalized for using them; there is still inequality at home with a women continuing to do a disproportionate share of child care and housework; and women tend to have mostly female networks, giving them less access to senior-level male sponsors.

And McKinsey is not alone. Best-selling author Sylvia Ann Hewlett and her team at The Centre for Talent and Innovation, who drive ground breaking research across the divides of gender, generation, geography, and culture, report that while women start their careers hungry to attain a powerful job, they lose their appetite as they get older and between thirty-five to fifty years of age perceive that the burdens of a powerful position outweigh the benefits. As *Reuters* declared around the globe, "Study finds women misunderstand what power affords."

Or how about Catalyst, the research and advisory organization committed to advancing women in business, who surveyed *Fortune* 1000 CEOs and women executives at the vice president level and above about the challenges women face in reaching the highest levels of corporate leadership and found that lack of general management or line experience was the primary obstacle. This lead the *Harvard Business Review* to conclude: "The main issue appears to be top leadership's failure to ensure that women get the profit-and-loss experience that would qualify them for the most senior positions."

Or the Pew Research Centre, a nonpartisan fact tank that informs the public about the issues, attitudes and trends shaping America and the world, who's study suggested that women are in short supply in leadership roles in business and government because they have to do more than their male counterparts to prove themselves and companies are not ready to put more women into leadership positions. As *The Economist* reported: "We still don't expect women to be able to do what men can do."

And we could go on and on and on. Be it the *New York Times* story that states unconscious bias is disadvantaging women's opportunities for hiring, compensation, performance, evaluation, and promotion decisions. *The World Economic Forum*, who report that women are still under-represented at every level in the corporate pipeline. *The Guardian's* observation, that the lack of female role models is leaving women directionless and lonely at work. Or, *The Times* article about how elite professional women are holding other women back. As we said, the list goes on.

We get it: the hurdles are many and varied

Clearly there are a number of significant structural hurdles, hidden cultural barriers and personal beliefs that need to be addressed if gender equality is to be achieved. While many organizations and governments have been open to finding ways to fix these problems, it turns out that as we saw in chapter three, turning a weakness into a strength is harder than it looks.

For example, in an effort to rewire individual, organizational, and societal stereotypes, workplaces have leaped into unconscious bias training for their people with both feet. The hope has been that when people realize that biases are widespread and the negative impact they're having, they will be more likely to overcome them. But as Dr. Iris Bohnet, author of *What Works: Gender Equality by Design*, and a professor of public policy at Harvard's Kennedy School of Government, reports that whilst we know bias holds us back, de-biasing people's minds has proven to be both difficult and expensive.

In a recent *Wall Street Journal* article, she states, "Diversity training programs have had limited success, and individual effort alone often invites backlash. Corporations, not-for-profit groups, and governments spend billions of dollars every year on diversity training, without knowing whether the programs work. A review of almost 1,000 studies on interventions aimed at reducing prejudice found that most programs weren't tested. For the few that were, including corporate-diversity training, the effects, wrote Elizabeth Levy Paluck of Princeton, and Donald P. Green of Yale in the Annual Review of Psychology (2009), remain unknown. It is hard to ignore the possibility that all the time and money devoted in recent decades to promoting diversity at our major institutions has largely been wasted."

And then, of course, there's the use of quotas, perhaps one of the most hotly debated areas of the gender diversity discussion. Different countries around the world have taken varying approaches to quotas: The Nordic countries have been leaders in implementing enforceable quotas, most notably Norway which was the first country in the world to mandate quotas at forty per cent for women on boards in 2003; following this approach Canada and Belgium have imposed quotas of fifty per cent; France, Spain, Finland and Iceland have set the number at forty per cent; Germany, the Netherlands, Italy and Malaysia have a thirty per cent quota; for state controlled firms, Brazil has a forty per cent quota and Kenya a thirty-three per cent quota; Indian companies must have at least one female director; Australia has a *disclose*, *comply* or *explain* approach, that has targets and diversity reporting requirements but not quotas; and whilst the United States hasn't adopted quotas, a growing number of large companies are setting discrete goals for hiring and retaining women and tying these to pay and performance.

But the jury is still out as to whether quotas impact long-term change and not one country has met its own quota targets yet, with many long past the due date they had set for themselves. And whilst the United Kingdom has shunned official quotas, opting for voluntary target setting instead, the country has recently made significant progress by increasing the number of women on boards from 12.5 per cent in 2011 to 22.8 per cent in 2015, without quotas.

When Germany agreed to opt in to mandatory quotas, German Chancellor Angela Merkel told parliament, "This law is an important step for equality because it will initiate cultural change in the workplace." And yet, cultural change may be the furthest thing from the minds of those in charge. As Kimberley Weisul reported in an article on *Fortune.com*, "In Norway, the rule was originally supposed to apply to about 500 companies. By the time the law went into effect, about one hundred of those companies had changed their corporate ownership structure so that the law no longer applied to them. Marianne Bertrand a professor at the University of Chicago's Booth School of Business, who has studied the Norwegian law extensively, says there's no proof that the Norwegian companies changed their ownership to avoid the law—but it sure does look that way."

As Harvard professor Max Bazerman, who studies the impact of goal setting on human behavior, notes in *The Wall Street Journal*, "Once given a goal people do lots of dysfunctional things to achieve that goal. The more people are checking off boxes, the less they're focusing on how to make this organization both fair and excellent." Not only have quotas been found to incent the wrong behavior and choices, but there is also the very real challenge of how they leave many women and men feeling. Often viewed as undemocratic and discriminatory women lament they rob them of the right to achieve success on their own merit, and men fume that they penalize them for their gender.

And while advocates of quotas hoped that by getting more women in board positions there would be a trickle down effect of pulling others through the pipeline, unfortunately, it seems this argument hasn't seen results either. In research published in The National Bureau of Economic Research, Bertrand and her colleagues found that whilst there may have been some incremental impact at the very top of organizations, there was no evidence of further impact on the gender wage gap, pipeline, or female representation in top positions.

Despite the good intentions and genuine effort, the truth as Sheryl Sandberg recently wrote in *The Wall Street Journal* is "At the current pace of progress, we are more than one hundred years away from gender equality in the C-suite. If NASA launched a person into space today, she could soar past Mars, travel all the way to Pluto and return to Earth ten times before women occupy half of C-suite offices. Yes, we're that far away."

What's the alternative?

Professor David Cooperrider one of the world's experts on creating systemic change, states that: "Change begins with the first question we ask." Sought out by world leaders including Jimmy Carter, Bill Clinton, Kofi Anan and the Dali Lama, Cooperrider's research has found that the seeds of change are sown by the questions we ask as they determine the answers that are discovered and consequently the future that is conceived and constructed.

The human brain's natural negativity bias has meant that traditionally most organizational change efforts have focused on identifying problems and their root causes, meaning that the first questions asked are usually deficit focused. What's not working? What's holding us back? Why aren't we meeting our numbers? We've all been asked these questions.

The challenge is that this approach helps to build a deeper understanding about the weaknesses that need fixing in our people, cultures and systems, but sheds no real light on the strengths upon which we could be building. And while research is yet to establish how long it might take to evolve an organizational weakness into an organizational strength, given studies suggest that seventy to eighty per cent of change projects fail it seems reasonable to conclude that this is no small feat.

We believe that a key reason we're struggling to reach gender equality, is that the conversation has become stuck because we are predominantly focused on all the reasons women are struggling at work, and as a result are missing important opportunities to learn more about the women who are thriving at work and how this can be replicated. You only have to look at the mainstream media headlines about women and work on any given day, to see the plethora of negatively biased articles. For example, try a simple Google search on what holds women back and you'll find more than 330,000,000 results, but search for what helps women succeed and you'll find only 168,000,000 results. While the ratio of 3:1 may not seem so bad, according to research in the change literature, as we will see shortly, this ratio sets us up for the poorest performing change efforts and in order to succeed, we would need to reverse this.

This is not to suggest that we should ignore the reality of all that has been reported previously, only that we might start making more progress towards the goal of gender equality if we spent as much time talking about what is working for women and men when it comes to feeling respected, valued and appreciated by each other at work. Because examples can be found everywhere when you start digging for them.

From the Canadian parliament where the Prime Minister has now appointed an equal number of men and women in cabinet; to the decision of ten of the world's leading companies (including Unilever, Barclays, Twitter, Vodafone and PwC) at Davos recently to start disclosing new workforce gender diversity figures in an effort to make radical change; the Male Champions of Change initiative in Australia lead by former Sex Discrimination Commissioner Elizabeth Broderick harnessing the collective positive intention and actions of dozens of the countries most powerful male leaders; the United Kingdom thirty per cent club, focusing on driving to thirty per cent representation of women in senior leadership and board positions; to the United Nations Women gender solidarity initiative HeForShe campaign.

Female leaders doing extraordinary things, as we saw at the start of this chapter, can be found everywhere, and gender diversity awards in different countries and industries around the world demonstrate case studies of what's working well that can be shared. Examples of positive change are abundantly available if we just open our eyes and pivot our focus to capture them.

Do you think we're being optimistically naïve? We understand you may be skeptical. Could just asking more appreciative questions about what's working well really create lasting changes? We were doubtful as well until we started to look at the research many years ago and discovered example after example of how questions that look for the true, the good and the possible in people, cultures and systems can accelerate sustainable positive changes.

Take the challenge of improving mental health. Following World War II, as funding surged around the treatment of mental illness, the field of psychology began to focus most of its attention and effort on healing people who were unwell. As a result Professor Martin Seligman from the University of Pennsylvania, one of the most cited psychologists of the 20th Century, concluded that psychologists can measure once-fuzzy concepts such as depression, schizophrenia, and alcoholism and know a good deal about their causes and fourteen mental illnesses can now be considerably relieved or cured. But psychologists also learned that the disease model of trying to fix what was wrong with people moved them no closer to the prevention of these serious problems.

Instead, as Seligman was taking the reigns as president of the American Psychological Association in 1998 he noted that the only progress really being made on the prevention of mental illness was coming from a small body of research on the recognition and cultivation of a set of strengths, competencies and virtues such as future-mindedness, hope, interpersonal skills, courage, perseverance, and the capacity for flow to name several. So, he made it his presidential mission to encourage psychological researchers and practitioners to become as concerned with the scientific study of strength as with weakness, as interested in building the best things in life as repairing the worst, and as concerned with making the lives of normal people fulfilling as with healing pathology. And the field of positive psychology was born.

For a proud, die-hard pessimist like Seligman it was an optimistic call. At the time, there was a seventeen to one negative-to-positive ratio of research in the field of psychology. In other words for every one study about happiness and thriving, there were seventeen studies on depression and disorder. And while the idea of positive psychology provoked derision and disdain from those who felt it would somehow ignore or dismiss the very real problems people face, researchers and practitioners around the world took up the invitation.

Based on in-depth research conducted by Professor Lea Waters and her colleagues at Melbourne University, it appears the scientific community has accepted the legitimacy of positive functioning as a topic worthy of investigation with this research now growing faster than psychological research as a whole. In fact, it's not just psychologists who are discovering the benefits of a strengths focus but neuroscientists, social scientists, economists, management, public health, sport scientists, political scientists, sustainability and educational researchers. They conclude that it appears the change in language used to talk about human behavior and experience, has resulted in a growing change in ideology and practices.

Right topic, wrong conversation?

Could it really be that we've spent decades having the wrong conversation when it comes to gender equality? The truth is as the example of positive psychology demonstrates, researchers have found that our words—individually and collectively—go a long way towards creating the world in which we live. After all, as we saw in chapter one these words shape our mindsets, the way we feel, the actions we take, and often make them a self-fulfilling prophecy.

The consistent exploration of why more women aren't in leadership roles has led to all sorts of discoveries about why historically, male-led and designed organizations don't work as well for women. But as we've seen this conversation isn't moving us very quickly towards preventing these problems in future, with little upward movement over the past decade. And with the World Economic Forum estimating it will take 117 years to reach gender parity, perhaps it's time to take a serious look at other approaches. We're not suggesting we throw the baby out with the bath water and abandon the current conversation altogether, but we are absolutely advocating that the time has come for this conversation to evolve and mature.

Surely we're ready to open our minds so we can equally acknowledge and learn from all that is working rather than just staying stuck in what isn't. Surely we're ready to not just talk about improving work for women, but to broaden the discussion to include improving workplaces for all. Surely we're ready to embrace a fresh mindset and methodologies, ones that discard rhetoric and divisiveness, that pit men against women, or that suggest that women should close our ranks. And surely we're ready to have a conversation that will dislodge us from our collective negativity bias, and look to practices that amplify the positive core of what works and what's possible. Surely we're ready for all of that. So where do we start?

How we create successful systemic change

Whilst we tend to think that organizational change happens from the top or in certain teams or initiatives, the truth is much more confronting; change happens when one individual, and then another, and then another, chooses to show up and act differently. From the top-down, from the bottom-up, and from all systems stakeholders. And while management researchers have traditionally taught us that the most effective way to create change is with a top-down group of eight to ten people who do all the planning and then begin the communications rollout and implementation, this micro approach generally fails to unite and harness the best in the people, cultures or systems it's changing.

Instead, as Cooperrider and Michelle write in their journal article on "*The Positive Arc of Systemic Strengths*" true innovation occurs when strong, multi-disciplinary groups come together, build a collaborative and appreciative interchange and explore the intersection of their different points of strengths. This macro-minded capability enables the connection of ideas, people, and resources from across boundaries of all kinds and paves the way for the kind of personal and collective commitment that is the key to powering sustainable change. While at first it may seem unimaginable that large groups of hundreds and sometimes thousands in the room can be effective in unleashing coherent system-wide strategies, designing rapid prototypes and taking action, this is exactly what is happening. Sounds complicated? Surprisingly it is exactly the opposite.

The reason Cooperrider is sought out by world leaders—besides the fact that he is one of the nicest people you could hope to meet—is because he pioneered and spent the last thirty years researching a systemic strengths-based approach to creating lasting change known as *appreciative inquiry*. His work has been instrumental in: accelerating the growth of the United Nations Global Compact from 1500 firms to 8000 of the world's largest corporations; improving energy efficiency across the Commonwealth of Massachusetts resulting in nearly nine billion dollars of benefits for residents and businesses; and bringing together the world's religious leaders to unite more than seven million people around the globe to try and build a better world. This is to name just a few of the systemic changes an appreciative inquiry approach has made possible.

How is this done? Grounded in the strengths-management philosophy, appreciative inquiry starts from the premise that you learn little about excellence by studying failure. Instead of talking more about *gender inequality* what might be possible if we started to explore *inclusive workplaces* or women who are thriving at work? Human systems have been found to grow in the directions about which they inquire, so making a careful, informed and thoughtful choice about the topic of conversation always sets the stage for what follows.

Appreciative inquiry is also underpinned by the knowledge that every action we take is preceded by a question. It's just that often we're so busy trying to get things done that we're completely unaware of the questions we're asking. But if you think about how you came to be reading this book you might start to notice that you asked yourself a whole lot of questions from: What's the book about? Who are Megan and Michelle? Would you get anything from reading this? Do you have the time to read it? What's it going to cost? Every action we take is preceded by a question.

To help us discover the strengths in people, cultures and systems, appreciative inquiry provides a framework of questions that seeks out the true, the good and the possible by:

- *Discovering* what's working to fuel a genuine sense of confidence and appreciation for the available strengths.
- *Dreaming* of what's possible if these strengths were consistently built upon to create a meaningful sense of connection and commitment to the change being proposed.
- *Designing* pathways forward to mobilize people's hope into clear actions for which they are volunteering.
- *Deploying* the promised actions by leveraging social support and social accountability to maintain momentum, navigate obstacles and celebrate what is being accomplished.

One methodology for applying this approach is an appreciative inquiry summit which wraps a whole system in these principles to create configurations and chemistries of strengths that simultaneously unite top-down, bottom-up, and everyone at the sides. Delivering a speed, dexterity and level of trust and collaboration often not experienced in most systems, its ability to bond opposing stakeholders around a common purpose, to motivate siloed leaders to pool their resources and to transform hard-nosed cynics into raving fans is why appreciative inquiry summits have steadily grown in popularity when it comes to creating lasting change.

For example, by 2007, the American dairy industry was coming under increasing pressure to reduce its carbon emissions. With little trust between dairy farmers, the processors and other stakeholders, to date sustainability had been viewed as a potential source of regulation to be complied with rather than an opportunity to improve their business. With no real progress being made to fix the industry's carbon emissions problem, the board of directors for Dairy Management Inc, decided to bring together more than 250 stakeholders from farms, academia, governmental and non-governmental agencies and food retailers to try and focus on opportunities to build consensus for ways to spark sustainability innovations that would strengthen farm businesses, reduce greenhouse emotions and increase business value.

As competitors who had previously been locked in a zero-sum game sat next to each other and explored their shared sustainability strengths, together they began to dream of what was possible by collaborating together, designed more than twenty prototypes with which to move forward and pledged their commitment to a constitution for sustainable dairy. Together they launched an unstoppable movement that has helped more than 6000 farmers get access to 287 million dollars in incentives to implement 222 air quality projects, 10,247 barn and manure nutrient management projects and 13,920 soil quality and fertility projects. In just two years they had achieved their target of reducing green house emissions by twenty-five per cent whilst increasing farm business value by more than 230 million dollars.

Nourishing strengths over weaknesses

While most of us have been conditioned to view organizations and the people within them as problems to be solved, this mechanistic view of our workplaces only feeds our inherent negativity bias and leaves us stuck trying to fix individual and organizational weaknesses. At best this approach tends to result in short-term compliance provided leaders enforce the required actions with promises of rewards or threats of punishment. After all, surely the point of quotas is that what gets measured, gets done.

Or does it? As we explored in chapter two, fixing our weaknesses is hard work that requires significant commitment, consistent effort, and time to embed. In our experience of leading change initiatives around the world for large organizations, traditional change management approaches work only as long as leaders give it their full attention. Then when people are no longer encouraged or coerced to comply, or when they adapt to the rewards and punishments on offer, they go back to what they were already doing. We think this is another reason why the momentum for gender equality has become stuck.

But by finding ways to elevate, align, and magnify the strengths of the whole system, at its best appreciative inquiry tends to result in long-term commitment by people across the organization. It turns out that confidence, a sense of purpose, social support, and accountability are far more sustainable motivators than just measurement.

Investing in what works

Two years after introducing gender targets across management roles, the technology division of one of Australia's largest banks approached Megan and Michelle, for additional help in advancing their women. Taking an appreciative approach to how women in technology were thriving in leadership roles, we all worked together to design a program that would help to: Develop the women professionally and personally; connect the women better so they could support each other; provide experiences that would broaden their thinking and horizons; and encourage them to take an active role in addressing the systemic diversity challenges in their business and the information technology industry. Embedded in the heart of the program was the *Lead Like A Woman* journey, which was taught at large forums and through coaching circles, involving more than 1000 participants.

In the first year, the program focused exclusively on women, but by the second year as the impact of the work began to spread, both the women and men in technology were eager to make the experience more inclusive. An independent exploration and evaluation of the program recently found considerable evidence that: The program plays a substantial role in encouraging and supporting women to pursue new career opportunities; contributes to systemic and cultural change by shifting attitudes towards gender diversity and workplace flexibility; influences recruitment practices and showcases career opportunities in technology to other women in the bank. The program was so impactful that it won The Chairman's Award for Best Diversity Initiative across the bank.

At an individual level, the researchers found that the women reported a range of personal outcomes including personal growth, increased confidence, and more self-acceptance. They also described a range of relational benefits including increased networks, increased quality of relationships, and an enhanced sense of community. And they were using the knowledge they gained to enact change in their lives and felt the program had equipped them with tools, strategies, and networks to help them cope with difficulties and deal with uncertainty. As one participant said: "It has had a significantly profound effect on me as a human being and as a leader."

This doesn't mean that an appreciative inquiry approach works for every person, every organization, or every system. After all, it's just one of many tools for change and not a magic wand. Nor does it mean that deficit-based problem solving approaches should never be used. Like any good tool, each approach will work best when chosen for the situations and outcomes for which it is most suited. In our experience, it also helps when an experienced pair of hands can guide it.

So if you're OK with short-term compliance and you're willing to ensure leadership attention is focused on the potential rewards and punishments, then a deficit-based approach may be an effective short-term way to enforce change. But it's important that we be realistic about the need to ward off the brains tendency for adaptation by being willing to increase the size of the carrots and sticks we're using over time. Of course, if what you really want is long-term commitment then an appreciative approach to change is likely to be far more effective when it comes to sustaining people's confidence, energy, and motivation.

What might this mean for gender conversations?

Researcher Linda Robson found that when it comes to creating change in workplaces the poorest performing change efforts have a 1:4 deficit-bias. But the highest performing change efforts have a positively biased strengths imbalance of over 4:1. So, where would you place the balance of your organization's current gender diversity conversation? And where do you think it needs to be to truly move your efforts forward at a reasonable pace?

Taking a more strengths-orientated approach starts with you. Throughout this book, we've provided you with appreciate questions for reflection at the end of each chapter. If you look at them you can see the four-step appreciative inquiry framework helping you to: *Discover* what's worked in the past; *dream* of what's possible if you consistently built on these strengths; *design* pathways to move you toward these hopes; *deploy* actions to deliver on your desired change. This simple framework can be used to help create all kinds of changes in your life. So when you think about how you'd like to be a more inclusive leader, where might you start?

This same approach can be used in coaching conversations with others. Make sure you have an appreciative topic to shape your questions, instead of *removing unconscious bias* maybe try *valuing people's differences*. Remember don't get stuck in a conversation about what you want to fix or to stop, try to focus on what you want to grow and see more of. Even if the likelihood of what's working is tiny, compared to all the things that are not, it's still the strength upon which you're far more likely to see a quicker and lasting return.

For example if the topic of your coaching conversation was *valuing people's differences* you might ask:

- *(Discover)* Tell me about your best and most surprising experience of working alongside someone of the opposite sex. Who was the person? What were you working on? What were you able to achieve? Why is this experience so memorable? What did you learn about working with the opposite sex?

- *(Dream)* If you could consistently apply this learning and achieve this kind of outcome going forward, how might it shape your interactions with colleagues of the opposite sex over the coming months at work? What might you be able to achieve as a result? How would you feel about yourself? Why would women and men in this company admire the changes you'd made in your approach?
- *(Design)* If there were three things, within your control, that you could do to make this new approach part of the way you went about your work each day what would you do differently? What impact do you think these changes might have? What, if any, support would you need? How could you hold yourself accountable?
- *(Deliver)* Based on this conversation, if there was one action you could take in the next one to two days, what would you like to try?

Of course these questions are intended as suggestions only, not a script for you to use. Remember you're on the journey to being an authentic leader so we recommend you find the appreciative questions that feel most natural to you. For more examples of appreciative inquiry coaching questions visit www.leadlikeawoman.net/bookplaysheets and download the free guide.

Finally this same appreciative inquiry framework can be used in team workshops or in summits that connect your whole system of stakeholders—leaders, employees, clients, suppliers, investors, and other influences—together. These larger group conversations, which can include as few as four people or as many as several thousand, are usually best designed with the help of an appreciative inquiry practitioner to help you get the most out of these conversations and create practical plans and internal innovation teams to drive actions. You can learn about these formats and access a selection of free tools to help you at https://appreciativeinquiry.case.edu.

Just think about the mindset shift that may start to take place in your organization if hundreds, or even thousands of voices were sharing stories with each other about what's working well when it comes to inclusiveness or how women thrive in your workplace. Consider the richness of possibilities that might open up about the strengths you have to build upon, and the kind of return on investment you're likely to get if you had a highly motivated team of change champions across your workplace who were personally committed to putting them into action. And, just for a moment, try to really and vividly imagine the kind of difference this could make for the women and men in your organization. Isn't this the kind of legacy you want to be part of creating?

What will you do now?

Of course, an appreciative inquiry approach is not the only answer to being more strengths focused when it comes to gender equality approaches. Here are some additional thought starters to move you in the right direction based on our experience as researchers, business leaders, leadership experts, change agents, and diversity specialists. This is not meant to be an exhaustive set of solutions, as that would be a whole other book. Instead, our goal is to challenge your thinking, provide you with some ideas, and make it easier to start taking a fresh approach on gender, diversity, and leadership in your business. If you did nothing else in this chapter but pick one item and really work it until it works, then you will have made significant strides forward in helping women in your business to be more successful on their own terms.

Getting real about making change

Stop looking for band aid solutions – many organizations are seemingly on board with diversity programs like unconscious bias training, development programs for high potential women, or mentoring match ups, but have little skin in the game in actually driving real change through these initiatives. We must stop looking for quick fix solutions that may appease the bleeding, but don't in any way address the wound. Before you sign up to support another program or instigate a new initiative, ask yourself what problem you are actually trying to address, and will this really make a dent or just layer another mask over the issue. We need to get past the beauty contest mentality of diversity with stop gap programs and start driving holistic strategies designed to drive long term, sustainable change.

Be honest about what is and isn't working – as we have seen in research from the World Economic Forum and others, if there was ever a time to get real about women and work the time is now, when the call for new leadership has never been louder. We have to be honest about the strategies that work, and those that don't; about the programs driving real cultural change and removing barriers, and those that aren't, about why certain women in certain industries are striding forward, and why others can't. As we learned earlier in this chapter from Dr. Bohnet of Harvard the large majority of diversity and leadership programs have never been tested and funds are arguably being wasted. Understand the data in your business and analyze both the investments you are making and the shifts taking place. We must get past the political need to appear to be doing the right thing, and actually do the right thing, and measure the outcomes.

Stop the rhetoric about wanting to drive change – if you really want to drive change as a leader or an organization, then please do and commit yourself to it in the new ways as we are outlining in this book. If you don't, and we don't mean to sound overly harsh here, but please stop talking about it. All it does, if your heart or business objectives really aren't in it, is lift expectations and drive up hope that something better is coming, and in the end, you drive them both into the ground. As *Fast Company* states, it's like revving the engine with the parking break on. Please don't do that. Pick your battles, drive the change you are passionate about and lead by following through. The time for rhetoric on this discussion is long, long, past. It's time for real leaders who are willing to drive real change.

Managing for gender differences

Recognize, accept, and manage for gender differences – one of the most essential things you can do as a leader is to understand gender intelligence. We highly recommend you read *Work With Me: How Gender Intelligence Can Help You Succeed at Work and in Life*, by John Gray (of Men Are From Mars fame) and gender intelligence expert Barbara Annis. In this groundbreaking book, which draws on more than twenty-five years of research, they clearly detail the science of how men and women are wired differently, how they behave differently, and the real impact this makes in the workplace.

Often if you look closely in a team, you will see Mary sitting at her desk, head down, working away, whilst Mark is in the boss's office bragging about his latest client win. As we have seen, numerous research studies clearly tell us that women speak up less, talk more about we than me and share their accomplishments far less often than their male counterparts. When you understand gendered behavior, you can better support both your male and female employees achieve their goals. Once you educate yourself on the realities, which are not largely understood or discussed, you will be able to manage in ways that enhance not only individual performance but team and business success as well.

Recognize and value different models of success – what looks like success for Paul may not look like success for Sarah. Just as we outline with strengths in chapter two, people's definition of success and what they value is as individual as their strengths are. Don't assume that your female team members value money, power, or the top job as their beacon of happiness. They very well might. But, they also may place more value on contribution, collaboration, team success, and meaningful work. The point is, for all your employees, to ask, and then manage accordingly.

Value different leadership styles – different people make different contributions and add value in unique ways. Do you value the contribution of the team member who adds the strategic content to the presentation or the one who presents it and makes you look good in front of your boss? Do you consider everyone who participates in a meeting or workshop or just the person who speaks the loudest and longest? Do you place as much value on the quiet but supportive leadership style of one team member as you do on the driven, assertive, and confident leadership style of another? Start to check in with yourself on where you are placing value and if you have blinders on that are skewing your own leadership.

Changing the conversation

Start focusing on what you want to see more of – as we have outlined in this chapter, shifting your focus as a leader solely from what's not working, to all that can be possible, is a critical shift to drive effective change outcomes. What is it that you want to see more of when it comes to women in leadership, and diversity overall? Where are the wins happening that you can start to amplify, positive leaders that you can highlight and positive change that you can replicate? Challenge your own thinking and that of your teams. It can be as simple as asking for examples of what's working at the start of review meetings, instead of going straight to the things that need to be fixed.

Bring everyone into the conversation – for so long, the diversity conversation has been women talking to women about women, with few men to be seen. Initiatives like the Male Champions of Change, HeforShe and the thirty per cent club, are finally changing that. We need men to have both their voices and their skin in this game. Helping men more broadly understand the business and economic case for gender diversity is a good place to start. Making it personal by asking them to reflect on what their workplace would be like for their wife, sister or daughter is another. As technology company Dell found, encouraging male leaders to be reverse mentored by a female staff member so that they more deeply understand both the challenges and the triumphs proves exceptionally helpful. Engaging men in this new conversation about what is working and how we can collectively be more inclusive is critical in moving from diversity to true inclusiveness. The more we change workplaces for women, the better off men will be as well. We know time will play this out to be true.

Change happens in the middle – as Megan has seen in her work as a senior business executive and in leadership discussions with CEOs of dozens of organizations, we often think that if we get the CEO engaged in gender change strategies, all will be good and the job will be done. But it's not the case. Yes, you need the CEO on board to drive systemic change. But as research in the *Harvard Business Review* confirms, the hallmark of successful change programs is the involvement of middle managers. Real change happens in the middle; middle managers, their mindsets, and the decisions they make every day, are one of the most critical success factors to driving gender and cultural change in business. Look at how you are engaging your mid level managers in the change you want to drive, how they are empowered and enabled, and importantly, how they are measured on the outcomes you want to achieve.

What about the men?

Challenge gender norms and gendered leadership models – when it comes to gender norms, men are limited by them as much as women are. Whilst the ideal worker and ideal leader model were built by men for men, and can be limiting for women who don't fit the mold; they also keep men stuck in models that may no longer serve them either. How are you as a leader perpetuating gender norms? Are you invested in the notion that successful leadership looks dominant, always on, aggressive and masculine, and are men locked into this model? Or are you supporting those that also embrace feminine traits of empathy, collaboration, creativity, and openness, be they male or female? Do you call out gender bias when you see it, in recruitment processes, succession planning or performance reviews? Challenge perspectives, and amplify examples that move you and your team forward, not keep you stuck in old modes that have no place in a modern world.

Realize wellbeing is an issue for everyone (men just don't talk about it) – when we have done research looking at functioning versus flourishing with men and women, we were surprised to see the numbers were pretty much the same between genders, with as many men struggling as women. We shouldn't be surprised that wellbeing is a huge issue for men at work; we just haven't talked about it that much. How are the men in your team doing? Are they so stuck in a male gendered version of success that they don't have permission to find the balance for their wellbeing? What are the conversations you can have with your male employees to help them get the right mix of work and life for them? How are you sharing the stories and celebrating the men who are doing this well?

Invest in positive leadership and emotional agility for men – according to research published in McKinsey Quarterly, the United States alone spends fourteen billion dollars annually on leadership development. We need to ensure that whilst women are getting the benefits of programs like ours, that men are also given access to authentic leadership, strengths, mindset, purpose, wellbeing and grit training. To get to equality, we have to care as much about how men can thrive as we do about the challenges women face. And when we address limiting factors for women at work and amplify what's working, the waters rise for everyone.

Designing for change

Integrate gender diversity and inclusion into all business operations – in too many organizations, any discussion about diversity and inclusion happens on the sidelines or in a special committee, typically managed and populated primarily with women. In a recent study by Bain & Co, less than forty-five per cent of women felt that leadership made gender diversity a visible priority in the business. To drive systemic change, diversity needs to be made visible as a strategic priority and initiatives need to be woven into the fabric of every part of the business. From building a culture based on the values of inclusivity; to raising awareness of bias and conducting training that works; to recruitment, retention and succession planning processes; through to a pervasive conversation at all levels about what is working well in addition to what needs to be addressed, it needs to be taking place far and wide across the business. We need to get discussion and business practice on inclusivity out of the shadows and onto the agenda of everyone in the business.

Mainstream flexible work practices; all levels, gender neutral and visible – flexible work has long been something that has fitted under the unspoken umbrella of part-time work for women with children, taken up by working mothers who had no option other than to sideline their careers while they went on the mummy track. While many organizations now have policies in place that support flexible work, even all roles flex mandates, the take-up rate is low as both men and women often see it as career suicide. Look at who in your business is working flexibly. Does the CEO work from home on Friday's? Do male general managers take sales calls from alternate locations? Where are the men and women working flexibly, successfully, that you can shine a light on? We need to get to a discussion on mainstreaming flexibility for men and women, in all roles at all levels. The more high level, visible and gender neutral we can make it, the more people will feel permission to participate in work modes that increase productivity, satisfaction, wellbeing, and enables more women to stay active at work.

Focus on where diverse teams are succeeding – let's face it; business is a competitive sport. This is especially true when you peek inside an organization to its senior leadership team. Looking at how your business uses metrics, codes of behavior and reporting to express progress (or not) in getting to gender parity can be a powerful lever and motivating factor for leaders. Use a ranking system by business function in your organization to share where the most progress is being made on gender equality and building diverse teams. At the start of monthly leadership meetings, ask each leader to share an update on progress against targets, focusing on the positive and where those diverse teams are succeeding. Focusing on the positive highlights the success of these teams, so this becomes the new normal, not the exception.

As we have seen in this chapter, creating positive organizational change is complex. Whilst there are no quick fixes, when it comes to shifting the dial on gender parity, it's time to the change the conversation from one that is embedded and invested in all that isn't working, to one that also embraces all that is true, good and possible for women, work and leadership today. Whilst there is still so much to do, incredible progress is being made by individual women, engaged men, and organizations that are seizing the opportunity to drive change. Let us all commit to being part of the new conversation, embrace new possibilities, and become the authentic, positive leaders we know the world needs us to be, to create a better future for us all.

Afterword

Our Dream For You

Well here we are—you made it! You have reached the end of this book, but we know you are only just starting out on this next incredible stage of your life's journey. We have so much gratitude and respect for you being here, for your courage to show up and do the work, and for your willingness to open the door to all that is possible.

And we have big dreams for you too.

It is a gift to be a woman at this time, when the feminine is finally rising up in the world to creative positive change not just for ourselves, but for all. We dream that you awaken to this gift, that you fully step into your feminine power and own and honor every part of your being.

We dream that you show up with presence, authenticity, and the true confidence that will enable your wildest hopes for your leadership, career, and life.

We dream that you have vibrant wellbeing, that you move through your life with grace and ease, and that you have the grit to achieve the goals you hold most dear.

We dream that you go to work each day in an environment, and with people, who respect every aspect of your authentic self, bring out your strengths and foster your most unique gifts.

We dream that you live in a world of true diversity, equality, and peace, where women, men, and children live together in harmony, respect, and freedom.

We dream that you realize just how very special you are, that you have talents that the world needs, and that you have the courage to use them.

And we dream that this work that comes straight from our heart to yours, will support you unfolding into who you truly are, help you create everything you could ever want, and enable you to live a truly beautiful life.

Thank you for allowing us to be a part of your journey.

Acknowledgements

With heartfelt thanks

Our journey to write this book has been as rich as the content in it, and there have been many wonderful people who have contributed with their presence, love, and expertise.

Thank you to all of the amazing women who have trusted us to help guide them through our programs, workshops and coaching. It's not a small thing to show up with your vulnerability, your hopes, your dreams and even your fears, and ask someone to help guide your path. Each and every time we hear your stories we feel so incredibly privileged to contribute in some small way to the important difference you're making for yourself, your families, your friends, your workplaces and communities. This book would not exist without your courage, generosity, and inspiration.

Thank you also to the remarkable organizations who have given us the opportunity to be part of the vital work they are doing to better support their women and create the kind of world we all want to live in. We are so grateful for the trust you place in us to teach your leaders, and we are extremely proud of what we are achieving together.

In particular thank you to Dayle Stevens, Nicole DeVine and Nicola Le Poidevin at National Australia Bank. When our program was nothing more than a big hope in our hearts, you gave us our first big opportunity and brought us into your incredible Women In Technology network. You are three of the most authentic leaders we have ever had the joy to work with. You truly lead like women every day and as a result you have made such a difference to the lives of the hundreds of women you work with and for the technology community.

This book and our work would not be possible without the ongoing research of remarkable leaders, especially in the fields of social science, positive psychology and neuroscience. We want to give special thanks and acknowledgement to the women whose work has inspired so many of the practices featured in this book, as we know first-hand how challenging it can be for female researchers to thrive in the largely male dominated world of academia. So thank you to Brené Brown, Amy Cuddy, Carol Dweck, Karen Reivich, Kristin Neff, Laura Morgan Roberts, Jane Dutton, Angela Duckworth, and Kelly McGonigal. Thank you also to Adam Grant whose honesty and willingness to step forward and champion how men can better support women is opening up important new conversations in workplaces everywhere.

And to our team, we thank you for supporting our vision, especially Penny Dixon for your faith and commitment to take our work to the world.

From Michelle

I've been blessed throughout my career to work alongside women who taught me it was not only possible—but preferable—to lead like a woman in a male dominated world. Liz Merrick opened my eyes to the power of authenticity; Sophie Crawford-Jones showed me the value women bring; and when she was my boss (yes that's how it all began), Megan Dalla-Camina taught me to never doubt the difference we could make even when the system seemed stacked against us at times. Lea Waters, Anne Johnstone, Peggy Kern, Dianne Vella-Broderick, Miriam DeBaets, Kathryn Parker, Manuela Schmidt, Gabi Donovan, Anna Phillips, Helen Fitzpatrick, Lisa Lawry, Cath Greaves, Jo Fisher, Elise Morris, Anna Betts, Margie Warrell, and Margio Raftopoulus you inspire me every day with your beautiful examples of what it means to lead authentically.

Behind every authentic woman is an incredible team of support. Thank you to Rachel Caradine, Michelle Millichip, Caitlin Judd, Rachel Taylor, and Debbie Hindle for making my wildest dreams a reality. Thank you to Oenone Serle and Naomi Hill for your beautiful words. Thank you to the incredible sponsors and mentors, Paul Brasher, Andrew Muir, Peter Tanner, Luke Sayers, Gene Donnelly, Marty Seilgman, and David Cooperrider I would not be where I am or where I'm going without your generosity. Thank you to my friends and family who patiently waited for me to finish this book so we could go play more together, in particular to my ever-patient husband Patrick and our beautiful boys Charlie and Jamie.

Finally thank you to my best friend, my mentor, my business partner and constant source of inspiration Megan Dalla-Camina. Your vision, your passion, your creativity, and your love is what has ensured this book found its way into the world. I feel so grateful to see my name alongside yours on this cover. Thank you for believing in me and in every other woman we wrote this for.

From Megan

All roads, and the people I have met along the path, have led me here and contributed so greatly to this work. Jenny Castelino gave me my first real taste of feminine leadership for which I will always be thankful. Elizabeth Broderick showed me that you could collaborate with the most powerful men in the country by changing the conversation and leading like a woman. And my former CEOs and mentors, Glen Boreham and Andrew Stevens both live and breathe authentic leadership, and are true male champions of change.

To my teachers, women who have broken down barriers and created new paradigms, paths and conversations for women, I have the deepest gratitude; my friends Anne Summers and Naomi Wolf, Gloria Steinem, Marion Woodman, Maureen Murdock, Clarissa Pinkola-Estes, and Jean Shinoda Bolen. To Sheryl Sandberg, thank you for raising the volume on the conversation. And to Marianne Williamson, I am forever grateful for your light that guides my path.

Thank you to my wonderful team Caitlin Judd, Michelle Millichip, Nikki Hassett and my right hand miracle worker, Samantha Thomas. Thank you to the women in my life for your sisterhood, being the Goddesses that you are and for being such an important part of my journey; Taren, Lucy, Simone, Sally, Michelle, Lyrene, Louise, Justine, Avril, Claire, Ezzie, Julie, Lisa, Janelle, Marilyn, Nancy and Vanessa.

To my parents and my brother Jamie, I am so grateful for your love, support and the endless help. To my son Luca, you are my everything, and truly the most incredible, funny, cool and kind-hearted person I know. You make me a better person everyday, and I am so very proud to be your Mother.

And to Michelle McQuaid, my soul sister and teacher, you show me what is possible, that dreams are never too big, and that together we can create remarkable work that is changing lives. This book and project would not have happened without your belief, your talent, and your grit. Deep bow my friend for your brilliance, your heart and your love.

Notes

Introduction

Dr Brene Brown, best-selling author of books: Brown, B. (2012). *Daring greatly: How the courage to be vulnerable transforms the way we live, love, parent, and lead.* Penguin, UK; Brown, B. (2015). *Rising strong.* Vermilion, UK.

Chapter One
Being an Authentic Leader

Research on the dynamics of warmth and competence: Fisk, S., Cuddy, A. & Glick, P. Warmth and competence as universal dimensions of social perception: The stereotype content model and the BIAS map, *Advances in Experimental Social Psychology 40*, Edited by Zanna.

Contribution to this discussion is particularly compelling: Zenger, J., & Folkman, J. (2013). New research shows success doesn't make women less likable, *Harvard Business Review*, retrieved from https://hbr.org/2013/04/leaning-in-without-hesitation.

And in her new best-selling book: Cuddy, A. (2015). *Presence: Bringing your boldest self to your biggest challenges*. Hachette UK.

Women can't be both likeable and successful is Sheryl Sandberg, COO of Facebook and author of: Sandberg, S. (2013). *Lean in: Women, work, and the will to lead* (First edition.). New York: Alfred A. Knopf.

And according to the World Economic Forum, that will be for the next 117 years: World Economic Forum. (2015). *Global Gender Gap Report 2015*, retrieved from https://www.weforum.org/reports/global-gender-gap-report-2015/

Alia Crum a psychologist at Columbia University, has one thought that sits at the center of, and motivates, all of her research: Crum, Alia J., & Ellen J. Langer. 2007. Mind-set matters: Exercise and the placebo effect. *Psychological Science 18*, no. 2: 165-171.

Greg Walton is a psychologist at Stanford University: Kenthirarajah, D. & Walton, G. M. (2015). How brief social-psychological interventions can cause enduring effects. In R. Scott & S. Kosslyn (Eds.), *Emerging trends in the social and behavioral sciences,* Hoboken, NJ: John Wiley and Sons.

We then share the research we will cover shortly that shows which of these traits have been classified by 32,000 people: Gerzema, J., & D'Antonio, M. (2013). *The Athena Doctrine: How* *women and the men who think like them will rule the future.* John Wiley and Sons.

In 2014, *lack of values in leadership* was number seven out of ten: World Economic Forum (2014). *Outlook on the global agenda 2014*, retrieved from http://reports.weforum.org/outlook-14/top-ten-trends-category-page/7-a-lack-of-values-in-leadership/

But turn to the 2015 report, which calls out *lack of leadership*: World Economic Forum (2105). *Outlook on the global agenda 2015.* Retrieved from http://reports.weforum.org/outlook-global-agenda-2015/top-10-trends-of-2015/

Coming out of the global financial crisis in 2008: Gerzema, J., & D'Antonio, M. (2010). *Spend Shift: How the post crisis values revolution is changing the way we buy, sell, and live.* Jossey-Bass.

Consider a recent study from Stanford Business School, that examined the promotion rates of 132 MBA graduates: Rigoglioso, M. (2011). Researchers: How women can succeed in the workplace. *Stanford Business School.* Retrieved from https://www.gsb.stanford.edu/insights/researchers-how-women-can-succeed-workplace.

For example, Dr. Brené Brown, who we met earlier: Brown, B. (2012). *Daring greatly: How the courage to be vulnerable transforms the way we live, love, parent, and lead.* Penguin, UK.

Chapter Two
Closing the Confidence Gap

70 percent of men across all age groups report having high or quite high levels of self-confidence: Institute of Leadership & Management (2011). *Ambition and gender at work.* Retrieved from https://www.i-l-m.com/~/media/ILM%20Website/Downloads/Insight/Reports_from_ILM_website/ILM_Ambition_and_Gender_report_0211%20pdf.ashx

Ask four times less frequently for pay rises and negotiate salaries of 30 percent less: Babcock, L. (2003). Nice girls don't ask. *Harvard Business Review, 10.*

Won't put themselves forward for promotions unless they meet 100 percent of the necessary job qualifications: Lee, H.L. & Billington, C. (1995). The evolution of supply-chain-management models and practice at Hewlett Packard. *Interfaces, 25.* No. 5, 42-63.

30 percent more neurons firing at any one time: Amen, D. G. (2013). *Unleash the Power of the Female Brain: Supercharging Yours for Better Health, Energy, Mood, Focus, and Sex.* Harmony.

The cingulate gryus - the brain's "worry wart"- appears to be larger: Brizendine, L. (2006). *The female brain.* Random House LLC.

Higher levels of estrogen and lower levels of testosterone coursing through our veins: Brizendine, L. (2006). *The female brain*. Random House LLC.

Other researchers argue that women's lack of confidence: Dweck, C. (2012). *Mindset: How you can fulfil your potential.* Hachette UK.

The result is that studies suggest women often learn early on in life to avoid taking risks or making mistakes: Kay, K., & Shipman, C. (2014). The confidence gap. *The Atlantic, 14.*

Girls are six times more likely to drop out of team sports: Irick, E. (2012). NCAA Sponsorship and Participation Rates Report 1981 – 1982 – 2010 – 2011. *National Collegiate Athletics Association, 69.*

Some studies suggesting there is a direct link between playing sports in high-school and earning a bigger salary: Glass, A. (2012). Title IX At 40: Where Would Women Be Without Sports? *Forbes,* retrieved from http://www.forbes.com/sites/sportsmoney/2012/05/23/title-ix-at-40-where-would-women-be-without-sports/

Studies have found that while overweight men: Roehling, M. V. (1999). Weight-based discrimination in employment: psychological and legal aspects. *Personnel Psychology, 52*(4), 969-1016.

Only two percent of us actually describe ourselves as beautiful: Reel, J.J. (2013). Dove campaign for real beauty. *Eating Disorders: An Encyclopedia of Causes, Treatment and Prevention*. Greenwood Publishing Group.

Series of studies conducted by Zach Estes at the University of Milan: Estes, Z. (2003). Attributive and relational processes in nominal combination. *Journal of Memory and Language, 48* (2), 304-319.

Multiple studies in multiple industries that suggest women often judge their own performance as worse than it actually is: Sandberg, S. (2013). *Lean in: Women, work, and the will to lead* (First edition.). New York: Alfred A. Knopf.

Researchers have found that self-doubt becomes unhealthy for us: Arkin, R. M., Oleson, K. C., & Carroll, P. J. (Eds.). (2013). *Handbook of the uncertain self.* Psychology Press.

Concluded that confidence is within reach if we choose to practice: McQuaid, M (2014). Ladies, is a lack of confidence holding your career back? *The Huffington Post,* retrieved from http://www.huffingtonpost.com/michelle-mcquaid/ladies-is-a-lack-of-confidence-holding-your-career-back_b_5497503.html?ir=Australia

In fact, a growing body of research over the last decade is finding that when it comes to our careers developing our strengths is good for: McQuaid, M. and Lawn, E. (2014) *Your strengths blueprint: How to feel engaged, energized & happy at work.* Melbourne, Victoria: Michelle McQuaid Pty Ltd.

Some researchers suggest that it may take you as many as 8,000 to 10,000 hours of practice: Ericsson, K. A., Krampe, R. T., & Tesch-Römer, C. (1993). The role of deliberate practice in the acquisition of expert performance. *Psychological Review, 100*(3), 363-406.

Your brain is also wired with a negativity bias: Baumeister, R. F., Bratslavsky, E., Finkenauer, C., & Vohs, K. D. (2001). Bad is stronger than good. *Review of General Psychology*, *5*(4), 323.

Some studies even suggest that in most workplaces people spend around eighty per cent of their time focused on fixing weaknesses: Cooperrider, D. L., & McQuaid, M. (2012). The Positive Arc of Systemic Strengths: How Appreciative Inquiry and Sustainable Designing Can Bring Out the Best in Human Systems. *Journal of Corporate Citizenship*, *46,* 71-102.

Unfortunately, it appears that many of us are blind to our strengths: Hill, J. (2001). *How well do we know our strengths?* Paper presented at the British Psychological Society Centenary Conference, Glasgow, Scotland.

Research suggests that perfectionism hampers achievement: Brown, B. (2012). *Daring greatly: How the courage to be vulnerable transforms the way we live, love, parent, and lead.* New York, NY: Penguin.

Studies have found that while both men and women hear these stories, women are more critical of themselves: DeVore, R. (2013). Analysis of gender differences in self-statements and mood disorders. *McNair Scholars Research Journal, 9*, 7.

Doubts about our ability to copy, seem to make women more fragile: McQuaid, M. (2015). Are the beliefs of female leaders undermining their success? *Huffington Post,* retrieved from http://www.huffingtonpost.com/michelle-mcquaid/are-the-beliefs-of-female-leaders-undermining-their-success_b_5501415.html?ir=Australia

Psychologists have found some common patterns to our stories: Reivich, K., & Shatté, A. (2002). *The resilience factor: 7 essential skills for overcoming life's inevitable obstacles.* New York, NY: Broadway Books.

More than eleven million pieces of information coming at us every second, and our brains ability to only process forty bits per second: Zimmermann, M. (1986). Neurophysiology of sensory systems. In *Fundamentals of sensory physiology* (pp. 68-116). Springer Berlin Heidelberg.

Researchers suggest that tapping into our self-compassion helps to break the cycle of self-criticism: Neff, K.D., & Dahm, K.A. (in press). Self-Compassion: What it is, what it does, and how it relates to mindfulness. To appear in M.Robinson, B. Meier & B. Ostafin (Eds.) *Mindfulness and Self-Regulation.* New York, NY: Springer.

Stop our brains from narrowing in and spiralling downward: Garland, E. L., Fredrickson, B., Kring, A. M., Johnson, D. P., Meyer, P. S., & Penn, D. L. (2010). Upward spirals of positive emotions counter downward spirals of negativity: Insights from the broaden-and-build theory and affective neuroscience on the treatment of emotion dysfunctions and deficits in psychopathology. *Clinical psychology review, 30*(7), 849-864.

The discovery by researchers that the key to confidently taking action and ensuring that what we achieve professionally and personally never plateaus: Dweck, C. (2006). *Mindset: The new psychology of success.* New York, NY: Random House.

Researchers suggest this lack of naturally expanded body language is actually less about biology: Cuddy, A. (2015). *Presence: Bringing your boldest self to your biggest challenges.* Hachette UK.

Unfortunately, women generally have been found to show more submissive, contractive nonverbal behavior: La France, M., & Mayo, C. (1979). A review of nonverbal behaviors of women and men. *Western Journal of Communication (includes Communication*

Reports), *43*(2), 96-107.

Researchers suggest this lack of naturally expanded body language is actually less about biology: Galinsky, A., & Schweitzer, M. (2015). *Friend and Foe: When to cooperate, when to compete, and how to succeed at both.* Random House.

Social psychologist Dacher Keltner and his colleagues propose: Keltner, D., Gruenfeld, D. H., & Anderson, C. (2003). Power, approach, and inhibition. *Psychological Review, 110* (2), 265.

Chapter Three
Building Your Personal Brand

Since Megan wrote her best-selling book: Dalla-Camina, M. (2012). *Getting real about having it all: Be your best, love your career and bring back your sparkle.* Hay House.

For example, in one study, researchers found when we use other people's expectations to motivate us: Niemiec, C. P., Ryan, R. M., & Deci, E. L. (2009). The path taken: Consequences of attaining intrinsic and extrinsic aspirations in post-college life. *Journal of Research in Personality*, *73*(3), 291–306. http://doi.org/10.1016/j.jrp.2008.09.001

Consider the following example from a study by Yale psychologist Amy Wrzesniewski: Wrzesniewski, A., McCauley, C. R., Rozin, P., & Schwartz, B. (1997). Jobs, careers, and callings:

People's relations to their work. *Journal of Research in Personality, 31*, 21-33.

Simon Sinek is the author of: Sinek, S. (2011). *Start with why: How great leaders inspire everyone to take action.* Penguin; Sinek, S. (2014). *Leaders eat last: why some teams pull together and others don't.* Portfolio.

On Sinek's website, he has his team photo's and roles: https://www.startwithwhy.com/About.aspx

Megan found in her American research study: Dalla-Camina, M. (2014). *Getting Real About Women and Work*, study retrieved from http://www.megandallacamina.com/resources/

If you've started to realize that your brand is a long way from where you need it to be: Clark, D. (2013). *Reinventing you: Define your brand, imagine your future.* Harvard Business Review Press.

When Sylvia Ann Hewlett published her book: Hewlett, S. A. (2013) *Forget a mentor, find a sponsor: The new way to fast track your career.* Harvard Business Review Press.

And yet so few women, it seems, actually have a mentor. According to trend research report: Neal, S., Boatman, J., & Miller, L. *Women as mentors: Does she or doesn't she? A global study of businesswomen and mentoring*, DDI Media.

As reported by non-profit organization Catalyst in: Dinolfo, S., & Nugent, J. (2010). Making Mentoring Work, *Catalyst.*

But we're sorry to say that you'd be wrong for making these assumptions: Women and Men in U.S. Corporate Leadership: Same Workplace, Different Realities, (2014). *Catalyst.*

As Hewlett stated in a recent *Forbes* article: Schwabel, D. (2013). Find a mentor instead of a sponsor, *Forbes* retrieved from http://www.forbes.com/sites/danschawbel/2013/09/10/sylvia-ann-hewlett-find-a-sponsor-instead-of-a-mentor/#3151a3991da6

Once you have identified them, work out ways to build a relationship and demonstrate both your capability and your value. In her book: Hewlett, S. A. (2013) *Forget a mentor, find a sponsor: The new way to fast track your career.* Harvard Business Review Press.

For many women the idea of having to build a network remains challenging: Vongalis-Macrow, V. (2012). Two ways women can network more effectively based on research. *Harvard Business Review,* retrieved from https://hbr.org/2012/11/two-ways-women-can-network-more.

Your relationships with others have been found to impact your levels of wellbeing and performance: Dutton, J. E., & Heaphy, E. D. (2003). The power of high-quality connections. *Positive organizational scholarship: Foundations of a new discipline, 3,* 263-278.

The reality is that networks come with three major advantages: Uzzi, B. & Dunlap, H. (2005). How to build your network. *Harvard Business Review,* retrieved from https://hbr.org/2005/12/how-to-build-your-network.

Professor Adam Grant at Wharton Business School recently challenged some of the conventional stories we tell in organizations about what it takes to climb to the top of the success ladder: Grant, A. (2013). *Give and take: A revolutionary approach to success.* Hachette UK.

As a result givers build formal and informal teams that are cohesive and coordinated: Grant, Adam. (April, 2013) In the company of givers and takers. *Harvard Business Review,* retrieved from https://hbr.org/2013/04/in-the-company-of-givers-and-takers.

Some evidence to suggest that when compared with takers, on average, givers: Judge, T.A., Livingston, B.A., Hurst, C. (2012). Do Nice Guys – and Gals – really finish last? The joint effects of sex and agreeableness on income. *Journal of Personality and Social Psychology, 102*, 390- 407; Halevy, N., Chou, E.Y., Cohen, T.R. & Livingston, R.W. (2012). Status conferral in intergroup social dilemmas: behavioral antecedents and consequences of prestige and dominance. *Journal of Personality and Social Psychology, 102*, 251 - 366.

From sales teams to paper mill crews to restaurants the more giving group members do, the higher the quantity and quality of their group's products and services: Grant, A. (2013). *Give and take: A revolutionary approach to success*. Hachette UK.

Studies have found that over the course of a thirty-five year career each woman loses: Bowles, H. R., Babcock, L., & McGinn, K. L. (2005). Constraints and triggers: situational mechanics of gender in negotiation. *Journal of personality and social psychology, 89*(6), 951.

Hundreds of executives to seek advice on a major work project from two dormant ties: Levin, D. Z., Walter, J., & Murnighan, J. K. (2011). Dormant ties: The value of reconnecting. *Organization Science, 22*(4), 923-939.

Chapter Four
Mindfully maintaining your wellbeing

70% of us report that we actually spend most of our time somewhere between 'functioning' and 'flailing': Rath, T., & Harter, J. K. (2010). *Wellbeing: The five essential elements*. New York, NY: Gallup Press.

Arianna Huffington's story of waking up in a pool of blood: Huffington, A. (2014). *Thrive: The Third Metric to Redefining Success and Creating a Happier Life*. New York, NY: Random House.

Researchers suggest ninety-five per cent of us need somewhere between seven and nine hours of sleep: Jones, M. (2011, April 15). How little sleep can you get away with? *The New York Times.* Retrieved from http://www.nytimes.com/2011/04/17/magazine/mag-17Sleep-t.html

One study found that losing 90 minutes of sleep: Manber, R., Bootzin, R. R., Acebo, C., & Carskadon, M. A. (1996). The effects of regularizing sleep-wake schedules on daytime sleepiness. *Sleep, 19*(5), 432–441.

And according to another researcher, four hours of sleep loss produces:

Rueters (May 31, 2012). Sleepy drivers as dangerous as drunk ones. *Foxnews.com.* Retrieved from http://www.foxnews.com/health/2012/05/31/study-sleepy-drivers-equally-as-dangerous-as-drunken-drivers/

Particularly true of working mums who appear to be the most fatigued: National Sleep Foundation (November, 2015). *Women and sleep.* Retrieved from www.sleepfoundation.org.

Our bodies run best on a 24-hour circadian rhythm: Stuster, J. (2011). *Bold endeavors: Lessons from polar and space exploration.* Naval Institute Press.

Three small changes researchers have found can help you get your sleep back on track: Schwartz, T. (2011). Sleep is more important than food. *Harvard Business Review,* retrieved from https://hbr.org/2011/03/sleep-is-more-important-than-f/ ; Barker, E. (2015). Get better sleep: 5 powerful new tips from research. *Time Magazine.* Retrieved from http://time.com/3942487/better-sleep-tips-research/.

Social psychologist Ron Friedman explains: Friedman, R. (2014). What you eat affects your productivity. *Harvard Business Review.* Retrieved from https://hbr.org/2014/10/what-you-eat-affects-your-productivity/

Three approaches researchers suggest trying: Rath, T. (2013). *Eat, move sleep: How small choices lead to big changes.* New York, NY: Missionday.

Increasingly, researchers are finding that each of us is unique in the way we absorb and metabolize nutrients: Murphy, K. (2016). A personalized diet, better suited to you. *New York Times.* Retrieved from http://well.blogs.nytimes.com/2016/01/11/a-personalized-diet-better-suited-to-you/?_r=0.

The most underrated health threat of our time: Hellmich, N. (2012, August 13). Take a stand against sitting disease. *USA Today.* Retrieved from http://www.usatoday.com/news/health/story/2012-07-19/sitting-disease-questions-answers/57016756/1.

The problem with sitting is that it takes an immediate toll on our health: Rath, T. (2013). *Eat, move, sleep: How small choices* *lead to big changes*. New York, NY: Missionday.

Researchers suggest that this is a simple and effective way to keep track of just how much we're moving: Bravata, D. M., Smith-Spangler, C., Sundaram, V., Gienger, A. L., Lin, N., Lewis, R., Stave, C. D., Olkin, I., & Sirard, J. R. (2007). Using pedometers to increase physical activity and improve health: A systematic review. *Journal of the American Medical Association, 298*(19), 2296–2304. doi:10.1001/jama.298.19.2296

Researchers suggest 30 minutes of exercise five times a week: American Heart Association (2015). *American Heart Associations recommended physical activity in Adults.* Retrieved from http://www.heart.org/HEARTORG/GettingHealthy/PhysicalActivity/FitnessBasics/American-Heart-Association-Recommendations-for-Physical-Activity-in-Adults_UCM_307976_Article.jsp#.VkqwPoRWj8k

Three ways researchers suggest you can make moving regularly more effective: Rath, T. (2013). *Eat, move, sleep: How small choices lead to big changes*. New York, NY: Missionday; Doheny, K. (2009, May 29). Post-exercise "glow" may last 12 Hours, *US News and World Report*. Retrieved from http://health.usnews.com/health-news/family-health/brain-and-behavior/articles/2009/05/29/post-exercise-glow-may-last-12-hours ; Khan, A. (2015). Easy ways to get 10,000 steps per day. *US News*. Retrieved from http://health.usnews.com/health-news/health-wellness/slideshows/easy-ways-to-get-10-000-steps-per-day.

Chade-Meng Tan, Google's master of mindfulness, suggests: Tan, C. M. (2012). *Search inside yourself: increase productivity, creativity and happiness*. HarperCollins.

The truth is eighty-nine percent of us believe that tomorrow will be better than today: Lopez, S. J. (2013). *Making hope happen: Create the future you want for yourself and others*. Simon and Schuster.

Social psychologists have discovered that most of us have a limited supply of willpower: Baumeister, R. F., & Tierney, J. (2011). *Willpower: Rediscovering the greatest human strength*. Penguin.

Health psychologist Kelly McGonigal explains: McGonigal, K. (2011). *The willpower instinct: How self-control works, why it matters, and what you can do to get more of it*. Penguin.

Studies have found that hope gives you the energy to make this happen: Lopez, S. J. (2013). *Making hope happen: Create the future you want for yourself and others*. Simon and Schuster.

Researchers at Duke University estimate up to forty percent of your actions each day are not conscious choices but mere habits: Neal, D. T., Wood, W., & Quinn, J. M. (2006). Habits—A repeat performance. *Current Directions in Psychological Science*, *15*(4), 198-202.

Researchers at MIT have found that our habits run on a simple loop of: cue, routine and reward: Graybiel, A. M. (1998). The basal ganglia and chunking of action repertoires. *Neurobiology of learning and memory*, *70*(1), 119-136.

Psychologist Daniel Kahneman, defines nudges as: Kahneman, D. (2011). *Thinking, fast and slow*. Macmillan.

Nudges are thought to be effective for several reasons: Cuddy, A. (2015). *Presence: Bringing your boldest self to your biggest challenges*. Hachette UK; Wansink, Brian (2006) *Mindless eating: Why we eat more than we think.* Bantam Books.

Chapter Five
Cultivating Grit and Grace

Scientists' believe that we are wired to adapt more quickly to our positive experiences: Lyubomirsky, S. (2013) *The myths of happiness: What should make you happy, but doesn't, what shouldn't make you happy, but does*. Penguin.

Despite our best intentions researchers have found that when it comes to making lasting changes: Duckworth, A. (2016). *Grit: The power of passion and perseverance.* Scribner.

Associate Professor Angela Duckworth from the University of Pennsylvania has found: Duckworth, A. L., Peterson, C.,

Matthews, M. D., & Kelly, D. R. (2007). Grit: Perseverance and passion for long-term goals. *Journal of Personality and Social Psychology, 92*(6), 1087-1101

Researchers have found that because this is far more of a learned skill – than a heritable trait: Duckworth, A. (2016). *Grit: The power of passion and perseverance.* Scribner.

We tend to carry a 'naturalness bias': Tsay, C. J., & Banaji, M. R. (2011). Naturals and strivers: Preferences and beliefs about sources of achievement. *Journal of Experimental Social Psychology, 47*(2), 460-465.

As the German philosopher Nietzsche noted: Nietzsche, F., & Hollingdale, R. J. (1996). *Nietzsche: Human, all too human: A book for free spirits.* Cambridge University Press.

In one study of competitive swimmers researchers found: Chambliss, D. F. (2006). The mundanity of excellence. *Sociology: Exploring the Architecture of Everyday Life Readings, 29.*

Duckworth suggests talent matters because: Duckworth, A. (2016). *Grit: The power of passion and perseverance.* Scribner.

Duckworth suggests one way to understand this to envision a goal hierarchy: Duckworth, A.L., & Gross, J.J. (2014). Self-control and grit: Related but separable determinants of success. *Current Directions in Psychological Science, 23*(5), 319-325

In one study researchers gave participants a math game: Lucas, G. M., Gratch, J., Cheng, L., & Marsella, S. (2015). When the going gets tough: Grit predicts costly perseverance. *Journal of Research in Personality*, *59*, 15-22.

Best-selling author Caroline Adams Miller: Adams Miller, C. (2017) *Getting Grit: The evidence-based guide to cultivating passion, perseverance and purpose*. SoundsTrue.

Duckworth suggests that to be gritty we also need to invest day after week after year in challenging practice: Duckworth, A. (2016). *Grit: The power of passion and perseverance.* Scribner.

The research of cognitive psychologist Anders Ericsson: Ericsson, K. A., Krampe, R. T., & Tesch-Römer, C. (1993). The role of deliberate practice in the acquisition of expert performance. *Psychological review*, *100*(3), 363 and Ericsson, K. A., Charness, N., Feltovich, P. J., & Hoffman, R. R. (Eds.). (2006). *The Cambridge handbook of expertise and expert performance.* Cambridge University Press.

New research suggests the impact of deliberate practice on performance varies: Macnamara, B. N., Hambrick, D. Z., & Oswald, F. L. (2014). Deliberate practice and performance in music, games, sports, education, and professions a meta-analysis. *Psychological science*, *25*(8), 1608-1618.

It's a state extensively researched by renowned psychologist Mihaly Csikszentmihalyi: Csikszentmihalyi, M. (2000). *Beyond boredom and anxiety*. Jossey-Bass.

Duckworth has found that gritty people do more deliberate practice and experience more flow: Von Culin, K., Tsukayama, E., & Duckworth, A. L. (2014). Unpacking grit: Motivational correlates of perseverance and passion for long-term goals. *Journal of Positive Psychology*, *9*(4), 1-7.

Studies suggest that mastery is made up of a series of smaller peaks and plateaus that can be approximated into a S-curve: Ericsson, K. A., Krampe, R. T., & Tesch-Römer, C. (1993). The role of deliberate practice in the acquisition of expert performance. *Psychological review*, *100*(3), 363 and Johnson, W (2015). *Disrupt yourself: putting the power of disruptive innovation to work.* Brookline, MA; Bibliomotion, Inc.

Duckworth notes that to be gritty is to fall seven times, and rise eight: Duckworth, A. (2016). *Grit: The power of passion and perseverance.* Scribner.

As health psychologist Kelly McGonigal summarizes in her best-selling book The Upside of Stress: McGonigal, K. (2015). *The upside of stress: Why stress is good for you, and how to get good at it.* Penguin.

Nearly every system in our body – brain, heart, blood pressure, body temperature, hormone levels -- pulses in waves when it's healthy: Loehr, J., Loehr, J. E., & Schwartz, T. (2005). *The power of full engagement: Managing energy, not time, is the key to high performance and personal renewal.* Simon and Schuster.

Researchers have found that your attitude towards time shapes every part of you life: Kasser, T., & Sheldon, K. M. (2009). Time affluence as a path toward personal happiness and ethical business practice: Empirical evidence from four studies. *Journal of Business Ethics*, *84*(2), 243-255.

Scientists discover that playing energizes us, lifts us out of the mundane, eases our burdens, renews our optimism and opens us up to new possibilities: Brown, S. L. (2009). *Play: How it shapes the brain, opens the imagination, and invigorates the soul.* Penguin.

Chapter Six
Creating Positive Organizational Change

From an economic perspective the McKinsey Global Institute reports: McKinsey (2015). *The Power of Parity: How Advancing Women's Equality Can Add $12 Trillion To Global Growth.* Retrieved from: http://www.mckinsey.com/global-themes/employment-and-growth/how-advancing-womens-equality-can-add-12-trillion-to-global-growth.

There's a plethora of credible research reports that confirm the bottom line value of women's participation: McKinsey (2010), Women Matter: Women at the top of corporations: Making it happen, *McKinsey and Company*; McKinsey (2012), McKinsey Quarterly: Is there a payoff from top team diversity? *McKinsey and Company*; Catalyst (2011) Why diversity matters, *Catalyst,* New York; Carter, N. M., & Wagner, H. M., (2011), The bottom line: Corporate performance and women's representation on boards 2004-2008, *Catalyst.* WGEA, (2013), The business case for gender quality, *Workplace Gender Equality Agency.*

In a 2013 report by Catalyst outlining significant research to support the business case for gender diversity: Catalyst Information Center (2013). Why diversity matters. *Catalyst.* Retrieved from http://www.catalyst.org/system/files/why_diversity_matters_catalyst_0.pdf

Even McKinsey who have spent years leading research on ways to improve gender balance for themselves and others recently acknowledged that despite their best efforts they are still not where they want to be:

Barton, D., Devillard, S. & Hazelwood, J. (September 2015). Gender equality: Taking stock of where we are. *McKindsey Quarterly. R*etrieved from: http://www.mckinsey.com/business-functions/organization/our-insights/gender-equality-taking-stock-of-where-we-are

Just a sample of data points about women in leadership positions: Catalyst (2015). *"Women Ceos of the S&P 500."* Retrieved from: http://www.catalyst.org/knowledge/women-ceos-sp-500; Pew Research Centre (2015). Number of women leaders around the world has grown, but they're still a small group. Retrieved from http://www.pewresearch.org/fact-tank/2015/07/30/about-one-in-ten-of-todays-world-leaders-are-women/; Australian Government (November, 2015). *"Australia's Gender Equity Scorecard."* Retrieved from https://www.wgea.gov.au/sites/

default/files/2014-15-WGEA_SCORECARD.pdf; Rankin, J. (2015). Fewer women leading FTSE firms than men called John. *The Guardian.* Retrieved from: http://www.theguardian.com/business/2015/mar/06/johns-davids-and-ians-outnumber-female-chief-executives-in-ftse-100

The findings of the McKinsey's 2015 Women In The Workplace study of more than 30,000 employees were reported: Waller, N. & Lublin, J.S. (2015). What's holding women back in the workplace? *Wall Street Journal.* Retrieved from: http://www.wsj.com/articles/whats-holding-women-back-in-the-workplace-1443600242?mg=id-wsj; Kahn, N (2015). New data explains Why you can't get that promotion." *Elle.* Retrieved from: http://www.elle.com/culture/career-politics/news/a30922/women-in-the-workplace-study-promotion/.

Best-selling author Sylvia Ann Hewlett and her team: Centre for Talent and Innovation, (2014). *Women want 5 things.* Retrieved from: http://www.talentinnovation.org/_private/assets/WomenWant%20FiveThings_ExecSumm-CTI.pdf.

As Reuters declared around the world: Marketwired. (2014). Study finds women misunderstand what power affords. *Reuters.* Retrieved from: http://www.reuters.com/article/idUSnMKWNYswSa+1f2+MKW20141209.

How about Catalyst, a research and advisory organization committed to advancing women in business: Wellington, S., Kropf, M.B. & Gerkovich, P.R. (2003). What's holding women back. *Harvard Business Review.* Retrieved from: https://hbr.org/2003/06/whats-holding-women-back.

Or the Pew Research Centre, a nonpartisan fact tank that informs the public about the issues, attitudes and trends shaping America: Pew Research Centre (2014) *Women and leadership.* Retrieved from http://www.pewsocialtrends.org/2015/01/14/women-and-leadership/.

As The Economist reported: (2015) E.W. (2015) What's Holding Women Back? *The Economist.* Retrieved from http://www.economist.com/blogs/democracyinamerica/2015/01/women-and-work.

The New York Times story that states unconscious bias is disadvantaging women's opportunities: Grant, A. & Sandberg, S. (2015). When talking about bias backfires. *The New York Times.* Retrieved from: http://www.nytimes.com/2014/12/07/opinion/sunday/adam-grant-and-sheryl-sandberg-on-discrimination-at-work.html?_r=0

The World Economic Forum, who report that women are still under-represented: WEF (October, 2015). *6 things holding US women back at work.* Retrieved from: https://www.weforum.org/agenda/2015/10/6-things-holding-us-women-back-at-work/.

The Guardian's observation, that the lack of female role models is leaving women directionless: Stocking, B. (2015). What holds women back in the workplace? *The Guardian.* Retrieved from: http://www.theguardian.com/sustainable-business/womens-blog/2015/jan/13/workplace-fails-women.

The Times article about how elite professional women are holding other women back: Wolf, A. (2013). Elite female professionals hold back other women. *Time.* Retrieved from: http://ideas.time.com/2013/10/02/elite-female-professionals-hold-back-other-women/?iid=sr-link5.

Dr. Iris Bohnet, author of *What Works: Gender Equity By Design*, and a professor at Harvard's Kennedy School of Government: Bohnet, I. (2015) Real fixes for workplace bias. *The Wall Street Journal.* Retrieved from: http://www.wsj.com/articles/real-fixes-for-workplace-bias-1457713338?cb=logged0.681038255803287.

Different countries around the world have taken varying approaches to quotas: Catalyst (2015). *Legislative board diversity.* Retrieved from: http://www.catalyst.org/legislative-board-diversity.

Whilst the UK has shunned official quotas: Davidson, L. (2015). Proof that women in boardrooms quotas work. *The Telegraph.* Retrieved from: http://www.telegraph.co.uk/finance/newsbysector/banksandfinance/11341816/Proof-that-women-in-boardrooms-quotas-work.html.

German Chancellor Angela Merkel told parliament: BBC (2014). Germany agrees law on quotas for women on company boards. *BBC.* Retrieved from: http://www.bbc.com/news/business-30208400.

As Kimberly Weisul reported: Weisul, K. (2014). Women on boards: Are quotas really the answer? *Fortune.* Retrieved from: http://fortune.com/2014/12/05/women-on-boards-quotas/.

Marianne Betrand, a professor at the University of Chicago's Booth School of Business: Betrand, M., Black, S.E., Jensen, S. & Muney, A.L. (2014). Breaking the glass ceiling? The effect of board quotas on female labor market outcomes in Norway. *The National Bureau of Economic Research.* Retrieved from: http://www.nber.org/papers/w20256

Harvard Professor Max Bazerman: Feintzeig, R. (2015). More companies say targets are the key to diversity. *The Wall Street Journal.* Retrieved from: http://www.wsj.com/articles/more-companies-say-targets-are-the-key-to-diversity-1443600464.

Betrand and her colleagues found: Betrand, M., Black, S.E., Jensen, S. & Muney, A.L. (2014). Breaking the glass ceiling? The effect of board quotas on female labor market outcomes in Norway. *The National Bureau of Economic Research.* Retrieved from: http://www.nber.org/papers/w20256

As Sheryl Sandberg recently wrote: Sandberg, S. (2015). When women get stuck, corporate America gets stuck. *Wall Street Journal.* Retrieved from: http://www.wsj.com/articles/sheryl-sandberg-when-women-get-stuck-corporate-america-gets-stuck-1443600325.

Professor David Cooperrider, one of the world's experts on creating systemic change: Cooperrider, D., & Whitney, D. D. (2005). *Appreciative inquiry: A positive revolution in change.* Berrett-Koehler Publishers.

Canadian parliament where the prime minister has now appointed an equal number of men and women in cabinet: Ford, M. (2015). A Canadian cabinet for 2015. *The Atlantic.* Retrieved from: http://www.theatlantic.com/international/archive/2015/11/canada-cabinet-trudeau/414280/.

Decision of ten of the world's leading companies: Stevenson, A. (2016). A push for gender equity at the Davos World Economic Forum and beyond. *The New York Times.* Retrieved from: http://www.nytimes.com/2016/01/20/business/dealbook/a-push-for-gender-equality-at-the-world-economic-forum-and-beyond.html.

The Male Champions of Change initiative: Broderick, E. (2014). In defence of the male champions of change. *Women's Agenda.* Retrieved from: http://www.womensagenda.com.au/talking-about/top-stories/item/4953-in-defence-of-the-male-champions-of-change.

The UK's 30 per cent club: Hill, A., Plimmer, G. & Boulton, A. (2010). Club aspires to give women 30% role. *The Financial Times.* Retrieved from: http://www.ft.com/intl/cms/s/0/5bbf3712-f0ec-11df-bf4b-00144feab49a.html#axzz48iuNrn00

UN Women gender solidarity initiative: Watson, E. (20 September, 2014) : *Gender equality is your issue to.* Retrieved from: http://www.unwomen.org/en/news/stories/2014/9/emma-watson-gender-equality-is-your-issue-too.

Take the challenge of improving mental health: Seligman, M. E., & Csikszentmihalyi, M. (2000). Special issue: Positive psychology. *American Psychologist, 55*(1).

Based on in-depth research conducted by Professor Lea Waters and her colleagues: Rusk, R. D., & Waters, L. E. (2013). Tracing the size, reach, impact, and breadth of positive psychology. *The Journal of Positive Psychology, 8*(3), 207-221.

World Economic Forum estimating it will take 117 years: World Economic Forum. (2015). *Global Gender Gap Report 2015*, retrieved from https://www.weforum.org/reports/global-gender-gap-report-2015/

As Cooperrider and Michelle write in their journal article: Cooperrider, D. L., & McQuaid, M. (2012). The positive arc of systemic strengths: How appreciative inquiry and sustainable designing can bring out the best in human systems. *Journal of*

Corporate Citizenship, (46), 71-102.

An independent exploration and evaluation of the progress recently found: Norrish, J. & Vella-Broderick, (2016). *Building leadership capacity in women.* Melbourne, Australia.

Researcher Linda Robson found that when it comes to creating change in workplaces: Cooperrider & Goodwin (2015). Elevation-and-change: An eight-step platform for leading P.O.S.I.T.I.V.E. change." *AI Practitioner.* Retrieved from: http://www.aipractitioner.com/elevation-and-change-an-eight-step-platform-for-leading-p-o-s-i-t-i-v-e-change.

As *Fast Company* states, it's like revving the engine with the parking break on: Jay, J.K. (2014). Why most leadership development programs for women fail and how to change that, *Fast Company,* Retrieved from http://www.fastcompany.com/3035263/strong-female-lead/why-most-leadership-development-programs-for-women-fail-and-how-to-change

One of the most essential things you can do as a leader is to understand gender intelligence. We highly recommend you read: Gray. J., & Annis. B. (2013). *Work With Me: How Gender Intelligence Can Help You Succeed at Work and in Life.* St. Martin's Press.

As technology company Dell found: Reverse mentoring (2012), *Working Mums,* Retrieved from http://www.workingmums.co.uk/reverse-mentoring/

But as research in the *Harvard Business Review* confirms, the hallmark of successful change programs is the involvement of middle managers: Tabrizi, B. (2014). The key to change is middle management, *Harvard Business Review*, Retrieved from https://hbr.org/2014/10/the-key-to-change-is-middle-management

According to research published in *McKinsey Quarterly*, the United States alone spends fourteen billion dollars annually on leadership development: Gurdjian, P., Halbeisen, T., & Lane, K. (2014). Why leadership development programs fail, *McKinsey Quartely.*

In a recent study by Bain & Co, less than forty-five per cent of women felt that leadership made gender diversity a visible priority in the business: Sanders, M., Hrdlicka, J., Hellicar, M., Cottrell. D., & Knox. J. (2011). What stops women from reaching the top? Confronting the tough issues, *Bain & Company*, Retrieved from http://www.bain.com/offices/australia/en_us/publications/what-stops-women-from-reaching-the-top.aspx

Free Book Resources

Throughout this book you will have noted references to *playsheets,* which you were guided to download at www.leadlikeawoman.net/bookplaysheets.

To access your free resources, simply head to www.leadlikeawoman.net/bookplaysheets and use the code **LLAWPLAY** for immediate access to all the playsheets, plus the guided meditation referenced in this book.

We hope that the extra resources we have provided serve you well and support your journey.

About the Authors

Megan Dalla-Camina is a strategist, speaker, bestselling author, and researcher passionate about changing the conversation on women, leadership and work. She spent two decades as a senior executive in global organizations such as GE, PwC and IBM; most recently as head of strategy for IBM, including remits for gender diversity and organizational culture and change. She is committed to helping women step into their power, and enabling leaders and CEOs to create workplaces of the future where women (and men) can thrive. Megan holds Masters degrees in both Business Management and Wellness (Positive Psychology) and is currently researching her PhD in women, leadership and equality. She is the author of the bestselling book *Getting Real About Having It All* (Hay House).

Michelle McQuaid is a best-selling author, workplace wellbeing teacher and playful change activator. With more than a decade of senior leadership experience in large organizations around the world, she's passionate about translating cutting-edge research from positive psychology and neuroscience, into practical strategies for health, happiness, and business success.

An honorary fellow at Melbourne University's Graduate School of Education, Michelle holds a Masters in Applied Positive Psychology from the University of Pennsylvania, where she studied alongside the field's founder Professor Martin Seligman and is currently completing her PhD in Appreciative Inquiry. She is the author of the bestselling book *Your Strengths Blueprint.*

About the *Lead Like A Women* Program

If you have loved this book and want to go deeper, then we would love you to join us in the *Lead Like A Woman* program. Whether you are a woman who is seeking the tools to enhance your career and leadership journey, or a leader or organization looking to change the game for women in your business, we have the tools and support you need.

Lead Like A Woman is an evidence-based online program, uniquely designed to help women emerge with the kind of true confidence, career clarity and vibrant wellbeing that creates lasting leadership success.

Here is the journey map you have just been on, and that we delve further into, inside the program. You can get all the details of the online program and our other offerings at www.leadlikeawoman.net.

CPSIA information can be obtained at www.ICGtesting.com
Printed in the USA
BVOW04s0154150816

459036BV00002B/2/P